Knowledge in Modern Philosophy

The Philosophy of Knowledge: A History

General Editor, Stephen Hetherington

'*The Philosophy of Knowledge* is a truly remarkable work. In addition to its vast breadth, the set is commendable for the expertise of the contributors and the clarity and rigor of their essays. The set has three chief virtues: it provides a clear understanding of Western epistemology; each individual volume makes for an ideal resource for courses focusing on that period; and the individual essays themselves are perfect complements to primary works of the philosopher(s) addressed. Summing Up: Highly recommended. Lower-division undergraduates through faculty; general readers.' *CHOICE*

'This series of four volumes gives a reader the opportunity to take a fascinating voyage through the history of epistemology with an emphasis on the evolution of various theories of knowledge. The authors who contribute to the volumes are experts in their fields and the chapters in each volume are uniformly excellent.'

Richard Fumerton, F. Wendell Miller Professor of Philosophy,
University of Iowa, USA

'This ambitious fourfold work aims to provide an overview of Western epistemology, from the Greeks through contributions on the contemporary scene ... An invaluable resource on epistemological topics and on the development of Western thought about them.'

Ernest Sosa, Board of Governors Professor of Philosophy,
Rutgers University, USA

The Philosophy of Knowledge: A History presents the history of one of Western philosophy's greatest challenges: understanding the nature of knowledge. Divided chronologically, these four volumes follow conceptions of knowledge that have been proposed, defended, replaced, and proposed anew by ancient, medieval, modern, and contemporary philosophers.

Each volume is centred around two key questions. What conceptions of knowledge have been offered? Which ones have shaped epistemology in particular and philosophy in general? Together, these volumes trace the historical development of knowledge for the first time.

> **Volume I** *Knowledge in Ancient Philosophy*, edited by Nicholas D. Smith
> **Volume II** *Knowledge in Medieval Philosophy*, edited by Henrik Lagerlund
> **Volume III** *Knowledge in Modern Philosophy*, edited by Stephen Gaukroger
> **Volume IV** *Knowledge in Contemporary Philosophy*, edited by Stephen Hetherington and Markos Valaris

The Philosophy of Knowledge: A History

Volume III

Knowledge in Modern Philosophy

Edited by Stephen Gaukroger

BLOOMSBURY ACADEMIC
LONDON • NEW YORK • OXFORD • NEW DELHI • SYDNEY

BLOOMSBURY ACADEMIC
Bloomsbury Publishing Plc
50 Bedford Square, London, WC1B 3DP, UK
1385 Broadway, New York, NY 10018, USA
29 Earlsfort Terrace, Dublin 2, Ireland

BLOOMSBURY, BLOOMSBURY ACADEMIC and the Diana logo
are trademarks of Bloomsbury Publishing Plc

First published in Great Britain 2019
Paperback edition published 2024
Reprinted in 2024

Copyright © Stephen Gaukroger and Contributors, 2024

Stephen Gaukroger has asserted his right under the Copyright,
Designs and Patents Act, 1988, to be identified as Editor of this work.

Cover image © The Yellow Books, 1887 (oil on canvas), Gogh, Vincent van
(1853–90)/Private Collection/Bridgeman Images

All rights reserved. No part of this publication may be reproduced or
transmitted in any form or by any means, electronic or mechanical,
including photocopying, recording, or any information storage or retrieval
system, without prior permission in writing from the publishers.

Bloomsbury Publishing Plc does not have any control over, or responsibility for,
any third-party websites referred to or in this book. All internet addresses given
in this book were correct at the time of going to press. The author and publisher
regret any inconvenience caused if addresses have changed or sites have
ceased to exist, but can accept no responsibility for any such changes.

A catalogue record for this book is available from the British Library.

A catalog record for this book is available from the Library of Congress.

ISBN: PB: 978-1-3504-4662-5

Typeset by Jones Ltd, London
Printed and bound in Great Britain

To find out more about our authors and books visit www.bloomsbury.com
and sign up for our newsletters.

Contents

List of Contributors	vi
General Editor's Preface	vii
Introduction *Stephen Gaukroger*	1
1 Bacon *Matthew Sharpe*	7
2 Gassendi and Hobbes *Stewart Duncan and Antonia LoLordo*	27
3 Descartes *Anik Waldow*	45
4 Spinoza *Aaron Garrett*	63
5 Malebranche *Andrew Pyle*	79
6 Leibniz *Justin E. H. Smith*	97
7 Locke *Peter R. Anstey*	111
8 Hume *Margaret Schabas*	129
9 Kant *John Zammito*	147
10 German Idealism *Dean Moyar*	165
11 Whewell, Mill, and the Birth of the Philosophy of Science *Stephen Gaukroger*	185
Index	203

Contributors

Peter R. Anstey (University of Sydney, Australia)

Stewart Duncan (University of Florida, USA)

Aaron Garrett (Boston University, USA)

Stephen Gaukroger (University of Sydney, Australia)

Antonia LoLordo (University of Virginia, USA)

Dean Moyar (Johns Hopkins University, USA)

Andrew Pyle (University of Bristol, UK)

Margaret Schabas (University of British Columbia, Canada)

Matthew Sharpe (Deakin University, Australia)

Justin E. H. Smith (University of Paris 7 – Denis Diderot, France)

Anik Waldow (University of Sydney, Australia)

John Zammito (Rice University, USA)

General Editor's Preface

Stephen Hetherington

The Philosophy of Knowledge: Introduction to a History

Welcome to philosophy – to part of it, at any rate. A powerful and pivotal part of it, though: *epistemology*. Welcome to this survey – a tour, across four volumes – of a significant segment of epistemology's history. Western philosophy began in ancient Greece, before travelling far afield, still prospering. And whatever it is now is at least partly a consequence of whatever it has been. Within these four volumes, we meet much of whatever epistemology has been and is.

Why is this form of historical engagement philosophically important? Why is it important *now* to have some understanding of what epistemology has *been*? One reason is the possibility of current epistemology's being more similar to some or all of its former selves than it might at first seem to be, in productive and destructive ways. We should not merely be reinventing the epistemological wheel; nor should we repeat past epistemological mistakes – design flaws in earlier epistemological conveyances. To know epistemology's history is to know better what contemporary epistemology could be and perhaps should be – and what it need not be and perhaps ought not to be.

Epistemology is usually said to be the philosophy of knowledge and of kindred phenomena. But what makes it *the* philosophy of such matters? Well, epistemology has long been a collective endeavour – a gathering of individual efforts, by a plethora of epistemologists over oh-so-many years – to understand the nature of knowledge and those kindred phenomena. (Some of those efforts even ask whether there *is* a phenomenon of knowledge in the first place.)

How does that collective endeavour take shape? A first – a partial – answer is that epistemology is ineliminably *theoretical*. It is one theory, another theory, yet more theories, and so on. And so it is theories linking with, and departing from, other theories. It is theories living, developing, dying, reproducing, influencing, succeeding, failing. It is new themes replacing old ones. It is old themes replacing new ones.

And these four volumes will introduce you to such theories – competing conceptions of knowledge and those kindred phenomena, conceptions from across the ages. Volume I introduces us to theories from parts of the ancient world, the fount of all Western epistemology. Volumes II and III trace theories of knowledge as these arose over the following two millennia, late into the nineteenth century. Volume IV then tells a tale of the past century or so – while gesturing also at how epistemology might continue into at least the near future, taking us there from here. Not all of epistemology's past or present theorists and theories appear in these pages; but many do. The result is a grand story of sweeping intellectual vistas with striking conceptual foundations and ramifications. It is living philosophy. It is here, with you right now.

Introduction

Stephen Gaukroger

The study of the history of seventeenth- and eighteenth-century philosophy has been shaped by a standard historiographical template that is essentially Kantian-inspired. According to this template, philosophy underwent a long fallow period between classical antiquity and the early modern era, and was effectively reborn in the early seventeenth century. The rebirth changed the nature of philosophy, transforming it from metaphysics – an account of what kinds of things there are in the world and how they are related – into epistemology – an enquiry into the sources of our knowledge. With this transformation, the basic fault line that shaped philosophy was no longer that between the competing metaphysical systems of Plato and Aristotle, but rather between two competing and mutually exclusive epistemologies: rationalism, which based all knowledge on truths of reason, and empiricism, which based all knowledge on sensation. On this reading, the process started with Descartes, the founder of rationalism, was challenged with the empiricism of Locke and then Hume, and finally came to be resolved in Kant; or Hegel, depending on the version of the story. Finally, there is another hiatus between Hegel and classical German idealism, in the early decades of the nineteenth century, and Frege's revolution in philosophy at the end of the century, where epistemology becomes reformulated in terms of issues in the theory of meaning, and where, in a development of Kantian concerns about the standing of mathematical truths, problems in the philosophy of mathematics assume a central role.

In its reconstruction of philosophy in the seventeenth and eighteenth centuries, this picture, with its central rationalism/empiricism focus, tells us less about early modern philosophy than it does about how Kant projected his own interests onto his predecessors, for the resolution of the dichotomy between rationalism and empiricism, as he construed them, is constitutive of his project. But it also tells us much about twentieth-century Anglophone philosophy, which has taken the rationalism/empiricism model as its own genealogy.

There are insuperable problems with this way of thinking of seventeenth- and eighteenth-century philosophy in terms of rationalism and empiricism however. In the first place, it finds no room for the range of questions that motivated early modern philosophers. One of the most widely cited philosophers in the seventeenth century, for example, was Francis Bacon, whose primary concern was with the reformation of natural philosophy (what later became 'science'). His account of the obstacles to progress in natural philosophy – his doctrine of 'Idols' – was formulated in psychological terms rather than epistemological ones. The move from psychology to epistemology is a crucial one, wholly obscured by the idea that the distinctive feature of early modern philosophy is the move from metaphysics to epistemology. Second, Descartes did not pursue epistemology as the kind of pure 'a priori' discipline that one associates with Kant, for example. Physiology plays a crucial role in his thinking about epistemology, and natural philosophy – particularly mechanics, optics, and cosmology – lay at the centre of his concerns. As Descartes (1974–86: v. 165) himself remarks in his Conversation with Burman (1648):

> A point to note is that you should not devote so much attention to the *Meditations* and to metaphysical questions, or give them elaborate treatment in commentaries and the like ... They draw the mind too far away from physical and observable things, and make it unfit to study them. Yet it is precisely these physical studies that it is most desirable for men to pursue.

Descartes' successors, whether self-styled Cartesians, whether critical but sympathetic, or hostile, considered Descartes above all to be a natural philosopher. This is particularly the case with his Cartesian successors such as Rohault and Régis, whose understanding of Cartesianism led them to do away with epistemological and metaphysical foundations and to go straight to natural-philosophical questions in their textbooks.[1] Malebranche, Spinoza, and Leibniz each engaged Descartes at the level of natural philosophy.

The cases of Spinoza and Leibniz show how problematic the idea of a move from metaphysics to epistemology is. Descartes himself certainly put epistemology at the forefront of philosophy, and indeed to a large extent subordinated metaphysics to epistemology.[2] But Spinoza and Leibniz abandoned the idea of a sceptically driven epistemology and approached metaphysics more directly, whereas Malebranche's treatment of epistemology was resolutely physiological. It is of importance here that Malebranche was the most influential representative of Cartesianism, and indeed the conduit to Descartes' thought to the middle decades of the eighteenth century. By contrast with other treatments of the period, a chapter has been devoted to this crucial figure, a 'rationalist' whose crucial influence was on the 'empiricists' Berkeley and Hume.

Locke's philosophy was immensely influential in the early and middle decades of the eighteenth century, particularly in Britain and France. He was concerned above all with the sources of our knowledge of the world, and with what resources we could draw upon once the Cartesian doctrine of innate ideas had been abandoned. But his solution was not to base everything on sensation. On the contrary, his reaction to Descartes was as much to Cartesian foundationalism per se as it was to the specific form that that foundationalism took. Locke was particularly interested in the travel reports that showed that what his contemporaries were taking as innate were really culturally specific.

Hume's anti-foundationalism was even more radical than Locke's. In particular, he questioned the standing of philosophy generally as a form of meta-discourse that could pass judgement on other disciplines. In contrast to the traditional conception of the role of philosophy, for Hume philosophy (i.e. metaphysics/epistemology) was not something that could probe fundamental questions unaided: to do so led to ridiculous sceptical conclusions. Philosophy had a powerful role in helping us to stand back from our beliefs and subject them to scrutiny, but it did not provide us with answers in itself.

Given this complexity, we can ask how the idea that it was rationalism versus empiricism that was at issue in philosophy from Descartes up to Kant arose? The view turns on a particular understanding of epistemology: historically speaking, one that depends less on scepticism and more on Descartes' doctrine of innate ideas. Like scepticism, the doctrine of innate ideas was largely independent of questions in physiology. It was Locke who developed the most sustained criticism of this doctrine, and it was the French Lockeans – particularly Condillac and Diderot – who pursued the question in greatest detail. It is in this context that epistemology becomes transformed into a struggle between Descartes and Locke. In the 'Plan' of that bible of Enlightenment philosophy, Diderot and d'Alembert's *Encyclopédie* (1749), for example, d'Alembert (1752: 5–6) writes:

> The Multiplicity of these Sensations, the concurring Agreement of their Evidence, the Degrees we observe them in, the involuntary Affections they excite in us, compar'd with the voluntary Controul we have over our Ideas of Reflection, which operate only upon our sensations; all this, we find, produces in us an irresistible Impulse to ascertain the real Existence of external Objects; and to regard them as the Cause of our Sensations. Many philosophers have held this Impulse to be the Effect of a Supreme being, and the most convincing Argument of the real Existence of an external World. But as there is no relation,

that we know of, betwixt any single Sensation, and the Object thus suppos'd to occasion it, we cannot reason from the one to the other: and nothing but a kind of Instinct, more certain than reasoning itself, could oblige us to draw so remote a Conclusion.

What has happened here is that a profound and complex epistemological question about sense certainty has been translated into a simple choice between divine guarantee versus what might be termed psychological certainty. One element in Descartes' elaborate epistemological argument is held up as if it were the issue on which everything else hinged (which it certainly is not for Descartes), so that what is now at stake is a choice between religion and reason. This is a choice made easier by the fact that whatever epistemological rationale the divine guarantee may have had in the original Cartesian argument, its removal from the context of this argument robs it of any epistemological rationale, so that it now appears as devoid of epistemological function, and hence wholly gratuitous as a means of securing the veridicality of sense perception. D'Alembert (1752: 6) does not so much deny that there may be other epistemological questions at stake, as deny that consideration of them could be of any value, suggesting that for fear of 'obscuring a Truth acknowledg'd even by the Sceptics, when not heated in Dispute, we leave the capable Metaphysicians to discover the transcendental Cause in this Case'. Similarly with the question of God's existence. He does not deny this, telling us (10–11) that it follows from reflection: it is just that it can play no fundamental role in our cognitive or moral thinking, for the ideas that underlie these derive exclusively from natural sources, notwithstanding that revelation may occasionally 'serve as a Supplement to Natural Knowledge' (23).

On this reading, Descartes and Locke are treated as being concerned with essentially the same kinds of foundational questions, one offering divinely guaranteed innate ideas as the solution, and the other offering the immediate awareness inherent in sensation. Such a reading is that which Kant will take up and develop, offering his own solution to questions that, on his account, Descartes and Locke were manifestly unable to answer. For Kant, epistemology is a strictly a priori exercise, and this is the view that has been taken by the philosophical tradition since, at least up to the last decades of the twentieth century.

The most systematic a priori reading of epistemology and metaphysics was undoubtedly that proposed in late-eighteenth- and early-nineteenth-century German thought, where the Kantian project was reworked in terms of a thoroughgoing idealism. Kant had distinguished between things as they appear to us and things as they are in themselves. Knowledge on his account was a product of our applying various forms of structuring to experience: most basically, in terms of space and time, and in terms of causation. Knowing something involves bringing it under these forms of structuring. Unless we could structure experience in these ways, nothing would be knowable. This meant that things as they are in themselves, that is, prior to any kind of structuring in experience, are unknowable in their own right. As a result, for Kant, the material world and God were unknowable in any unmediated way. This was a move that Kant's idealist successors rejected as inviting scepticism. The idea of unknowable things in themselves was universally regarded as the most problematic aspect of Kantian metaphysics. Fichte was the first to offer a systematic response, abandoning the idea of things in themselves and arguing that knowledge, and consciousness more generally, cannot have any grounding in some supposed world to which we do not have access. Consciousness cannot be grounded in anything external to itself. The world as it appears to us *is* the world, and it is generated by self-consciousness: thinking and being are identical. Hegel too saw the key issue as overcoming the opposition between thinking and being, though he was adamant that that did not mean a reduction of being to thinking, as in Fichte. Consequently, although his system is usually referred to as 'objective idealism', in his later writings he himself preferred the term 'ideal-realism'.

The popularity of Hegelian philosophy peaked in the decade after his death, but collapsed after that. Although no one had a taste for things in themselves, and fewer and fewer were attracted by the various form of idealism, it was nevertheless Kant who set much of the terms of debate in the nineteenth century. This is true of England as much as Germany. In particular, there arose in England a formative debate over the nature of science initiated by William Whewell, whose reading of Kant shaped his views on the nature of scientific enquiry. The issues were prompted not by developments in science or in epistemology as such, however, but rather by new and unprecedented claims to scientific standing in what were termed the moral sciences, particularly ethics, in the form of consequentialism, and politics, in the form of Ricardian political economy. It was on this basis that Mill came to develop a comprehensive philosophy of science, and indeed it is in the dispute between Whewell and Mill on metascientific questions that that canonical modern discipline, the philosophy of science, is born.

Notes

1 See, for example, Verbeek (2000).
2 See Gaukroger (2002: ch. 3).

References

d'Alembert, J. le Rond (1752), *The Plan of the French Encyclopedia*, London: Hitch et al.
Descartes, R. (1974–86), *Oeuvres*, ed. C. Adam and P. Tannery, 2nd edn, 11 vols, Paris: Vrin.
Diderot, D. and d'Alembert, J. le Rond (1777–79), *Encyclopédie*, 2nd edn, 40 vols, Geneva: Pellet.
Gaukroger, S. (2002), *Descartes' System of Natural Philosophy*, Cambridge: Cambridge University Press.
Verbeek, T. (2000), 'The Invention of Nature: Regius and Descartes', in S. Gaukroger, J. Schuster, and J. Sutton (eds), *Descartes' Natural Philosophy*, London: Routledge.

1

Bacon

Matthew Sharpe

1. Introduction

It was the historian Stephen Beasley Linnard Penrose (1934: 1–2) who commented thus:

> Few philosophers have suffered greater variation in ... reputation ... throughout the history of modern philosophy than has Francis Bacon. Carried by eighteenth century thought to a commanding position as the 'greatest, the most universal, and the most eloquent of philosophers' he was plunged in the nineteenth century to the despicable status of a man whose scientific method was never used by any real scientist, whose effect upon the advancement of science was, if anything, detrimental ... The only philosopher who could come close to being favourably compared with him was Aristotle, or Plato; and yet there were few men in the history of philosophy who had not made greater contribution to knowledge than had Bacon.[1]

In the second half of the twentieth century, Bacon's stocks dropped even lower. The philosophical Lord Chancellor was now hailed by Adorno and Horkheimer (1989), then Caroline Merchant (2006), as the harbinger of the modern world's destructive, instrumental approach to understanding nature. The culmination of Baconianism on these views lay in totalitarian governance and environmental degradation. Bacon has been arraigned as a cold-hearted proponent of the Machiavellian claim that knowledge is power. It was Bacon who is supposed to have put an end to the ancient and medieval valuation of the contemplative ideal of inquiry (Sargent 1996). It was he who, by advocating for a collective form of natural philosophy, ended the classical tradition for which the pursuit of knowledge both requires and engenders ethical edification in inquirers.[2] Bacon was a naïve empiricist. His experimental idea of natural philosophy leads only to chaotic compilations of facts. Baconianism hopelessly undervalues the role of the formation and testing of hypotheses in scientific practice and progress.[3] Or else his 'scientific method' maintains, impossibly, 'that absolute truth can be discovered in science by applying a purely mechanical procedure' (Urbach 1982).

Bacon's divided reception reflects the complexity of the man. The author of essays on civic and moral subjects, of a book of apothegms and one devoted to classical mythology, an elegant stylist and a celebrated orator, hymned by contemporaries as the 'tenth muse' to bring the choir together (Rawley 1626), Bacon stands as an uncanny colossus astride the straits adjoining the modern world and the renaissance, the new sciences and classical letters.

Francis Bacon was born in 1561, the son of the Lord Keeper of the Privy Seal. He was educated for a career in the law and served as a member of Parliament. Yet the young Bacon soon bridled at the prospect of an exclusively active, public life. In a famous letter to his patron, Lord Burley, in 1592, Bacon (1753) confesses that 'I have as vast contemplative ends, as I have moderate civil ends: for I have taken all knowledge to be my province ... This, whether it be curiosity, or vain glory, or nature, or (if one take it favourably) *philanthropia*, is so fixed in my mind as it cannot be removed'. Moreover, Bacon seems to have developed from his time at Cambridge University a lively sense of the limitations of the education on offer there, led by Aristotle and the schoolmen. Bacon's famous 1603 'Proem' to *Thoughts on the Interpretation of Nature* tells us that it was as a young man that he conceived the need for, and vision of, a radical renewal of learning. Bacon (1893: 35) was struck by the deficiencies of the present understandings of natural philosophy, and their failure to have produced almost any new inventions since Archimedes that ministered to 'the glory of the creator and the relief of man's estate'. It was perhaps as early as the 1560s, then, that Bacon (1868: 84–5) began to envisage what became his '*novum organum*' for understanding the natural world, to replace the old Aristotelian *organon*:

> [A]bove all, if a man could succeed, not in striking out some particular invention, however useful, but in kindling a light in nature – a light which should in its very rising touch and illuminate all the border-regions that confine upon the circle of our present knowledge; and so spreading further and further should presently disclose and bring into sight all that is most hidden and secret in the world – that man (I thought) would be the benefactor indeed of the human race.

Nevertheless, Bacon (1869: Bk 1, sec. 120) published no writings before around 1600 devoted to his vision of 'laying a foundation in the human understanding for a holy Temple after the model of the World': what he calls 'the great instauration'. A series of earlier, unpublished drafts survive, in which Bacon (1964: 43) experiments with different literary forms to communicate and win sponsors for his radical program: 'He tries Latin, he tries English. He wonders if a dramatic monologue will not be more effective than a straight exposition. At one moment he is violently polemical, at the next urbane. He wonders whether it would not be best to suppress his own name and write under a pseudonym.' Bacon's entire oeuvre remains fragmented and pointedly incomplete. This adds considerably to the difficulty of achieving a comprehensive understanding of his theory of knowledge, or his persona more widely. Bacon's two most famous, systematic philosophical works are *The Advancement of Learning* of 1605 (expanded and translated into Latin in 1623 as *De Augmentis Scientiarum*) and the *Novum Organum* of 1620. The first work represents the first of six projected parts of the *Great Instauration*, the second work (which remained incomplete) as its second part. Book II of the *Novum Organum* contains Bacon's fullest extant account of his new 'organon' for the 'art of interpreting Nature'. It is accompanied by the much shorter *Parasceve*. This work provides a series of instructions for the compiling of newly systematic forms of natural history. It thus speaks to the third part of the projected *Great Instauration*. Bacon himself completed several such natural histories in the last decade of his life, including histories on the winds, the prolongation of life, and density and rarity. There is also the intriguing collection of 1,000 experimental observations known as the *Sylva Sylvarum* (Bacon's most popular work in the seventeenth century).

At least five interconnected projects are undertaken in Bacon's philosophical works. The first, achieved centrally in *The Advancement of Learning/De Augmentis*, is a comprehensive critical survey of all existing branches of human and divine knowledge. These Bacon (1893: 69) groups into forms of history (which he aligns with the human memory), poesy (aligned with imagination), and philosophy (aligned with reason). The second is an explanation of the deficiencies in extant learning disclosed by this magisterial survey. For these deficiencies, Bacon (1869: Bk 1, secs 38–91) seeks out what he terms 'signs' and causes, both in the institutions and practices of established forms of learning, and in the human mind itself. Third, and of arguably most enduring significance, is Bacon's account of induction in *Novum Organum* II, alongside his rules for the compilation of natural histories. Fourth are Bacon's own attempts at what we would call scientific inquiries into specific phenomena. Finally, there are Bacon's own speculative physical and metaphysical claims, including a post-Aristotelian theory of forms and of kinds of natural motion (Bk 1, secs 1–10; Bk 2, sec. 48), which Bacon sometimes aligns with forms of atomistic pre-Socratic natural philosophy.[4]

In the introductory account of Bacon's 'epistemology' that follows, we will focus preeminently on the second and third of these projects. Section 2 looks at Bacon's critique of existing forms of philosophizing, in particular natural philosophy. The culmination of this *pars destruens* comes in Bacon's famous delineation of four 'idols of the mind'. This is what we might call an 'epistemic psychology' which hearkens back to the *Advancement* and earlier texts (Bacon 1869: Bk 1, secs 42–65). Section 3 looks at Bacon's account of induction in the *Novum Organum* book II, alongside the prescriptions concerning the compilation of natural histories in the *Parasceve* and elsewhere. As we proceed, we shall introduce readers to some of the debates, and correct several of the false impressions surrounding Bacon's oeuvre that have arisen at different times: what Dana Jalobeanu (2013) has called 'the idols of Baconian scholarship'.

2. *Pars destruens*: anticipations of nature and the idols of the mind

In aphorism III of *Novum Organum* book I, Francis Bacon (1869: Bk 1, sec. 3) makes the famous pronouncement that '[k]nowledge and human power are synonymous'. This Baconian oracle seems to wholly politicize inquiry. Or else it seems to reduce all epistemic pursuits to so many branches of technical, even mechanical activity. It is true that Bacon admired aspects of the mechanical arts. One 'sign' of the limitations of premodern natural philosophy, for Bacon (Bk 1, secs 69–77), was that it had generated no new inventions of practical utility since the Roman imperium, save the printing press, compass, and canon. Like the mechanical philosophy simultaneously being forged by Galilei Galileo on the continent, Bacon (1893: 70–1) challenges the ancient oppositions of mind versus hand, and natural versus artificial (manufactured) things. 'The sun enters alike the palace and the privy', he echoes the Cynics. And 'that which is deserving of existence is deserving of knowledge, the image of existence' (Bacon 1869: Bk 1, sec. 120).

Bacon admired the cumulative progress of the mechanical trades, with expertise being passed down the generations. This he favourably contrasts with many other branches of learning that have not progressed beyond commentary on ancient masters. Nevertheless, it is untrue to Bacon (1863a) to pursue this thought too far. 'I care little about the mechanical arts themselves', he clarifies, 'only about those things which they contribute to the equipment of philosophy' (381). The mechanic arts as they stand 'take but small light from natural philosophy', Bacon (1955a: 393) writes in a characteristic passage in the *Filum Labarynthi* (c. 1607), 'and do but spin on their own little threads'. In a celebrated analogy (1869: Bk 1, sec. 90), he positions these mechanics, alongside the alchemists, as like 'ants' that collect information more or less blindly, without any larger orientation. 'The present method of experiment is blind and stupid', *Novum Organum* complains (Bk 1, sec. 70): 'hence men wandering and roaming without any determined course, and consulting mere chance, are hurried about to various points, and advance but little'. Bacon's epistemology then does not, *contra* some images, praise the unordered collections of facts as a sufficient goal of inquiry.

Bacon is better known for his criticism of Aristotle and his medieval and early modern scholastic admirers (Bk 1, sec. 90): less ants than 'spiders [that] spin out their own webs'. As with the mechanicals, Aristotle's model of natural philosophy rests on a basis of inadequate observation of the natural world. Above all, the theoretical account of 'induction' or *epagôgê* in *Posterior Analytic* II 19 is radically deficient, as an account of how we can discover new axioms or principles about the natural world – although Bacon (1964: 42) can express admiration for Aristotle's *History of Animals*. In line with this inadequate account of how we adduce our first principles, Aristotelian *epistêmê* overvalues deduction and dialectical reasoning. Accordingly, it illustrates what he will call in the *Novum Organum* an 'idol of the cave', the extrapolation of a mode of inquiry beyond its proper bounds: 'and I appeal to your memories, son, and ask whether in his *Physics* and *Metaphysics* you do not hear the voice of dialectic more often than the voice of nature' (112). This criticism informs one of Bacon's (1893: 66) several concerns with the University teaching of his time: 'which is, that scholars in universities come too soon and too unripe to logic and rhetoric'. At base, Bacon charges Aristotle with confusing invention in argument (a canon of rhetoric, and a dialectical technique modelled in the *Topics*) with the invention or discovery of natural principles (1–6). A valid argument may not be sound. One resting on a 'first digestion' of false or undiscerning premises can only yield erroneous conclusions: 'The syllogism consists of propositions; propositions of words; words are the signs of notions. If, therefore, the notions (which form the basis of the whole) be confused and carelessly abstracted from things, there is no solidity in the superstructure' (1869: Bk 1, sec. 14). Bacon comments that 'this art of [deductive] judgment is but the reduction of propositions to principles in a middle term' – as in the syllogism, 'Socrates is a man; *all men are mortal*; so,

Socrates is mortal.' If we do not have adequate procedures assuring us then that our middle terms capture real forms in nature, 'the principles to be agreed by all [are] exempted from argument; the middle term to be elected at the liberty of every man's invention' (1893: 130).

Bacon coins the term 'anticipations of nature' in the *Novum Organum* I for the kinds of inadequate principles that he saw as shaping the alchemical and peripatetic natural philosophies alike gleaned from too little or too unsystematic forms of observation. 'The axioms now in use', Bacon (1869: Bk 1, sec. 25) claims, 'are derived from a scanty handful … of experience, and a few particulars of frequent occurrence, whence they are of much the same dimensions or extent as their origin'. They force assent, but do not reflect or shape things (Bk 1, sec. 29).

It is against the background of this fundamental criticism of the natural philosophies of his day that Bacon does concede a good deal of ground in book I of *The Advancement of Learning* to criticisms of the life of the mind proffered by *politiques*: that scholarship makes men impractical, pedantic, and unsociable, and tenders to no public good. His argument there is indeed that these criticisms hit their mark, if it comes to many extant, deficiently carried-out, forms of inquiry, and the *personae* that they engender. It is first in this context that Bacon proffers his justly famous and powerful account of the 'tincture' of the human mind. This 'epistemic psychology' or 'virtue epistemology', as we might call it today, aims at explaining the very deep, innate sources of our tendencies to form erroneous judgements of things.

Bacon agrees with classical sources that the mind is 'the form of forms' (1893: 122): and that 'knowledge is a double of that which is; the truth of being and the truth of knowing is all one' (2008: 34). *Contra* strong instrumentalist readings of his position, Bacon is what we would call an empirical realist. Yet, reflecting contemporary Augustinian accounts of the mind's epistemic faculties having been damaged by the fall, Bacon (1893: 122) maintains that, without a strict methodological regimen, 'the human mind resembles those uneven mirrors which impart their own properties to different objects, from which rays are emitted and distort and disfigure them'. It is like 'an enchanted glass, full of superstition and imposture, if it be not delivered and reduced' (132). As he develops different drafts of the 'great instauration', Bacon develops different enumerations of the kinds and sources of error to which he sees the human mind as being naturally prey. In *Advancement* II, this work is situated as a necessary addendum to Aristotle's *Refutation of Sophistries*, and advertised as treating 'a yet much more important and profound kind of fallacies in the mind of man, which I find not observed or inquired at all ... false appearances which are imposed upon us by the general nature of the mind' (9).

In *Advancement* I, in medicinal language, Bacon hence delineates three diseases of the mind (fantastical, contentious, and delicate learning), accompanied by ten 'peccant humours'. By the time of *Novum Organum* I, fifteen years later, these epistemic maladies have been collected under the biblically resonant header of four genii of 'idols of the mind'. So deeply set are these *idola* in our mental makeup that Bacon (1869: Bk 1, sec. 38) cautions that 'even when access is obtained [to them they] will again meet and trouble us in the instauration of the sciences'. Nevertheless, by diagnosing them, and (as we shall examine in Section 3) by prescribing a new manner of proceeding in natural philosophy, Bacon hopes to philosophically both forewarn and forearm inquirers against them.

The first genus is the 'idols of the tribe'. Bacon divides several different species, all 'inherent in human nature and the very tribe or race of man' (Bk 1, sec. 41). Today, these might be described as forms of 'confirmation bias'. The human mind works by attributing order to experience. However, because of this natural tendency, we very often attribute 'a greater degree of order and equality in things than [we] really find [there]' (Bk 1, sec. 45). Having generated such an 'anticipation of nature', we then tend to seek out and 'see' confirmations of it everywhere: a phenomenon that Bacon thinks underlies the eternal appeal of astrology. The flipside is that we are naturally loath to confront 'negative' or 'contradictory instances': '[W]hen any proposition has been once laid down [the mind] forces everything else to add fresh support and confirmation; and although most cogent and abundant instances may exist to the contrary, yet [the mind] either does not observe or despises them, or gets rid of and rejects them by some distinction, [even] with violent and injurious prejudice' (Bk 1, sec. 46).

Contesting the intellectually flattering notion that the kind of abstract thought generic to philosophers is most difficult and refined, Bacon claims that 'the mind is fond of starting off to generalities, that it may avoid labour, and after dwelling a little on a subject is fatigued by experiment' (Bk 1, sec. 20). Indeed, it is of the nature of our minds 'to delight in the spacious liberty of generalities' (1893: 55). This delight Bacon assigns to a certain fallen pride. He sees it writ large in the schoolmen:

> [A]s in the inquiry of the divine truth, their pride inclined to leave the oracle of God's word, and to vanish in the mixture of their own inventions; so in the inquisition of nature, they ever left the oracle of God's works, and adored the

deceiving and deformed images which the unequal mirror of their own minds, or a few received authors or principles, did represent unto them. (27–8)

Bacon also challenges the Aristotelian supposition that it is only practical reasoning that works to temper the passions. The mind is no dry light, Bacon analogizes. It is 'moistened' and 'clouded' by the passions (122). For this reason, 'man always believes more readily that which he prefers', even in matters of *theoria*. As Bacon (1869: Bk 1, sec. 49) continues, in one of his majestic sequences of periods:

> He rejects difficulties for want of patience in investigation; sobriety, because it limits his hope; the depths of nature, from superstition; the light of experiment, from arrogance and pride, lest his mind should appear to be occupied with common and varying objects; paradoxes, from a fear of the opinion of the vulgar; in short, his feelings imbue and corrupt his understanding in innumerable and sometimes imperceptible ways.

The idols of the cave or den are again universal to all humans (Bk 1, secs 62–8). But these *idola* reflect our individual predispositions. Each of us has our own 'individual den or cavern, which intercepts and corrupts the light of nature', Bacon contends: '[E]ither from his own peculiar and singular disposition, or from his education and intercourse with others, or from his reading, and the authority acquired by those whom he reverences and admires, or from the different impressions produced on the mind, as it happens to be preoccupied and predisposed, or equable and tranquil, and the like' (Bk 1, sec. 42). Some people are more analytically minded, especially adept at finding and handling fine distinctions. Others (those today more attracted to 'continental' forms of theory, we might say) 'are sublime and discursive [and] recognize and compare even the most delicate and general resemblances' (Bk 1, sec. 55). Some men, again, are inclined to admiration of what is old and tested, scorning novelty. Others seek out the new, and scorn what is established as dull or staid. Students who have been trained to expertise in one field, or who have spent the longest time mastering some difficult author, tend to surmise a greater scope and importance for that discipline or thinker than things themselves merit. Each of us, for Bacon, has a natural tendency to scorn the modes of inquiry we find difficult or dry. What is ideal, by his lights, seems close to his autobiographical intellectual portrait, that of 'a mind nimble and versatile enough to catch the resemblances of things (which is the chief point), and at the same time steady enough to fix and distinguish their subtler differences; … that neither affects what is new nor admires what is old, and that hates every kind of imposture' (1868: 84–5).

The third idol of the mind anticipates the formative claims of later philosophies of language. Bacon (1869: Bk 1, sec. 59) opines that 'the great and solemn disputes of learned men often terminate in controversies about words and names'. Yet the words that circulate in natural languages trail inherited notions about things 'hastily and irregularly abstracted from things'. Some terms signify phantasms that don't exist. Most describe medium-sized objects and actions immediately accessible to our unaided senses. Many others (Bacon uses the example of 'moist') ambiguously condense a range of different meanings. In short, here as elsewhere pointing a way towards later distinctions between primary (objective or real) and secondary (subjective and apparent) qualities, Bacon (1869: Bk 1, sec. 59) worries that '[w]ords are generally formed in a popular sense, and define things by those broad lines which are most obvious to the vulgar mind; but when a more acute understanding or more diligent observation is anxious ... to adapt them more accurately to nature, words oppose it'.

The final genus of *idola* of the mind are 'idols of the theatre'. These are none other than the established, competing, philosophical, and theological systems that have accumulated and been handed down to us since antiquity. Bacon (1869: Bk 1, sec. 62) sees that, absent a more incisive manner of inquiry into things, an underdetermination of theory by the data abides: '[f]or as many imaginary theories of the heavens can be deduced from the phenomena of the sky, so it is even more easy to found many dogmas upon the phenomena of philosophy'. Bacon compares the resulting, incommensurable, systems to the sui generis worlds laid out before us in stage plays – except that the worlds presented 'for the stage are more consistent, elegant, and pleasurable than those taken from real history' (Bk 1, sec. 62).

And so, at this point of *Novum Organum*, Bacon is ready to give us a summative threefold typology of the kinds of 'anticipatory' philosophical 'theatre plays' that his promised interpretation of nature aspires to supersede. Each, we can now see, gives different forms to the *idola* of the human mind:

- *The sophistics*, who 'take too much from too little', spinning systematic theories, spider-like, from a limited set of observed regularities (Aristotle and the schoolmen belong here: so many Ixions who, hoping to bed divine Hera, couple with clouds and beget chimeras) (ibid.).
- *The 'empirics'*, who, ant-like, 'take too little from too much'. They multiply disordered experiments but, for want of method, draw erroneous claims from them, lured by promises of fame (the mechanics and alchemists belong here) (Bk 1, sec. 70).

- *The superstitious*, led by Pythagoreans and Platonists, who would derive principles in natural philosophy from theological or supernatural premises. These theoretical theatre-plays Bacon warns his readers off especially (Bk 1, sec. 65): 'for the apotheosis of error is the greatest evil of all, and when folly is worshipped, it is … a plague spot upon the understanding' engendering 'heretical religion … from the absurd mixture of matters divine and human'.

3. *Pars construens*: Bacon's prescriptions for new natural histories and the inductive natural philosophy

The heart of Bacon's (1869: Bk 1, sec. 14) project for the advancement of learning was his claim to have discovered a new form of *'inductio'*. This new form of inquiry, the philosopher Lord Chancellor famously maintained, promised to correct for the deficiencies of earlier forms of natural philosophy. Given Bacon's epistemic psychology, we shall see that his *organon* was also recommended, quite explicitly, as a medicinal regimen for the innately idolatrous tendencies of the human mind,[5] which 'take for the groundwork of their philosophy either too much from a few topics, or too little from many; in either case [founding] their philosophy … on too narrow a basis of experiment and natural history, and deciding [*sic*] on too scanty grounds' (Bk 1, sec. 62).

Bacon divides natural philosophy in *The Advancement of Learning* into three parts: natural history (which gathers information about natural phenomena, and phenomena 'wrought' by human crafts [1893: 70]), physics (which aims at the material and efficient causes of phenomena), and metaphysics (which aims at deciphering the 'alphabet' of formal causes or true forms of things in nature [90–8]). It is important, given continuing misrepresentations of Bacon as out to reduce knowledge to utility or power, to emphasize that each part has a speculative, as well as an operative role (90–1). Nature to be commanded, must first be obeyed, 'for the chain of causes cannot by any force be loosened' (2012: 45). Its workings need to be understood, before they can be harnessed. Unlike Atalanta (1869: Bk 1, sec. 70), who put aside the chase of Hippomenes to pick up the golden apples strewn in his path,

> there is another thing to be remembered – namely, that all industry in experimenting has an unseasonable eagerness; it has sought … experiments of fruit, not experiments of light, not imitating the divine procedure, which in its first day's work created light only and assigned to it one entire day, on which day

it produced no material work, but proceeded to that on the days following. (Bk 1, secs 70, 121)[6]

Bacon's most detailed prescriptions for the compilation of new forms of natural history come in the *Parasceve*. This is a short work (1863b) appended to the *Novum Organum*. These 'histories' (inquiries) serve to provide aids to the senses, as the tables of instances they give rise to will aid the memory, and the new eliminative induction assist our reason. This is the place to again underscore that, despite continuing images of him as a naïve empiricist, Bacon nominates the limitations of the senses as one of the causes of the 'idols of the tribe'. He has warm things to say (1869: Bk 1, secs 37, 40, 50, 52) about the ancient sceptics' criticisms of 'the incompetence of the senses'. But 'we derogate not from the senses but assist them' (Bk 1, sec. 126). Many real objects escape our sense, Bacon summarizes in *Novum Organum*,

> either on account of [their] distance; or on account of the interposition of intermediate bodies; or because it is not fitted for making an impression on the sense; or because it is not sufficient in quantity to strike the sense; or because there is not time enough for it to act on the sense; or because the impression of the object is such as the sense cannot bear; or because the sense has been previously filled and occupied by another object, so that there is not room for a new motion. (Bk 2, sec. 40)

As such, Bacon prescribes five different 'instances of the lamp' to minister to these limitations: notably including the use of instruments to 'strengthen, enlargen, [or] rectify' our immediate sense perceptions, like lenses and telescopes; 'dissecting instances' to see into the hidden and minute workings of nature, like microscopes; and what he calls 'instances of the road' to monitor slow processes over long periods, like time-lapse photography today (Bk 2, secs 38, 434, 41, respectively).

The new natural histories which will be needed if natural philosophy is to be renewed, Bacon tells us, are to serve as a compendious stockpile of observations of phenomena under investigation, including those gathered through the use of instruments. As previous natural philosophy had scorned minute or common phenomena, the Baconian inquirer must document even the basest, illiberal things: for 'to the pure all things are pure'. S/he should not overlook things usually considered trifling or childish; nor things which appear subtle and useless (Bk 1, secs 99, 119, 120). All natural bodies should be measured, numbered, weighed (Bk 2, sec. 44). We should note all doubtful observations as doubtful; weigh the different sources, and reliability, of different testimonies; raise questions that come to mind at each point of the investigation (1963b: 368–9); and document any experimental procedures that are undertaken so that others may repeat or develop these. All 'philological matters' touching the interpretations of books, not things, should be eschewed (or be noted with due caution): 'let antiquities be done away with, works, citations, assents of authors, altercations and disputations' (368). Only the simplest unadorned language should be used: 'all eloquences [are] likewise to be cast aside' (ibid.). Any interpretations that suggest themselves should be adduced 'sparingly' and in a provisional manner, withholding final assent: 'for they are useful, if not altogether true' (1863c: 377).

Yet such histories, which Bacon models for us in his own *History of Dense and Rare* and his *Sylva Sylvarum*, are only the first component of Bacon's account of how true 'interpretations of nature' might be arrived at. As Parasceve precedes the Sabbath, they are as 'a granary and storehouse of matters, not meant to be pleasant to stay or live in, but only to be entered as occasion requires, when anything is wanted for the work of the *Interpreter*, which follows' (1963b: 360).

Book II of *Novum Organum* sets out the heart of this 'work of the Interpreter', and by what means it should proceed. We should never lose sight of the fact that what Bacon is aiming at is a new 'logic', which he calls inductive. We saw above that it was Aristotle's negligence of an adequate account of *epigôgê* that most attracted Bacon's ire. We saw also that Bacon believed that the human mind has a natural tendency to leap too quickly to generalizations, then scorn 'negative instances' contradicting its 'anticipations of nature'. The disciplines for compiling natural histories minister to this first tendency. The account of induction enshrines a regimen of actively seeking out negative instances to eliminate candidate explanations of phenomena. It is clearly designed to counteract the latter, pervasive, human propensity.

Book II of the *Novum Organum* brings its own interpretive difficulties for the reader who goes to it looking for anything like a systematic, step-by-step 'discourse on method' for conducting any particular induction. Only ten out of fifty-two sections of the text cover eliminative induction. Thirty-one sections by contrast enumerate twenty-seven 'prerogative instances' which are presented as 'aids' to the induction of true axiomata, defining the true metaphysical forms in nature (1869: Bk 2, secs 1–10). Yet leading commentators still divide on just what that 'aid' consists in.[7]

'[N]atural and experimental history is so various and diffuse that it confounds and distracts the understanding, unless it be ranged and presented to view in a suitable order', Bacon comments in *Novum Organum* (Bk 2, sec. 10). The observations collected concerning the phenomena at issue – to use Bacon's famous example, heat – should accordingly be tabulated. Three tables should be drawn up. First, there is an exhaustive 'positive' table. This should list all known phenomena in which heat is present in nature. Bacon inventories twenty-eight such examples of hot things, from celestial (the sun, fiery meteors) to terrestrial phenomena (fire, sparks, air confined in caverns, vitreous substances, quicklime sprinkled with water, etc.). Next, and more decisively, a table of negative instances should be compiled. This 'subjoins' to each of the confirming instances of the first table matching 'negative' examples of phenomena in which one might expect heat to be present, but wherein – despite our anticipations – it is *not* found: 'and the absence of the given nature inquired of in those subjects ... that are most akin to the others in which it is present and forthcoming' (Bk 2, sec. 12). The third 'table of degrees' collects that host of phenomena wherein the form at issue is present in different degrees: from objects which seem unable to bear any degree of heat (like snow, to continue Bacon's example); through objects readily able to be heated, like sulphur or naphtha; flames of varying kinds and temperatures.

The goal of the process of tabulation is to enable an exhaustive, ordered review of the instances from our natural histories. We are then to seek out, by this survey, such a 'nature' as is always present or absent with the sought-after form. It should also 'always decrease when the nature in question decreases, and in like manner always increase when the nature in question increases' (Bk 2, sec. 13). In this search, it is the second table of 'negative instances' that does the most work: '[f]or wherever a case is established of negation, privation, or exclusion, there is some light given towards the invention of Forms' (2011: 419). When we see that heat both *is and is not sometimes* present in different heavenly bodies, elements, liquids, admixtures, the expansion of whole bodies, motion, destruction, and so on we can successfully 'tick these' off as candidates for what heat essentially must be, as a natural form. The true form of heat (for Bacon, the rapid, expansive, upwards movement of microscopic constituents of bodies) is the last candidate explanation standing, as it were. It alone always accompanies heat, is never absent when heat is present, and always increases and decreases in direct relation to the increase and decrease of warmth. Rather than forming an anticipation of nature and trying then to either force or explain away apparently contradictory data, we see that this approach proceeds 'by negatives and exclusions elicited and brought forth as it were out of darkness and night', in stages towards a true explanation. 'To God, truly, the Giver and Architect of Forms, and it may be to the angels and higher intelligences, it belongs to have an affirmative knowledge of forms immediately', Bacon (1869: Bk 2, sec.

15) muses: 'But this assuredly is more than man can do, to whom it is granted only to proceed at first by negatives, and at last to end in affirmatives after exclusion has been exhausted.'

The prerogative instances that follow the sections dedicated to this induction by exclusion are adduced by Bacon as aids to speeding the eliminative inductive work. In Stephen Gaukroger's (2001: 153-4) telling assessment, they

> enable one to seek out the most informative kinds of case, avoid dead-ends, collect the clearest and most unambiguous evidence, and so on ... They show the different probative values, degrees of relevance, and heuristic values that different kinds of observation have, and are an invaluable guide as a detailed account of observational and experimental practice without precedent and unparalleled in detail and scope not only in Bacon's times but since.

With that said, most leading commentators devote little space to their analysis (excluding 'the instance of the fingerpost' or *instantiae crucis* [1869: Bk 2, sec. 36]).[8] Bacon does not make things easier by announcing (Bk 2, sec. 21) that these instances are the first of some eight further parts of his organon, which he never then presents. The definition of heat that he develops in the sections of the text on eliminative induction is also qualified as a 'first vintage', not a full exemplar of Baconian induction (Bk 1, sec. 20). The instances themselves are also grouped into three genii. Five are 'aids to the senses', not induction per se. A further seven are aids to 'operation', not the discovery of forms at all.

Finally, the five numerically central of the fifteen speculative instances adduced to aid the understanding (the instances number six to ten) are described by Bacon in terms that clearly mark these off as involving exercises to educate inquirers, preliminary to their inductive seeking out of particular forms. 'A collection of them should be begun at once, as a sort of particular history', Bacon comments (Bk 2, sec. 32). His reasoning is therapeutic or pedagogical. It points back to the epistemic psychology that we examined in Section 2.[9] Learning to observe 'conformable instances' between apparently disparate phenomena (like the structures of our ears and caverns, eyes and looking glasses); or 'bordering instances' like moss or platypi that seem to conjoin features of different genii; or singular 'deviating' prodigies within species, are therefore recommended as 'purgatives' to 'withdraw [*sic*] the understanding from things to which it is accustomed'; or for 'correcting erroneous impressions created by ordinary phenomena' and 'curing' the understanding that has been 'depraved by ordinary custom and the common course of things'; or for 'raising and elevating

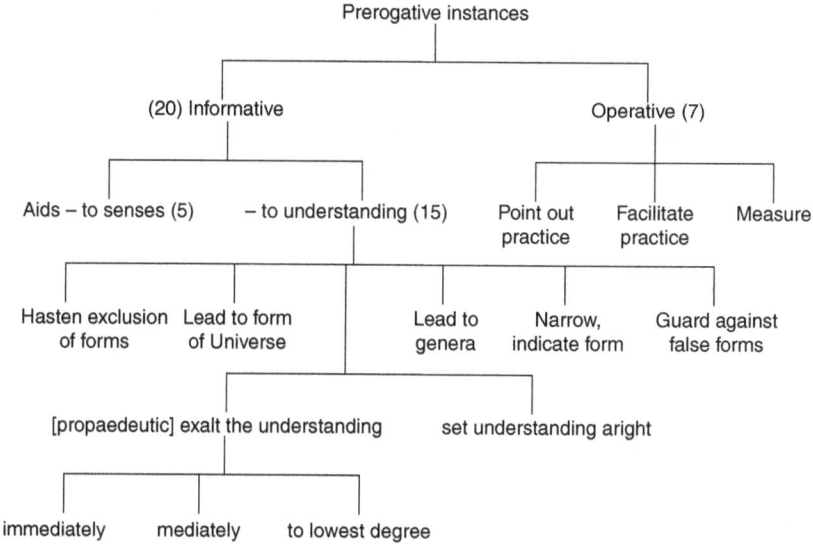

Figure 1.1 *Diviso* of prerogatives from NO II LI 348–9, relative to different epistemic ends.

understanding from specific differences to *genera*, and … dispelling phantoms and false images of things' (Bk 2, secs 32, 38, 35, respectively).

These passages clearly underscore the limits of Bacon's rhetorical boast in the Preface to *Novum Organum* (Bk 1, sec. 16) that 'the course I propose for the discovery of sciences' is almost mechanical, 'leaving but little to the acuteness and strength of wits'. They speak to the strength of the interpretation of figures like Sorana Corneanu that situate Bacon's regulative epistemology as operating within and transforming a tradition of *medicina animi*, looking sideways to contemporary Augustinian and neo-Stoic texts, and backwards to the classical conception of philosophy as a way of life. Certainly, even among the ten prerogative instances adduced as aids to the eliminative induction of true, particular forms in nature, it is remarkable how they direct us again and again to the limits, variations, genesis, dissolution, comparisons, and *conjuncta* of apparent natural forms. It is just as if this new *organon* is recommended by Bacon as much as a machinery to challenge and reform 'idolatrous' intellectual habits in inquirers, as it is also and above all a means to enable the true induction of natural forms. Thus, 'clandestine instances' show us the power of given genii (for instance, the force of attraction between bodies) at their lowest degrees (Bk 2, sec. 25); 'subjunctive instances' direct us to the greatest instance of a form (like whales among mammals), showing the extremes of which nature is capable (Bk 2, sec. 34); 'migratory instances' direct our attention to forms in their genesis and disappearance (Bk 2, sec. 28); 'singular instances' like comets among heavenly bodies challenge established genera (here, heavenly versus terrestrial forms of motion); and 'solitary instances' 'exhibit the nature in question in subjects which have nothing in common', like coloured reflections cast ghostlike on a wall, as against the colours seemingly inherent in different substances' (Bk 2, sec. 22).

While Bacon's *inductio* in these ways takes on and transforms inherited intellectual traditions, it does have to be stressed that the Lord Verulam undoubtedly also does stand at the beginning of the modern conception of a collective, cumulative, and intergenerational natural philosophy (Bk 1, secs 57, 108, 113; Sargent 1996: 147–71). The sheer scope of Baconian natural histories, and the variety of the information they register, recommends the collectivization of research:

> But after having collected and prepared an abundance and store of natural history, and of the experience required for the operations of the understanding or philosophy, still the understanding is as incapable of acting on such materials of itself, with the aid of memory alone, as any person would be of retaining and achieving, by memory, the computation of an almanac. Yet meditation has hitherto done more for discovery than writing, and no experiments have been committed to paper. We cannot, however, approve of any mode of discovery without writing, and when that comes into more general use, we may have further hopes. (1869: Bk 1, sec. 101)

Bacon's emphasis on documentation and the written tabulation of instances also point to this 'externalization' of knowledge (Yeo 2007). A true natural philosophy's means and its benefits alike point, for Bacon, beyond the edification of the inquirers themselves. For knowledge of true natural causes, he reasons, must bring an enlarged capacity to anticipate and generate effects (1893: 90). His goal is a new wedding of theory and practice, contemplation and action (34–5):

> Neither is my meaning, as was spoken of Socrates, to call philosophy down from heaven to converse upon the earth – that is, to leave natural philosophy aside, and to apply knowledge only to manners and policy. But as both heaven and earth do conspire and contribute to the use and benefit of man, so the end ought to be, from both philosophies to separate and reject vain speculations … that knowledge may not be as a courtesan, for pleasure and vanity only, or as a bondwoman, to acquire and gain to her master's use; but as a spouse, for generation, fruit, and comfort.

One reason for hope that the new *organon* can win followers in *Novum Organum* I likewise lies in Bacon's appeal (1869: Bk 2, sec. 113) to how much could be expected 'from united minds and successive ages'. In a famous letter to Playfer, Bacon (1841: 27) had expressed the humble hope that he might sound the bell that called other wits together. The Proem to book II of *Advancement* likewise calls for new communities of inquiry in natural philosophy and more widely: 'For as the proficience of learning consisteth much in the orders and institutions of universities in the same states and kingdoms, so it would be yet more advanced, if there were more intelligence mutual between the universities of Europe than now there is' (1893: 67).

4. Concluding remarks

As we opened by reflecting, the extent and shape of the influence of Francis Bacon's philosophy is disputed. His metaphysics of forms was soon passed over, and its own nature remains contested.[10] Some of his physical claims, like those concerning fire, have proved prescient. Bacon also posited a force of attraction between bodies (allegedly encrypted in the ancient fable of Cupid [Bacon 1857]) whose effects Newton would mathematically formalize later in the seventeenth century. Bacon's work on the methodology of natural histories, alongside his more enigmatic *New Atlantis* (1626), inspired the Royal Society. His theory of induction has been widely accepted as a key progenitor of what later became 'the scientific method', although again its exact nature and influence on later scientific practitioners remains debatable.

This chapter has examined Bacon's criticisms of previous philosophies and conceptions of knowledge (Section 2). We then reconstructed the 'aids' to the senses and memory enshrined in his prescriptions for the compilation and tabulation of natural histories, and the aids to the understanding for the induction of true axioms concerning natural forms of *Novum Organum* II: Bacon's new logic (Section 3). As we proceeded, we have shown that he was not the naïve empiricist he is still widely depicted as having been. We have seen also that he was what we would call an empirical realist, not an instrumentalist in epistemology. It is the sacred marriage of knowledge and the world for which Bacon hopes. This alone, he thinks (1893: 34–5), can beget an offspring of bountiful works ministering to human need. Bacon certainly challenges the contemplative conception of knowledge hailing back to Aristotle – claiming that 'this is that which will indeed dignify and exalt knowledge, if contemplation and action may be more nearly and straitly conjoined and united together than they have been' (35). But this challenge doubly does not bespeak a daemonic exaltation of power. On one hand, it is a charitable motive set deep in the Christian and hermetic traditions that underlies Bacon's hope for new forms of natural philosophy,[11] 'and the effects are of more value as pledges of truth than from the benefit they confer on men' (1869: Bk 1, sec. 124). On the other hand, Bacon insists that a true contemplation of the intricacy and glory of God's works requires more veridical conceptions of the natural world. Otherwise, men can only continue to adore the creations of their own understandings: 'Let men learn (as we have said above) the difference that exists between the idols of the human mind and the ideas of the divine mind. The former are mere arbitrary abstractions; the latter the true marks of the Creator on his creatures, as they are imprinted on, and defined in matter, by true and exquisite touches' (ibid.).

Notes

1 See Jalobeanu (2013: 5–27).
2 See, for example, Harrison (2015: 106–107, 122–4).
3 See Popper (2005: 279).
4 See Giglioni et al. (2016).
5 See Corneanu (2011).
6 See Bacon (1955b: 416; 2012: 39).
7 Cf. Urbach (1987: 163–9), Pérez-Ramos (1989: 243–54), Malherbe (1996: 87), and Gaukroger (2001).
8 The famous 'instances of the fingerpost' stage actions that promise to decide finally between two competing hypotheses (1869: Bk 2, sec. 32). We can think of Galileo's dropping a cannonball and a lighter object from the top of the leaning Tower to test which is true: either (a) the Aristotelian notion of specific weights, or (b) a notion according to which all objects heavier than air fall at the same, or nearly identical, rates.
9 Again see, especially, Corneanu (2011: 14–45).
10 See Pérez-Ramos (1989).
11 See, for example, Cordell (2011).

References

Adorno, T. and Horkheimer, M. (1989), *The Dialectic of Enlightenment*, New York: Continuum.

Bacon, F. (1753), 'VII. To My Lord Treasurer Lord Burghley, 1591', in *Works of Francis Bacon, Volume II*, London: D. Midwinter et al.

Bacon, F. (1841), 'Sir Francis Bacon: His Letter of Request to Doctor Playfer, to Translate the Book of Advancement of Learning into Latin', in B. Montagu (ed.), *The Works of Francis Bacon. A New Edition: With a Biography by Basil Montagu, Volume III*, Philadelphia: Carey & Hart.

Bacon, F. (1857), 'XXVII. Cupid, or the Atom', in *Wisdom of the Ancients*, London: Heinemann, at http://www.bartleby.com/82/17.html.

Bacon, F. (1863a), 'Catalogue of Particular Histories by Titles', in J. Spedding, R. L. Ellis, and D. D. Heath (eds and trans.), *The Works of Francis Bacon, Volume VIII*, Boston: Houghton, Mifflin & Co.

Bacon, F. (1863b), 'Preparative for a Natural and Experimental History [Parasceve]', in J. Spedding, R. L. Ellis, and D. D. Heath (eds and trans.), *The Works of Francis Bacon, Volume VIII*, Boston: Houghton, Mifflin & Co.

Bacon, F. (1863c), 'Rule of the Present History', in J. Spedding, R. L. Ellis, and D. D. Heath (eds and trans.), *The Works of Francis Bacon, Volume IX*, Boston: Houghton, Mifflin & Co.

Bacon, F. (1868), 'Preface for *De Interpretatione Naturae*', in J. Spedding, R. L. Ellis, and D. D. Heath (eds and trans.), *The Letters and the Life of Francis Bacon, including His Occasional Writings, Volume III*, London: Longmans, Green, Reader, and Dyer.

Bacon, F. (1869), *Novum Organum*, in J. Spedding, R. L. Ellis, and D. D. Heath (eds and trans.), *The Works of Francis Bacon: Volume VIII*, New York: Hurd and Houghton.

Bacon, F. (1893), *Advancement of Learning*, ed. H. Morley, London: Cassell.

Bacon, F. (1955a), 'Clue to the Maze (ca. 1607)', in H. G. Dick (ed.), *Selected Writings of Francis Bacon*, New York: Random House.

Bacon, F. (1955b) 'Atalanta; or Profit', in H. G. Dick (ed.), *Selected Writings of Francis Bacon*, New York: Random House.

Bacon, F. (1964), 'The Refutation of Philosophies', in B. Farrington, *The Philosophy of Francis Bacon*, Chicago: University of Chicago Press.

Bacon, F. (2008), 'Of Tribute: The Praise of Knowledge', in B. Vickers (ed.), *Francis Bacon: The Major Works*, Oxford: Oxford University Press.

Bacon, F. (2011), *De Augmentis Scientiarum*, in J. Spedding, R. L. Ellis, and D. D. Heath (eds and trans.), *The Works of Francis Bacon, Volume IV: The Philosophical Works in Translation*, Cambridge: Cambridge University Press.

Bacon, F. (2012), 'Plan of the Work', *Francis of Verulam's Great Instauration*, in F. Rees and M. Wakely (ed. and trans.), *The Oxford Francis Bacon XI. The Instauratia Magna II: Novum Organum and Associated Texts*, Oxford: Oxford University Press.

Cordell, J. (2011), 'Baconian Apologetics: Knowledge and Charity in *The Advancement of Learning*', *Studies in Philology*, 108: 86–107.

Corneanu, S. (2011), *Regimens of the Mind: Boyle, Locke, and the Early Modern* Cultura Animi *Tradition*, Chicago: University of Chicago Press.

Gaukroger, S. (2001), *Francis Bacon and the Transformation of Early-Modern Philosophy*, Cambridge: Cambridge University Press.

Giglioni, G., Lancaster, J. A. T., Corneanu, S., and Jalobeanu, D. (eds) (2016), *Francis Bacon on Motion and Power*, Dordrecht: Springer International.

Harrison, P. (2015), *The Territories of Science and Religion*, Chicago: University of Chicago Press.

Jalobeanu, D. (2013), 'Francis Bacon, Early Modern Baconians, and the Idols of Baconian Scholarship', *Society and Politics*, 7: 5–27.

Malherbe, M. (1996), 'Bacon's Method of Science', in Markko Peltonen (ed.), *The Cambridge Companion to Francis Bacon*, Cambridge: Cambridge University Press.

Merchant, C. (2006), 'The Scientific Revolution and the Death of Nature', *Isis* (Special Focus section on Carolyn Merchant's *The Death of Nature*), 97: 513–33.

Penrose, S. B. L. (1934), *The Reputation and Influence of Francis Bacon in the Seventeenth Century*, New York: Columbia University Press.

Pérez-Ramos, A. (1989), *Francis Bacon's Idea of Science and the Maker's Knowledge Tradition*, Oxford: Oxford University Press.

Popper, K. R. (2005), *The Logic of Scientific Discovery*, London: Routledge.

Rawley, W. (1626), *Manes Verulamiani: Sacred to the Memory of The Right Honourable Lord Francis Baron Verulam, Viscount St. Albans* (London, 1626): at www-site http://hiwaay.net/~paul/bacon/manes/verulam.html, last accessed November 2016.

Sargent, R.-M. (1996), 'Bacon as an Advocate for Cooperative Scientific Research', in Markku Peltone (ed.), *The Cambridge Companion to Bacon*, Cambridge: Cambridge University Press.

Urbach, P. (1982), 'Francis Bacon as Precursor to Popper', *British Journal of Philosophy of Science*, 33: 113–32.

Urbach, P. (1987), *Francis Bacon's Philosophy of Science: An Account and a Reappraisal*, La Salle, IL: Open Court.

Yeo, R. (2007), 'Between Memory and Paper Books: Baconianism and Natural History in Seventeenth-Century England', *History of Science*, 45: 1–46.

2

Gassendi and Hobbes

Stewart Duncan and Antonia LoLordo

1. Introduction

Thomas Hobbes was born in 1688 in Malmesbury, England. Four years later, Pierre Gassendi was born in Champtercier in France. The two men, both of whom had notable philosophical careers, met in Paris in the early 1640s, where they were part of a philosophical group centred on Marin Mersenne (Malcolm 2002: 17). There is little detailed evidence of the personal relationship between Gassendi and Hobbes, largely because almost none of their correspondence survives: just two short letters, one from 1649 and one from 1654 (Hobbes 1994a: letters 62, 66).[1] There are, however, clear similarities between the philosophical approaches of the two men in their published work.[2]

Both Hobbes and Gassendi are often considered materialists.[3] Both wrote a set of *Objections* to Descartes' *Meditations*. Both argued against the Cartesian doctrine of innate ideas and for the claim that all knowledge ultimately derives from the senses. Both were nominalists. And both paid a great deal of attention to method in their discussions of knowledge.

The two philosophers differ, however, in their methodology. Gassendi writes in typical humanist fashion, identifying and explaining a wide variety of past views before going on to present his own alternative. Hobbes just tells the reader what he thinks. The content and orientation of their views is very different as well – in particular, the content and orientation of their epistemologies. Gassendi (1964: iii, 192b) began his career as a sceptic, and although he soon came to reject scepticism, he also rejected the Aristotelian notion of *scientia*, arguing that there is no 'certain and evident cognition of a thing, obtained through an acquaintance with its necessary cause, or by a proof'. In its place, Gassendi presented a probabilistic view that shows us how we can move on in the absence of certain and evident knowledge.

For Hobbes, in contrast, discussion of knowledge is by and large discussion of how to achieve *scientia*, where to have *scientia* of something is to know it through its causes. In his discussion of knowledge, if not elsewhere, Hobbes is roughly Aristotelian: he argues that we should revise our understanding of what *scientia* consists in rather than abandoning the search for *scientia* altogether.

2. Gassendi's attacks on the Aristotelians and on Descartes

In his first published work, the *Exercitationes paradoxicae adversus Aristoteleos* (*Exercises in the Form of Paradoxes against the Aristotelians*), Gassendi uses material drawn from ancient scepticism to attack the doctrine of *scientia*. He relies heavily on the Ten Modes – various ways to show (as he explains in the later *Syntagma*) that 'one and the same thing can appear in different ways to different animals and different men, and even to one and the same man according to his various senses and his various affections' (Gassendi 1964: i, 84a). In the *Exercitationes*, Gassendi uses traditional examples in which 'the judgments of different men concerning the things that are perceived by the senses are very different' (iii, 197b), which he understands as evidence that 'men do not know the inner natures of things' (iii, 203a). The same wine, for instance, tastes sweet to some people and bitter to others (iii, 198ff). How can we know what the wine in itself is truly like? We cannot say that how the wine tastes to a healthy man is how it really is (as healthy men disagree), or that the way the wine tastes to the majority is the way it really is (because there is no reason to assume the majority is right), and so on. Hence, Gassendi concludes (at least at this early, sceptical point in his career), the testimony of the senses cannot be trusted to inform us about the inner natures of things.

This forms the basis for a critique of Aristotelian *scientia*. Gassendi shares the consensus view that 'all of our knowledge either is sensation or proceeds from the senses', and notes that it follows from this 'that we cannot make a judgment about anything unless the senses have first given testimony of it' (iii, 192b). Hence there is no 'knowledge as Aristotle conceived it' (iii, 192a) – that is, no 'certain and evident cognition of a thing, obtained through an acquaintance with its necessary cause, or by a proof' (iii, 192b).

We tend to think of demonstration via causes as the hallmark of Aristotelian *scientia*, but this is not Gassendi's main focus. He is chiefly concerned with another element of the Aristotelian conception of knowledge: that knowledge involves both certainty and evidentness. This was also part of Descartes' conception of knowledge – clear and distinct perception is certain and evident – and Gassendi expressed similar concerns about Descartes' view. A central theme of Gassendi's *Fifth Objections* to Descartes' *Meditations* and his long *Counter-Objections* is that clear and distinct perception cannot do what Descartes wants it to do, namely, serve as a criterion of truth that is immune to sceptical doubt.[4]

Gassendi has two main lines of objection to the Cartesian doctrine of clear and distinct perception. The first is familiar: he claims that Descartes' argument for the veracity of clear and distinct perception relies on a premise concerning the existence of God, while his argument for the existence of God relies on a premise concerning the veracity of clear and distinct perception. But Gassendi also has another, less familiar, concern about clear and distinct perception. Is there, he asks, a distinction between perceptions that are *genuinely* clear and distinct and those that merely *seem* to be clear and distinct? Are we supposed to determine which of our perceptions are genuinely clear and distinct on the basis of the phenomenology alone, or is there something else to which we can appeal?

Whichever way Descartes responds, he faces an insuperable difficulty. Suppose he says that clarity and distinctness involve something more than mere phenomenology – that there's a distinction between genuinely clear and distinct perception, and perception that just seems clear and distinct. If so, Gassendi argues, then we need a criterion to distinguish genuine clarity and distinctness from merely apparent clarity and distinctness. But, he continues, Descartes has no such criterion to offer. Hence, clarity and distinctness cannot be the criterion of truth.

Suppose, however, that Descartes denies that perceptions can seem clear and distinct without being genuinely clear and distinct. In other words, suppose that we can determine whether a perception is genuinely clear and distinct just by introspecting. If so, Gassendi argues, we will be faced with the existence of inconsistent clear and distinct perceptions. Disagreement is rampant, and different people – all of whom are honest, and all of whom have thought carefully about the matter at hand – perceive different and incompatible things with apparent clarity and distinctness (Gassendi 1964: iii, 315a). Worse, an individual may clearly and distinctly perceive that *p* at one time and that *not-p* at another. For instance, Gassendi says, as a youth he clearly and distinctly perceived that two lines that continually approached each other more closely must eventually meet. Later he learned about asymptotes and came to perceive, with equal clarity and distinctness, that they might not intersect (iii, 314b).

Descartes in fact holds the second view. Anything that seems clear and distinct *is* clear and distinct, at least if you have properly cleared your mind of preconceived notions (1996: vii, 739; 1984: ii, 26). He responds to Gassendi's objection with impatience, insisting (1996: vii, 361; 1984: ii, 249–50) that these inconsistent perceptions are not all genuinely clear and distinct. It is typical of Gassendi that he finds this response impossible to take seriously. Our evidence that different people can perceive inconsistent things with apparent clarity and distinctness is extremely strong: 'the fact that men go to meet death for the sake of some opinion seems to be a perspicuous argument that they perceive it clearly and distinctly' (Gassendi 1964: iii, 317a). Descartes cannot escape the existence of inconsistent clear and distinct perception unless he allows a distinction between genuine clarity and distinctness and merely apparent clarity and distinctness. And if he allows such a distinction, his alleged criterion becomes useless.

3. Gassendi's middle way

In his magnum opus, the enormous *Syntagma philosophicum*, Gassendi (1964: i, 79b) outlines his own epistemology:

> [A] certain middle way between the sceptics ... and the dogmatists should be followed. For the dogmatists do not really know all the things they suppose they know, and they do not have an appropriate criterion for judging those things. However, it does not seem that all the things that are thrown into dispute by the sceptics are so unknown that we cannot have some criterion for judging them. And because the majority of the things that the dogmatists suppose they know are really unknown, too often in physics the occasion arises for declaring that we are fortunate when we arrive not at what is true but at what is probable.

This middle way between dogmatism and scepticism has been called mitigated or constructive scepticism (Popkin 2003: 112–27). Its central claim is that although we cannot know the essences of things in the way the Aristotelians and Cartesians hoped, or achieve the sort of certainty they wanted, we can still have some genuine knowledge. This knowledge is sufficient for everyday life and for meaningful scientific enquiry, although it does not rise to the level of *scientia*. Popkin, introducing this view, connects it in particular with Mersenne and Gassendi (112).[5] Later, he also associates Hobbes with it.[6] There are some reasons to be cautious about the term 'mitigated scepticism' – the position involved is often not what today's epistemologists would label 'scepticism'. Nevertheless, Gassendi did attempt to find a position between the extremes of scepticism and dogmatism.

Gassendi's (1964: i, 85b) middle way offers a new kind of criterion:

> [W]henever someone objects that there ... is no criterion ... because anyone who says that there is does so either without a demonstration or with one, but that either way, etc., it can be said, first, that we have some demonstration. Although it is not an Aristotelian demonstration or a demonstration which requires a precise investigation of some previous sign or criterion or the like, it is the sort of demonstration that men who are prudent, intelligent, and furnished with good sense will generally accept as a proper reason and which cannot be contradicted except out of sheer contrariness.

Gassendi is referring to the Two Modes of ancient scepticism:

> [W]hen Pyrrhonism was revived, some other Modes were added ... The first is what can be called *regressus in infinitum*, where what has been put forward to confirm something, is said to require confirmation by another thing, and that again by another, so that no way out can be found. The second is *diallelus* ... where it is shown that someone who is giving a proof asserts one thing in order to establish a second, and asserts the second in order to establish the first ... The last is *hypothetical*, or *from supposition*, where, after something has been supposed, someone asserts that he is permitted to make the contrary supposition. (i, 75b; emphases in the original)

Say that the sceptic's interlocutor asserts that p. The sceptic then asks whether she has a demonstration that p. If she says no, then we have no reason to believe that p. If she says yes – that p is demonstrated by q – then the sceptic asks whether she has a demonstration that q. If the interlocutor replies that q is demonstrated by p, we have a circle and again no reason to believe that p. If she replies that q is demonstrated by r, then the same question is raised about r; and so on, and again we have no reason to believe that p.

Gassendi does not think that we can escape the Two Modes once we are entangled in them, but he does think that we can avoid entanglement in the first place. We can offer a demonstration without having to then show that this demonstration is itself valid, so long as the demonstration is generally accepted by reasonable people and we are not presented with a reason to reject it. For, Gassendi claims, the mere fact that someone can pretend to doubt a demonstration does not call it into question. Only genuine, sincere disagreement does that:

> [A]lthough it is countered that someone who simply makes a declaration and does not prove it should not be believed, and that that the opposite can be

asserted hypothetically and claimed as true by anyone ... who wishes to maintain the other side, it is clear that this can indeed be done in doubtful matters, where neither experience nor some convincing and reasonable argument comes to our support, but it cannot be done without folly in other cases. (i, 86a)

Thus Gassendi treats the Ten Modes and the Two Modes very differently. He takes the Ten Modes seriously because they involve actual disagreement and actual conflicting evidence. Since the Two Modes do not, he sees no reason to entangle ourselves in them. They could be used to achieve universal suspension of judgement, but this would be folly.

4. Gassendi's two criteria

Gassendi offers two criteria of truth – reason and the senses. They apply to different domains. The senses are the criterion of truth for the appearances. My sense of taste, for instance, is the criterion by which I know that honey appears sweet. Gassendi does not spend much time defending this criterion, because he thinks that even the ancient sceptics accepted it. Indeed, he thinks that even *Descartes* accepts it, since Descartes concedes that the sceptical hypotheses of the First Meditation are supposed to affect us only within a limited context and only for a short time.

The second criterion, reason,[7] has a different domain: it informs us about the 'hidden' truths that are 'lurking under the appearances' (Gassendi 1964: i, 80b).[8] This is a form of inference to the best explanation. Appearances are signs of the hidden because they can only exist if there is some appropriate hidden cause. Motion is a sign of the void, for instance, because we observe motion and infer that there must be some empty space for moving bodies to move into (i, 81a). Various cognitive capacities are signs of the existence of a soul (i, 82b). The fact that iron is attracted by a magnet is a sign that there is some power in the magnet (ibid.). The order apparent in the universe is a sign that God exists and created the universe (ibid.). And so on.

In general, Gassendi treats appearances as signs of the internal corpuscular structure of the things that appear to us. When I taste the sweetness of honey, I can thereby know that honey has an internal corpuscular structure that is fitted to produce the sensation of sweetness in me, under current circumstances. This move enables him to show that much of the conflict gestured at in the Ten Modes is illusory. Honey is not by nature sweet or bitter – by nature it has the power to produce the sensation of sweetness in sense organs disposed one way, and bitterness in sense organs disposed another way:

> It seems that one and the same thing can appear in different ways to different animals and different men, and even to one and the same man according to his various senses and his various affections ... But although so many various *Phantasiae* or appearances are created, nevertheless it's clear that there is in the thing or object some general cause that suffices for all the things which are manifest. And so, to whatever extent the effects are not like each other, nevertheless there are two things that are certain and can be proven ... One is that there is a cause in the thing itself, or the object, and the other is that there is a different disposition in the faculties that encounter it. (i, 84a)

Consider the action of the sun, which melts wax but hardens clay. We know that there is something in the sun that enables it to cause both the melting of the wax and the hardening of the clay. And we know that there is some difference between the wax and the clay that explains why the sun melts the first but hardens the second. We know this by the use of reason, just as we know by the use of reason that there must be pores in the skin else sweat could not occur (i, 68b).

This last example is particularly significant for Gassendi. He points out that, although we used to have only inferential knowledge of the pores in the skin, we now know their existence by the senses, using the microscope. Similarly, we used to infer that mites have feet from the way they move, and now we see their feet; we used to infer that the Milky Way is made up of stars and can now see the individual stars that compose it through telescopes (i, 82a). Gassendi imagines that 'many of the things ... which we until now perceive only by understanding will one day, by some instrument thought up by our descendants, will become ... perceived by the senses' (ibid.). This provides sensory evidence that inference to the best explanation is a legitimate source of knowledge. In other words, it shows – using the one criterion that is not, Gassendi thinks, in dispute – that reason too can serve as a criterion.

5. Certainty and probability

The examples of knowledge that Gassendi provides typically do not involve absolute certainty or evidentness. I could be wrong that I am tasting something with an internal corpuscular structure that gives it the power to produce the sensation of sweetness in me. Perhaps I am dreaming, and not actually tasting anything at all. Gassendi accepts this possibility, and grants that if I am in fact dreaming and there is no honey, then the belief I arrive at using reason will be false. The same goes for beliefs arrived at using the senses alone. However, he denies that the possibility of error undermines the epistemic credentials of the beliefs I have when I'm *not* dreaming or otherwise in error. Consider another example:

> [T]he sense of pain which still appears to be in a foot or hand after the limbs have been amputated can sometimes deceive ... but those who are whole are so certain that they feel pain in the foot or hand which they see pricked that they cannot doubt it. In the same way, because while we live we are alternately awake and asleep, we may be deceived by a dream ... but nevertheless we are not always asleep, and when we are really awake we cannot doubt whether we are awake or asleep. (Gassendi 1964: iii, 388a-b)

Let us reconstruct Gassendi's view in somewhat anachronistic terms. My belief that my foot is injured is justified by my experience of pain in my foot. Now, there may be cases where I have the same experience even though the belief in question is false: cases of phantom limb pain. But this does not show that my experience of pain in my foot cannot justify the belief that my foot is injured. It simply shows that justification does not entail truth.

Gassendi thinks that Descartes' first big mistake is his failure to recognize this. Descartes insists that it is impossible for something I perceive clearly and distinctly to be false. Gassendi objects that if we insist on a justification that entails truth for there to be knowledge, then we will have no knowledge. And he also objects that no such justification is necessary. We can have good reason to believe something even if it could turn out to be false.

This view is part of what has been called Gassendi's mitigated scepticism. It's important to see that Gassendi is sceptical about *scientia* and Cartesian absolute certainty, but not about knowledge in general. In this respect he's in agreement with most contemporary epistemologists who do not consider themselves sceptics of any kind.

6. Hobbes and scepticism

Unlike Gassendi, Hobbes did not engage with scepticism at length in his writing.[9] Indeed, he barely mentioned it.[10] He did, however, respond to possibly the most famous use of sceptical arguments in seventeenth-century European philosophy: Descartes' First Meditation. Hobbes' comment on the First Meditation in his Objections is as follows:

> From what is said in this Meditation it is clear enough that there is no criterion enabling us to distinguish our dreams from the waking state and from veridical sensations. And hence the images we have when we are awake and having sensations are not accidents that inhere in external objects, and are no proof that any such external object exists at all. So if we follow our senses, without exercising our reason in any way, we shall be justified in doubting whether anything exists. I acknowledge the correctness of this Meditation. But since Plato and other ancient philosophers discussed this uncertainty in the objects of the senses, and since the difficulty of distinguishing the waking state from dreams is commonly pointed out, I am sorry that the author, who is so outstanding in the field of original speculations, should be publishing this ancient material. (Descartes 1996: vii, 171; 1984: ii, 121)

One might at first suspect that Hobbes, though he clearly was aware of sceptical arguments, just did not see the point of what Descartes was doing in the First Meditation. But in fact he seems, at least in outline, to agree with Descartes – at least to agree that doubts arise 'if we follow our senses, without exercising our reason in any way'.

The solution, for Hobbes as for Descartes, is to make appropriate use of reason.[11] The difference between them lies in what that appropriate use of reason is. Hobbes, like Gassendi, rejected Descartes' method of discovering essences via clear and distinct intellectual perception. However, unlike Gassendi, Hobbes did not deny that there was such a thing as *scientia*, which was the best sort of knowledge.

Though Hobbes shows little explicit concern with scepticism, it does make sense to think of him as a sceptic about various specific topics. For instance, we might well describe Hobbes as a sort of religious sceptic. In several texts he argues that our knowledge of God – indeed, the very manner in which we can conceive of him – is severely limited. Hobbes argues that our thoughts about God are like the thoughts that a man born blind can have of fire.[12] That man can conceive of fire only as the cause of the warmth he feels, and we can conceive of God only as the cause of everything around us. Though such restricted views about what we can think and know about God are hardly unknown, they are in a sense sceptical, for they deny that we have, or can have, knowledge which many people take us to have.[13]

7. Hobbes, perception, and 'the modern philosophy'

Perhaps the most prominent part of Hobbes' theory of knowledge is his theory of perception. This appears in chapter 1 of *Leviathan*, and chapter 2 of the *Elements of Law*. In these works, Hobbes begins with views about individual human beings, before moving on to views about groups of humans (i.e. political philosophy). The first part of the theory he presents is his theory of sense. This theory is also presented in chapter 25 of *De Corpore*. Though the three presentations differ slightly, the central views are the same in each case – the differences seem to arise from differences in which Hobbes wanted to emphasize in each context, rather than from any change in his view on these issues between the early 1640s and the mid-1650s.

We might relate Hobbes here to a general view about what was distinctive about modern philosophy. Hume (2000: I.iv.4.) states it as follows: 'The fundamental principle of that philosophy is the opinion concerning colours, sounds, tastes, smells, heat and cold; which it asserts to be nothing but impressions in the mind, deriv'd from the operation of external objects, and without any resemblance to the qualities of the objects.'[14] Looking at Hobbes' (1994b: ii, 4) accounts of sense, we find him arguing, as he puts it in the *Elements of Law*,

(1) That the subject wherein colour and image are inherent, is not the object or thing seen.
(2) That that is nothing without us really which we call an image or colour.
(3) That the said image or colour is but an apparition unto us of that motion, agitation, or alteration which the object worketh in the brain or spirits, or some internal substance of the head.
(4) That as in conception by vision, so also in the conceptions that arise from other senses, the subject of their inherence is not the object, but the sentient.

Thus Hobbes argues that colour is an appearance, or a feature of appearances, not a feature of any external object.[15] The perceived colour is (merely) causally related to the perceived object. Hobbes is, in this sense, modern. Gassendi, with his views about appearances as signs of corpuscular structure, is similarly modern.[16]

How far did Hobbes take this view? Certainly he held it about the qualities commonly called secondary, such as colour. Indeed, colour is his main example in chapter 2 of the *Elements of Law*. Did Hobbes also hold this view about other perceived qualities? Though it is not entirely clear, in the above passage, what 'image' refers to, earlier in *Elements* 2.4 it seems clear that Hobbes wants to treat shape as well as colour. And later in the chapter, he says more:

> And from thence also it followeth, that whatsoever accidents or qualities our senses make us think there be in the world, they are not there, but are seemings and apparitions only. The things that really are in the world without us, are those motions by which these seemings are caused. And this is the great deception of sense, which also is by sense to be corrected. (ii, 10)

All of our perceptions of qualities are apparently on a par here. The accidents and qualities we seem to perceive are 'not there' in 'the world', but only in us. Motion is a special case. But even then we cannot perceive all of the relevant motions (such as the ones that give rise to the perceptions of particular colours). There is indeed a great 'deception'. Some might want to apply the word 'scepticism' here, but Hobbes does not.

Indeed, Hobbes does not suggest that we lack of knowledge of the object, even if our perceptions do not present it as having the same features it really has. Rather he thinks we can, using a combination of sense and reason, learn that we should not identify the features of appearances and the features of objects, and learn that the appearances are caused by motions, not by qualities that resemble the appearances.

8. Knowledge and scientific knowledge

That account of sense is only part of Hobbes' more general account of knowledge. Another thing we need to acknowledge is that Hobbes thought there were different kinds of knowledge. Consider what he says in the first paragraph of chapter 6 of *De Corpore* (the chapter on method):

> Philosophy is knowledge [*cognitio*], acquired through correct reasoning, of the phenomena or apparent effects from the conceived production or a certain possible generation, and of the production which was or could be from the conceived apparent effect. The *method* of philosophizing *is therefore the shortest investigation of effects through known causes, or of causes through known effects.* Moreover then, we are said *to know* an effect *scientifically* [*scire*] when we know [*cognoscimus*] *of its causes that they are, and in what subject they inhere, and in what subject they introduce the effect, and in what manner they produce it.* And accordingly, scientific knowledge [*scientia*] is τοῦ διότι or of causes; all other

knowledge [*cognitio*], which is called τοῦ ὅτι, is either sense, or imagination or memory remaining after sense.[17]

Hobbes here distinguishes between two things we might call knowledge – both of which, indeed, his seventeenth-century English translator called knowledge.[18] These are, in Latin, *scientia* and *cognitio*. *Scientia* – which we might call scientific knowledge, though this too has potentially misleading connotations – is the best sort of knowledge. *Cognitio* is, or at least can be, a sort of knowledge, but falls short of *scientia*.

Consider here the account of the human mind that Hobbes (1994c) builds up in the early chapters of *Leviathan*. As he develops this account, he discusses sense and memory and experience. He does grant that there is knowledge here, though it is not of the best sort: 'sense and memory are but knowledge of fact' (v, 17). Building on those, he gives an account of prudence, which is a sort of correct prediction, based on experience:

> Sometime a man desires to know the event of an action; and then he thinketh of some like action past, and the events thereof one after another; supposing like events will follow like actions ... Which kind of thoughts is called *foresight*, and *prudence*, or *providence*; and sometimes *wisdom*; though such conjecture, through the difficulty of observing all circumstances, be very fallacious ... it be called prudence, when the event answereth our expectation. (iii, 7; emphases in the original)

Prudence, then, is a sort of correct prediction, based on experience. But for all the value of sense and memory and indeed prudence, Hobbes nevertheless contrasts them with science.

This Hobbesian science (or *scientia*) does not include everything we might call science. For one thing, Hobbes is often talking about a sort of knowledge, rather than an area of enquiry. Moreover, Hobbes thinks that *scientia* is not possible in some of the fields we might regard as sciences. Thus he excludes both natural and political history from philosophy, because they are 'but experience, or authority, and not ratiocination'.[19]

Hobbes develops this sort of categorization further in chapter 9 of *Leviathan*. There, after distinguishing science from history, he distinguishes different sciences by their subject matter. Hobbes here appears to be approaching the notion of a science as an area of enquiry, rather than of a kind of knowledge, though that second notion is certainly at work too. His list of sciences includes geometry, astronomy, meteorology, and optics, but also some more surprising examples (in particular, astrology).[20]

That gives us an idea of areas in which we might hope to have *scientia*. But what is *scientia* (other than simply being a good sort of knowledge) and why is it so good? In chapter 6 of *De Corpore*, Hobbes discusses method, the correct way to try to achieve *scientia*. Here we focus on one important aspect of Hobbes' view: the role of causes. Scientific knowledge, Hobbes says, is of causes. And we '*know* an effect *scientifically when we know of its causes that they are, and in what subject they inhere, and in what subject they introduce the effect, and in what manner they produce it*'.[21] The best sort of knowledge, for Hobbes, is causal understanding.

There has been considerable debate about how these views relate to Hobbes' other views about method.[22] However exactly we resolve this debate, it remains clear that Hobbes' account of *scientia* focuses on causal explanation. That itself suggests the question of when and how we can know what the causes are. Hobbes himself was aware of this, and suggests a restrictive answer. We can and do know the causes, and thus have *scientia*, in geometry and in civil science (political philosophy). Elsewhere, however (even in proper philosophical or scientific investigation), our grasp on causes is less secure, and we lack *scientia*.

Seeing Hobbes' positive evaluation of geometry here, we might associate him with a general trend among early modern philosophers to praise the successes of mathematics and look for a way, through method, to associate philosophy more closely with mathematics.[23] Hobbes' (1839) approach to that is to place civil science – which is to say, his own political philosophy – on the same footing as geometry. For there, as in geometry, we can really know the causes:

> Geometry therefore is demonstrable; for the lines and figures from which we reason are drawn and described by ourselves; and civil philosophy is demonstrable, because we make the commonwealth ourselves. But because of natural bodies we know not the construction, but seek it from the effects, there lies no demonstration of what the causes be we seek for, but only of what they may be. (vii, 184)

In the geometrical and political cases, we ourselves make the things we are investigating, so we know their causes. In other cases – say we want to investigate the workings of the tides – we can suggest what the causes might be, but cannot be so sure of what they are.

Hobbes' views about causal explanation connect to another important aspect of his view, an emphasis on definitions.[24] In the Epistle Dedicatory to *De Corpore*, Hobbes said that he was 'confident ... that in the three former parts of this book all that I have said is sufficiently demonstrated from definitions; and all in the fourth part from suppositions not absurd' (i, xi). Part I is on 'Computation or Logic', Part II on 'The First Grounds of Philosophy', Part III on 'Proportions of Motions and Magnitudes', and Part IV on 'Physics, or the Phenomena of Nature'. Thus, Hobbes thought that all of his system, from logic through metaphysics, and through geometry to the account of refraction and reflection at the end of Part III, was grounded in definitions. Once we leave geometry for physics, and the realm in which we do not know the causes, we also lack definitions.

Explaining by citing causes, and explaining by deducing from definitions, seem however to be different enterprises. Ultimately, one wants an account of how these two aspects of Hobbes' method are related. In several cases, though not all, the connection appears to be that the definitions state causes. Consider, for example, the definitions of 'line', 'length', and 'point': 'Though there be no body which has not some magnitude, yet if, when any body is moved, the magnitude of it be not at all considered, the way it makes is called a *line*, or one single dimension; and the space, through which it passeth, is called *length*; and the body itself, a *point*.'[25] Each of those key geometrical notions is defined by describing what causes such a thing.

There are also non-geometrical examples. For example, at the point in chapter 17 of *Leviathan* – 'Of the Causes, Generation, and Definition of a Commonwealth' – where we might expect a definition of 'commonwealth', and where Hobbes (1994c: xvii, 13) emphasizes the word in the text, as if he has defined it, what he has actually done is state how a commonwealth is caused:

> This is more than consent, or concord; it is a real unity of them all, in one and the same person, made by covenant of every man with every man, in such manner, as if every man should say to every man *I authorise and give up my right of governing myself to this man, or to this assembly of men, on this condition, that thou give up thy right to him, and authorize all his actions in like manner*. This done, the multitude so united in one person is called a COMMONWEALTH, in Latin CIVITAS. (Emphasis in the original)

Scientia is, for Hobbes, the best sort of knowledge, and is possible for us, but seemingly only in limited realms.[26] Though there is nothing about the subject matter of physics per se that means we cannot have *scientia* there, we are in practice unable to know what the causes of many physical phenomena are, and so cannot have *scientia* of them. *Scientia* remains in Hobbes' account, unlike Gassendi's, and Hobbes thinks it is present in two important sciences. But he also finds it to be absent in all other sciences. So, perhaps there is a way in which, on this issue, Hobbes and Gassendi are closer than they first appear.

Notes

1. Gassendi is also mentioned in Hobbes' other correspondence, largely that with Samuel Sorbière, who in 1661 recalled 'delightful conversations with Mersenne, Gassendi, and yourself' (Hobbes 1994a: letter 142).
2. In the Epistle Dedicatory to *De Corpore*, Hobbes (1839: i, p. ix) praised the way that astronomy and natural philosophy had 'been extraordinarily advanced by Johannes Keplerus, Petrus Gassendus, and Marinus Mersennus'.
3. In Gassendi's case, inaccurately. In the *Fifth Objections* to the *Meditations*, he argues that Descartes has not ruled out the materialist alternative. But in his *Counter-Objections* (1964: iii, 369a) he makes clear that he does not himself accept the materialist view: 'I hold by faith that the mind is incorporeal.' And in the *Syntagma*, he gives arguments for the immateriality of the mind (iii, 441b-2.451b).
4. Gassendi was so upset by the condescending tone of Descartes' *Replies* that he answered them with a book-length set of *Counter-Objections*; the whole exchange was published as the *Disquisitio Metaphysica* – now in volume 3 of Gassendi (1964).
5. On Mersenne and mitigated scepticism, see Dear (1984: 173–205) and Popkin (2003: 113–20).
6. 'Both Hobbes' and Gassendi's answers to Descartes are part of their efforts to present new views for the new science in terms of a "mitigated" or "post-" sceptical attitude' (Popkin 2003: 192).
7. Calling reason the criterion may surprise some readers, who are used to thinking of Gassendi as an empiricist. But notice that what reason is doing here is making an inference from what is observed: the source of knowledge here is reason plus the senses.
8. These hidden truths are contrasted both with things that are only circumstantially hidden (e.g. a fire that is too far in the distance for us to see) and with things that are entirely hidden, in the sense that humans cannot possibly come to know them (Gassendi 1964: i, 68b-69a).
9. Some scholars think that scepticism forms an important context to Hobbes' work. Even if that were the case, it would still be notable that explicit engagement is largely absent. Here see Tuck (1988a,b), Popkin (1992: 8–49; 2003: 189–207), and Paganini (2003a,b, 2015).
10. Popkin (1992) notes only one passage in *De Corpore* (Hobbes 1839: i, 63) and one in the *Six Lessons* (vii, 184). Popkin (2003: 207) describes Hobbes as 'almost oblivious to his contemporary epistemological sceptics, and far more cautious than his contemporary religious ones'.
11. Cf. Laird (1968: 160): 'In the main, therefore, Hobbes was a joyful rationalist, relying confidently upon individual insight.'

12 See the fifth of Hobbes' *Objections* to Descartes' *Meditations* (Descartes 1996: vii, 179–80; 1984: ii, 126–7) and Hobbes (1994c: 11.25). We cite passages in *Leviathan*, *De Corpore*, and the *Elements of Law* by chapter and paragraph.
13 Popkin (1992) discusses the 'religious scepticism' of denying that Moses was the author of all the Pentateuch. On this issue, see also Malcolm (2002: 383–431).
14 See also the description of what the 'new philosophy' holds in the speech of the second *abbé*, 'a good philosopher', in note B to the article 'Pyrrho' in Bayle's *Dictionary* (1991: 196–7).
15 On discussions of such Galilean ideas by Hobbes, Gassendi, and other members of the Mersenne circle, see Tuck (1988a).
16 See Section 3 above.
17 This translation is based upon, but modifies, that of Hattab (2014: 469–70); emphases in the original.
18 On the translation, see Hattab (2014: esp. 469–70).
19 Hobbes, *De Corpore* 1.8, in Hobbes (1839: I, 11). Hobbes also there excludes, for various reasons, theology, 'the doctrine of angels', knowledge acquired by divine revelation, and 'the doctrine of *God's worship*'. Some will no doubt suspect that these exclusions are a cover for atheism. But on the face of it Hobbes is saying that there is such possible knowledge, but it is not the same sort of knowledge as one seeks in philosophy.
20 Hobbes lists astronomy as a science in this chapter in the 1651 English edition, but not in the rather different chapter in the 1668 Latin edition.
21 Hobbes, *De Corpore* 6.1, in Hobbes (1839: i, 66); emphasis in the original.
22 For a very helpful recent discussion, see Hattab (2014).
23 Gassendi is an exception here: despite his admiration for Galileo, his physics is rarely quantitative and he expresses no desire to emulate the alleged certainty of mathematics.
24 For a recent discussion of the role of definitions in Hobbes' view, see Adams (2014).
25 Hobbes, *De Corpore* 8.12, in Hobbes (1839: I, 111).
26 See Jesseph (2009).

References

Adams, M. P. (2014), 'Hobbes, Definitions, and Simplest Conceptions', *Hobbes Studies*, 27: 35–60.

Bayle, P. (1991), *Historical and Critical Dictionary: Selections*, trans. R. H. Popkin, Indianapolis: Hackett.

Dear, P. R. (1984), 'Marin Mersenne and the Probabilistic Roots of "Mitigated Scepticism"', *Journal of the History of Philosophy*, 22: 173–205.

Descartes, R. (1984), *The Philosophical Writings of Descartes*, 3 vols, ed. and trans. J. Cottingham, R. Stoothoff, and D. Murdoch, Cambridge: Cambridge University Press.
Descartes, R. (1996), *Oeuvres de Descartes*, 11 vols, ed. C. Adam and P. Tannery, Paris: Léopold Cerf.
Gassendi, P. (1964), *Petri Gassendi Opera Omnia in sex tomos divisa*, 6 vols, Stuttgart-Bad Canstatt: Frommann-Holzboog.
Hattab, H. (2014), 'Hobbes's and Zabarella's Methods: A Missing Link', *Journal of the History of Philosophy*, 52: 461–85.
Hobbes, T. (1839), *The English Works of Thomas Hobbes*, ed. Sir W. Molesworth, London: Bohn.
Hobbes, T. (1994a), *The Correspondence of Thomas Hobbes*, ed. N. Malcolm, Oxford: Oxford University Press.
Hobbes, T. (1994b), *The Elements of Law*, ed. J. C. A. Gaskin, Oxford: Oxford University Press.
Hobbes, T. (1994c), *Leviathan*, ed. E. Curley, Indianapolis: Hackett.
Hume, D. (2000), *A Treatise of Human Nature*, ed. D. F. Norton and M. J. Norton, Oxford: Oxford University Press.
Jesseph, D. (2009), '*Scientia* in Hobbes', in T. Sorell, G. A. J. Rogers, and J. Kraye (eds), *Scientia in Early Modern Philosophy*, Dordrecht: Springer.
Laird, J. (1968), *Hobbes*, New York: Russell & Russell.
Malcolm, N. (2002), *Aspects of Hobbes*, Oxford: Oxford University Press.
Paganini, G. (2003a), 'Hobbes among Ancient and Modern Sceptics: Phenomena and Bodies', in G. Paganini (ed.), *The Return of Scepticism: From Hobbes and Descartes to Bayle*, Dordrecht: Springer.
Paganini, G. (2003b), 'Hobbes and the Continental Tradition of Scepticism', in J. R. M. Neto and R. H. Popkin (eds), *Scepticism in Renaissance and Post-Renaissance Thought: New Interpretations*, Amherst, NY: Humanity.
Paganini, G. (2015), 'Hobbes and the French Skeptics', in J. C. Laursen and G. Paganini (eds), *Scepticism and Political Thought in the Seventeenth and Eighteenth Centuries*, Toronto: University of Toronto Press.
Popkin, R. H. (1992), *The Third Force in Seventeenth-Century Thought*, Leiden: Brill.
Popkin, R. H. (2003), *The History of Scepticism: From Savonarola to Bayle*, Oxford: Oxford University Press.
Tuck, R. (1988a), 'Optics and Sceptics: The Philosophical Foundations of Hobbes's Political Thought', in E. Leites (ed.), *Conscience and Casuistry in Early Modern Europe*, Cambridge: Cambridge University Press.
Tuck, R. (1988b), 'Hobbes and Descartes', in G. A. J. Rogers and A. Ryan (eds), *Perspectives on Thomas Hobbes*, Oxford: Oxford University Press.

3

Descartes

Anik Waldow

1. Introduction

Descartes' *Meditations on First Philosophy* (1641) aim to establish the foundation of knowledge, but before this happens they take the reader on a journey that leaves nothing as it is. Already a few paragraphs into Meditation I, some of the most firmly established beliefs no longer seem certain, not even the belief that the meditator exists as the embodied being he takes himself to be: 'Suppose that I am dreaming, and that these particulars – that my eyes are open, that I am moving my head and stretching out my hands – are not true. Perhaps indeed I do not even have such hands or such a body at all' (1964–76: vii, 19; 1984: ii, 13). Casting doubt on our ability to know that we exist as bodies within the world of matter is not a mean feat. It goes to the heart of who we think we are and what it is that constitutes our lives. After all, if my own body cannot be known to exist in the way in which I perceive it, then it cannot be known either whether I have embodied senses capable of revealing to me what exists in the world, and apart from the inner events that I take to be my thoughts and feelings. So what comes under scrutiny is not just whether or not I have a body, but whether there is a self that has senses through which it can connect with reality.

Radical as this argumentative move is, the meditator's all-absorbing doubt does not last for much longer. Already in Meditation II, he feels compelled to acknowledge that he exists as a thinking thing: 'I am then in a strict sense only a thing that thinks; that is, I am a mind, or intelligence, or intellect, or reason thinking thing – words whose meaning I have been ignorant of until now. But for all that I am a thing which is real and which truly exists. But what kind of thing? As I have just said – a thinking thing' (1964–76: vii, 27; 1984: ii, 18). Given that in this passage all that counts is the self's *thinking*, it seems natural to assume that, for Descartes, the question of whether or not the self has a body that supports the production of thought is irrelevant to his conception of the self.

This chapter seeks to complicate this standard picture of what the Cartesian self is by placing the *Meditations*' dream argument into the wider context of Descartes' earlier and later discussions of the concept of dreaming. More specifically, it will be argued that, for Descartes, dreaming is a mental process during which the body takes over control, so that references to dream states must be understood as indicating that the mind fails to actively guide its thoughts and, because of this, counts as passive. What follows from this account is that dreaming can take place when we are asleep or awake, since all it depends on is passivity of mind. Learning to use the mind actively thus becomes paramount, not only in order to be able to wake up, but also, as will be argued below, in order to be able to actualize ourselves as humans who are distinguished from all other animals through their capacity to organize their lives actively.

Once we understand that, for Descartes, dreaming stands for passivity of mind, it becomes clear that in the *Meditations* more is at stake than the sceptical worry that nothing can be known. It is a work that draws us in, startles and shocks us with madness, solitude, and uncertainty. As such, it offers the perfect opportunity for us to become active in our thinking. This happens when we embark, together with the meditator, on a reflective journey and we learn to use our mental powers in a self-determined way. The ultimate goal is here constituted by the ideal of self-actualization that manifests itself in a life of willed reflection and active self-determinacy. Knowing the truth, of course, also matters for the purpose of the *Meditations*, but, on the interpretation advanced here, it counts as a by-product of a specific use of mind that, besides enabling knowledge, also makes it possible for us to lead a genuinely human life.[1]

Section 2 will show that the knowledge of the self in Meditation II remains incomplete: what is lacking from it is awareness of the fact that many of the ideas investigated at this stage of the *Meditations* are ideas that are grounded in bodily processes. Section 3 will join these insights with Descartes' conception of dreaming as a passive state of mind during which bodily mechanisms hold us firmly in their grip. It will here turn out that, strictly speaking, it is our lack of control in guiding passively produced thoughts, rather than the mere fact that we have a body, that poses the problem for a thoroughly active stance. Section 4 will apply these findings to the *Meditations* in order to show that an activation of the mind is what enables us to escape from the Cartesian dream scenario.

2. Dreaming and the embodied self

As we have seen, Meditation I invokes a concept of dreaming that problematizes the belief in our body by questioning whether the body that we perceive to be ours exists in this manner. Curiously, in his earlier and later writings, Descartes approaches the concept of dreaming from a different angle. Here he treats dreaming as an activity of the imagination, while the imagination is primarily understood as a bodily faculty (1964–76: xi, 27; 1984: i, 104–105).[2] Thus, in the *Treatise on Man* (written during the years 1629–33), he explains that the imagination has its seat in the brain where it produces 'the forms or images' to which the rational soul united with the machine of the body applies itself 'when it imagines some object or perceives it by the senses' (1964–76: xi, 177; 1984: i, 107).[3] This passage tells us that the main task of the imagination consists in producing physical representations in the brain (Gaukroger 1995: 163, 281–5) that then function as the basis of those ideas that the soul forms when it represents empirical objects. (Descartes tends to use the concepts of mind and soul synonymously, and I will follow this usage in this chapter.) Importantly, for Descartes, perceiving and imagining are both processes facilitated by the corporeal imagination. In order to be able to tell whether the mind is perceiving or merely imagining, it is therefore necessary to determine whether or not the represented object is present or instead absent. If it is present, the object acts as the trigger of movements in the brain and, through this, qualifies the resulting mental process as an act of perception. If the object is absent, and lacks this trigger function, the resulting process counts as dreaming, fantasizing, or merely thinking of something that may or may not exist (1964–76: xi, 173–8; 1984: i, 104–107).

A similar account of dreaming is given in Descartes' 1637 *Discourse on the Method*. He here states (ibid.) that it is through the 'corporeal imagination' and the movements of the animal spirits – the smallest particles of the blood – that pass through the brain and impress certain patterns in its fibres that representations of objects can be formed. While the *Treatise* account was more concerned with a reconstruction of what is happening in 'waking, sleep, and dream' (1964–76: vi, 56; 1984: i, 139), Descartes' discussion in the *Discourse* refers to bodily processes in order to show that the human body is not unlike that of an animal, given that it can move 'without being guided by the will' (ibid.). This last point about the will and its lack of guidance will become important in Section 3, when considering the difference between passive and active states of mind, and I will return to it when taking up this question.

As mentioned above, the *Meditations* begin with an account of dreaming that seems to leave aside the role of the embodied imagination, and yet, as soon as we move to Meditation II, it seems to be back in place, as the following consideration will show (cf. Almog 2002; Shapiro 2005). When reflecting on the epistemic status of ideas that represent the meditator as an embodied being (he here refers to 'the structure of limbs that is called a human body') (1964-76: vii, 27; 1984: ii, 18), he notes: 'If the "I" is understood strictly as we have been taking it [viz., as a thinking thing], then it is quite certain that knowledge of it does not depend on things of *whose existence I am as yet unaware*; so it cannot depend on any of the things which I *invent in my imagination*' (1964-76: vii, 27-8; 1984: ii, 18-19; emphases added). 'Inventing something' here stands for a state in which the perceived thing – in this case, the human body – may or may not be there, as the meditator suggests when saying that this 'invention' is of something of which he is 'as yet unaware'. With this reference to the possible existence, and related trigger function of the object that, in the perceptual case, sets the corporeal imagination in motion and thus leads to the representation of an object that is really there, Descartes implicitly relies on the accounts presented in the *Treatise* and the *Discourse*. For here, as much as in these earlier works, it is the question of whether the represented object is present or absent that determines what kind of representational process takes place (i.e. perceiving or rather dreaming/hallucinating/imagining something fictitious).

As we know, in Meditation VI it will be possible for the meditator to be certain that he can trust his senses. What seems to follow from this establishment of the veridicality of the senses is that the bodily images that the meditator encountered at an earlier stage of his investigations – namely, in Meditation II – were in fact veridical perceptions that correctly represented the meditator's body, and as such did not stand for something that he merely imagined. But, of course, in Meditation II this kind of knowledge is not available, so that using the images of his bodily existence to understand what he is would amount to simply accepting what needs to be rejected as dubitable. To flag this point, the meditator compares trusting the imagination, which produces the relevant sensory images of his body, to falling asleep again:

> I know for certain that I exist and at the same time that all such images and, in general, everything relating to the nature of body, could be mere dreams <and chimera>. Once this point has been grasped to say 'I will use my imagination to get to know more distinctly what I am' would seem to be as silly as saying 'I am now awake, and see some truth; but since my vision is not yet clear enough,

I will deliberately fall asleep so that my dreams may provide a truer and clearer representation.' (1964-76: vii, 28; 1984: ii, 19)

The point that deserves our attention here is not simply that being awake brings with it the possibility of seeing the truth. We also need to understand *why* sensing and perceiving the body can be interpreted as types of dreaming. As mentioned above, the primary reason for this is that, in Meditation II, we cannot be sure that the represented thing (the meditator's body) is really present or instead absent. Yet if we knew this, we would be able to say that the meditator *perceives* that he has a body rather than merely *imagines* it to be so. On the basis of this knowledge, the meditator could then scrutinize the perception of his body, similarly to how he scrutinizes the idea of a piece of wax (1964-76: vii, 30-1; 1984: ii, 20-1), to understand better what the images of his bodily existence tell him about his existence as a self.

To say that the meditator's images of the body could in principle be used to better understand what he takes himself to be is, of course, not to argue that the claim that the meditator is a thinking thing is false, or that it does not amount to knowledge proper. For the meditator is rather explicit that this claim is necessarily true and that the images of his body are irrelevant with respect to establishing it (1964-76: v, 25, vii, 28; 1984: ii, 19 and ii, 17). Yet we need to understand that the meditator's knowledge accumulates as the investigation proceeds. Insights gained in Meditation II must therefore be regarded in relation to the stage of investigation at which the meditator finds himself: they stand for what can be known at *that* particular moment, not what is the case as such. Since this is so, the temporarily unknown – in our case, the existence of the embodied self – should not simply be ignored, since it stands for what will become knowledge at a later stage: namely, that the thinking thing is instantiated in the world of matter and that the majority of its thoughts are facilitated by its body.

To make clear what is at stake here, let us turn to the analysis of the thoughts that the meditator encounters in Meditation II, when trying to comprehend better what a thinking thing is. These thoughts are about empirical objects such as wax, hats, and coats of the people on the street (1964-76: vii, 30-2; 1984: ii, 20-1). With respect to the first, the meditator states: 'If I judge that the wax exists from the fact that I touch it, the same result follows, namely that I exist. If I judge from the fact that I imagine it, or for any other reason, exactly the same thing follows' (1964-76: vii, 33; 1984: ii, 22). Thoughts about empirical objects are thus taken to confirm what has been understood before – namely, that processes of thinking, or mental activity more generally (i.e. judging and imagining), reveal that the self exists as a thinking thing. What does not matter in this specific context is whether or not the objects in question are perceived or imagined (in the sense of invented/hallucinated/dreamt).

As we have seen, in works written before the *Meditations* the capacity to represent empirical objects – in our case, a piece of wax – involves the corporeal imagination that, as Descartes writes in the *Treatise*, produces the 'forms or images' (1964–76: xi, 177; 1984: i, 107) to which the mind applies itself when it judges the object in question. Of course, in Meditation II the meditator cannot embrace this physiological theory of representation because he does not even know that he has a body. So we cannot expect him to *know* the fact that he has an idea of wax before his mind requires a brain in which movements of animal spirits, strings, and nerves produce physical representations. Yet Meditation VI renders explicit what has implicitly been suggested since Meditation II – namely, that Descartes remains faithful to his earlier theory of representation. Drawing on the same mechanistic vocabulary as in the *Treatise* and *Discourse*, he here writes:

> When the nerves in the foot are set in motion in a violent and unusual manner, this motion by way of the spinal cord, reaches the inner parts of the brain, and there gives the mind its signal for having a certain sensation, namely the sensation of a pain as occurring in the foot. This stimulates the mind to do its best to get rid of the cause of pain. (1964–76: vii, 88; 1984: ii, 60)

Importantly, in Meditation VI the meditator has already learnt to use his capacities in such a way that he can perceive the truth; how to do this is established in Meditation IV (I will say more about this below). The Meditation VI statement that the human body is involved in processes of perceptual cognition and the production of ideas of corporeal things therefore has the status of a claim that counts as true; which means that it holds, irrespective of whether or not the meditator knows it to be true in Meditation II.

With this in mind, let us now return to the question of what kind of knowledge is given in Meditation II, where the meditator understands himself as a thinking thing. This knowledge remains incomplete: not only does it lack awareness of the fact that the meditator's thinking is instantiated in the material world through his union of body and mind; it also lacks the more general knowledge – the truth of which is stated in Meditation VI – of what is involved in being able to have certain thoughts, such as the thought that there is a piece of wax in front of one. In order to have these thoughts, the meditator has to have a body that, qua imprints in the brain, facilitates the relevant representational process. Crucially, in this particular context thoughts about corporeal things like wax are treated not as random thoughts, but rather as thoughts that the meditator uses to specify what he is: a thinking thing. Failing to see what is required for the production of these thoughts therefore amounts to failing to grasp the full extent of what it is to be a thinking thing.

The purpose of this section was to reveal that the discovery of the self in Meditation II does not exhaustively capture all there is to be known about the meditator's self. What eludes his grasp is the intricate relationship of body and mind in the production of thought. Placed in a more general context of Descartes' writings, this tells us that we have to rethink what it means for him to be embodied and what the challenges of Cartesian selves are when they try to understand their place in the world. In the next section, we will see that one of the major challenges for a creature with a body and a mind is the passivity to which its bodily mechanisms tend to confine it. Activating one's mind here becomes the task that not only promises support in situations in which we find ourselves exposed to body-induced sufferings, but also holds the key to realizing ourselves as the agents of our thoughts and actions.

3. Passivity of mind

As we have seen, for Descartes, dream thoughts are a species of imagined thoughts, while the corporeal imagination is understood as facilitating processes of perception, thinking, inventing, and hallucinating alike. Given this tight link between these various cognitive capacities, it is little surprise that, for Descartes, we can dream even when we are awake. In his correspondence with Princess Elisabeth of Bohemia, he writes in 1645: 'Those [thoughts] which depend only on what the preceding impressions left in the memory and the ordinary agitation of the spirits are dreams, whether they come while asleep or when one is awake, and the soul, determining itself to nothing on its own, follows nonchalantly the impressions found in the brain' (1964–76: iv. 311; 2007: 118–19). Apart from merely stating that we can have dreams while being awake, Descartes here also gives us important clues about what exactly happens when we are dreaming. Thus, he tells us that dreaming consists in the experience of a state of mind that is produced when the soul simply *responds* to what is occurring in the brain, and does not *initiate* actions on its own. Passivity thus seems to lie at the heart of Descartes' concept of dreaming/imagining, and ties it in with his concept of perception, that, as he states in Meditation VI, is also characterized by this passivity: 'There is in me a passive faculty of sensory perception, that is a faculty for receiving and recognizing the ideas of sensible objects; ... these ideas in question are produced without my cooperation and often even against my will' (1964–76: vii, 79; 1984: ii, 55).

We gain a more nuanced picture of what it means to be passive, and thus to be dreaming, if we turn to Descartes' letter to Elisabeth from a few weeks earlier, where he notes: 'There is no one who does not desire to make himself happy [*heureux*], but many do not know the means to do so, and often a bodily indisposition prevents the will from being free. Something similar happens when we sleep, for the most philosophical person in the world, does not know how to prevent himself from bad dreams' (1964–76: iv. 282; 2007: 107). When we have dreams during sleep, he here tells us, we cannot use our will freely, which is also what happens when we are ill. The reason for this is that in dreams, as much as in illness, bodily operations govern our thoughts and leave little or no room for the will to express itself.[4]

Curiously, the context in which Descartes discusses the mechanical character of thought-formation during illness and sleep is provided by Elisabeth's poor health, which Descartes regards as a consequence of the sorrow that she suffers on account of her family's repeated blows of fate. The reason for conceiving of bodily diseases in this way is that, for Descartes, thoughts typically manifest themselves in the movements of animal spirits, hence in bodily phenomena that can then become obstacles to the smooth functioning of other bodily mechanisms. Thus, he writes that a person 'who sees continually represented before her tragedies full of sadness and pity ... accustoms her heart to close itself up and to emit sighs' (1964–76: iv. 219; 2007: 91). The physical consequence of this is that 'the circulation of the blood' becomes 'blocked and slowed'. In this state 'the largest particles of the blood, attaching one to the other, could easily grind up the spleen by getting caught and stopping in its pores' such that the 'more subtle particles, retaining their agitation could alter the lungs and cause a cough'.

Since there is this fundamental connectedness between bodily and mental processes,[5] Descartes recommends to Elisabeth that she treat her melancholia by engaging in intellectually stimulating activities (1964–76: iv. 218; 2007: 91). The aim of this is to divert attention from 'one's imagination and one's senses' and to attend to 'one's understanding alone' (ibid.). Crucially, this form of control does not seek to suppress the pains that we passively receive when our perceptual apparatus and the embodied imagination respond to bad news or disconcerting images with the production of negative thoughts and feelings; rather, it aims to *supplement* passively received mental states with thoughts generated of our own accord, so that it becomes possible for us to feel content in the midst of misery caused by our affective receptivity to the world and other persons.

But what, precisely, does it means to generate thoughts of our own accord? To answer this question, it is useful to have a closer look at Descartes' definition of the difference between actions and passions. In the *Passions of the Soul* (1649) he writes thus:

> Having thus considered all the functions belonging solely to the body, it is easy to recognize that there is nothing in us which we must attribute to our soul except our thoughts. These are of *two principle kinds, some being actions of the soul, others its passions. Those I call its actions are all our volitions*, for we experience them as proceeding directly from our soul and as seeming to depend on it alone. On the other hand, the various perceptions and modes of knowledge present in us may be called its passions, in a general sense, for *it is often not our soul which makes them such as they ar*e, and *the soul always receives them* from the things that are represented by them. (1964–76: xi, 342; 1984: i, 335; emphases added)

This passage states that having passions amounts to receiving ideas that are produced when our perceptual apparatus is affected, while being active stands for an activity of the soul, during which it does not merely *follow* what the body presents to it but actively wills its own course of action. Drawing on this contrast between passively received and wilfully produced thoughts, we thus gain the picture that having thoughts of one's own accord means being active, which in turn denotes a state in which the will gives one's thinking a self-determined direction.

It is important to note here that being active does not require us to abandon our passions. In *Passions of the Soul*, art.107, Descartes states that it is possible for the soul to 'join itself willingly' (1964–76: xi, 408; 1984: i, 366) to certain bodily occurrences, such as in love, which then creates the disposition to experience these occurrences in a specific way: 'Our soul and body are so linked that once we have joined some bodily action with a certain thought, the one does not occur afterwards without the other occurring too' (1964–76: xi, 407; 1984: i, 365). So, the union of body and mind can in fact actively generate passions by involving the will in the channelling of its experiences (Shapiro 2003).[6] More generally, this means that, in order for a mental state to count as active and self-determined, it is not necessary that affective and bodily elements be absent. What really matters is that such elements are part and parcel of a process that involves volition.

At this point it might be objected that, for Descartes, ordinary sense perception involves the judgement of what we see and feel: consider the example of the piece of wax or the perception of people on the street in Meditation II (1964–76: vii, 31–3; 1984: ii, 20–2). The specifically active aspect of judging would here be constituted by the will's affirmation of what the intellect perceives in representations produced by the body, so that perceptions, too, would count as active.[7] To counter this objection, which seems to remove the contrast between perceptions as passive mental states and actively generated thoughts, we only need to remember what Descartes says in the passage cited above – namely, that in perception the soul is in its *receptive* mode. This tells us that there is an important difference between thoughts that come to us passively – in the sense of being triggered by events in our surroundings that we perceive via our perceptual apparatus – and those mental episodes (including rational as well as passionate thoughts, such as intellectual pleasures) that we actively generate by involving the will to a more substantial degree than simply by judging what it is that we perceive.

To be sure, Descartes calls *any* kind of mental state that the mind passively receives a passion, but he also tells us that 'a passion in the soul is usually an action in the body' (1964–76: ix. 328; 1984: i, 328). His claim that 'everything that is not action is passion' (1964–76: iv. 310; 2007: 118) is therefore slightly misleading, because it suggests that activity and passivity are mutually exclusive categories, although both can coexist – namely, as activity in the body and passivity in the mind, or vice versa (Hoffman 1990). Yet, according to what has been said above, it is clear that, for Descartes, bodily activity is fundamentally different from the kind of activity that we encounter in the mind. The reason for this is that typically the first is mechanically triggered and follows fixed causal patterns, while the second is guided by the will.

With this in mind, we have everything in place to fully understand what is at stake when Descartes tells us that dreams are mental states that arise when the soul responds to what it finds within the brain, and *without* determining its thoughts on its own. This statement directly points us to the fact that humans, who exist as unions of body and mind, are at risk of leading the lives of dreamers. This is the case when they simply respond to the deliverances of the body and do not use their will to give their thoughts a self-determined direction. Being a dreamer thus stands for a failure: the failure to make most of the fact that we have a soul that does not only enable us to consciously experience what the body delivers to us via sense and embodied imagination, but also gives us will and reason, and through this the power to manage our thoughts and feelings in an active way. While the will can help us to focus our attention on certain activities, such as the study of intellectually stimulating books that Descartes recommends to Elisabeth, reason makes it possible for us to bring our actions in line with the understanding.[8]

In the next section, I will argue that the concept of dreaming as a passive state of mind, and the demand to become active in one's thinking, lies at the heart of the *Meditations* and crucially shapes the aim of this work. So, what is at stake is not simply the attempt to demonstrate that knowledge can be had, but also the more fundamental aim of transforming the manner in which we think, act, and live. Approached from this angle, it becomes evident that practical questions mix in with Descartes' epistemological queries, thus revealing that the *Meditations* possess a genuinely moral dimension.

4. Activation and self-discovery

In the opening paragraph of Meditation I, the meditator declares that he wants to rid himself of 'a large number of falsehoods' that he 'had accepted as true in [his] childhood' (1964–76: vii, 17; 1984: ii, 12). While in the *Meditations* Descartes gives no reasons for the emergence of false beliefs, in the *Principles of Philosophy* (1644) he explains that so-called childhood prejudices result from the mind's inability to distance itself from body-produced thoughts: 'In our early childhood the mind was so closely tied to the body that it had no leisure for any thoughts except those by means of which it had sensory awareness of what was happening in the body' (1964–76: viiiA. 35; 1984: i, 218). Prejudices thus emerge as states of mind that are *caused* via the perceptual mechanisms of the body. They thereby neatly fit the description of dream states that, as has been argued above, are also characterized by the fact that in dreams the soul simply follows what is placed before it when bodily processes unfold within the brain: the soul thus passively responds to the body and, because of this, can be seen as being caused to behave in a certain way. Notably, prejudices instilled in us by other persons, in principle, also fall under this description; for when we uncritically accept what we hear, see, or read, we passively receive through the perceptual apparatus of the body whatever is placed before us and *without* actively organizing our thinking.

To be sure, Descartes not only invokes prejudices towards the beginning of the *Meditations*, but also leads the reader to a point where the meditator starts speculating about the possibility of being caught up in an eternal dream. In line with the interpretation advanced above, this fear in principle constitutes a variation of the worry already articulated in the opening lines of the First Meditation. This is the fear that, up to this point in the meditator's life, all of his beliefs were passively received rather than actively generated. One important function of the dream hypothesis thus seems to consist in rendering explicit – in a very gripping way – what is implicitly contained in the fear that the mind is governed by prejudices. To claim this is, of course, not to say that the dream hypothesis does not possess all of the other argumentative functions usually attributed to it, such as its challenging the belief that sensory perceptions veridically represent reality.[9] Yet it is important to realize that there is an *additional* function: by confronting the *Meditations*' readers with very uncomfortable thoughts, the dream hypothesis shakes us up and activates passive minds trapped in the slumber of their received opinions.

Now, if it is true that Descartes uses references to dreams in order to flag mental passivity, the possibility of exiting our supposedly endless dream would seem to consist in becoming an active thinker, because only actively formed thoughts do not, in the strict sense of the term, count as dream thoughts.[10] The success of the *Meditations* as a whole would thus depend on how well they succeed in mobilizing active thoughts in their readers, because it is the mind's active participation, rather than the passive absorption of a given set of truths, that counts. Taking his analysis in a similar direction, Daniel Garber (2001: 283) stresses that, for Descartes, 'learning cannot be a spectator sport, a passive absorption of what the teacher has to tell' but must be conceived as a certain form of experience through which truth can be intuited. Gary Hatfield (1986: 50–1) agrees with Garber that it is by way of an active participation in the meditator's reflections that Descartes wants to lead the minds of his readers on the path of truth. However, in Hatfield's discussion the value of becoming active is first and foremost defined in relation to the question of how this activity enables the perception of truth, so that questions about an active use of the mind are treated as being subordinate to questions of knowledge acquisition.

In contrast, on the interpretation advanced here, beliefs ensuing from an engagement with the *Meditations* count as meritorious not simply because they are true, but rather because they have been generated by an active process of thinking. Through this, activity of mind is conceived of as a value that can stand, quite independently of whether or not it leads to true insights – which of course is what usually happens when the mind actively uses its powers of reason and will. An example of what this active use involves is given in Meditation IV, where we learn that, in order to avoid error, we need to actively restrict the will, so that it affirms only what the intellect clearly and distinctly perceives (1964–76: vii,

59–62; 1984: ii, 41–3); otherwise, the will dashes ahead and leads to false beliefs. Apart from establishing that the possibility of having true beliefs requires an active control of the will, Meditation IV thus also clarifies that, in order to overcome the kind of dreaming that, in the context of the *Meditations*, takes the form of being deluded by one's passive state of mind, it is not enough to simply will a certain course of thinking. What needs to be achieved instead is an active attunement of the will to the insights delivered by the intellect.

One of the advantages of stressing that the *Meditations* seek to activate the mind, rather than merely to establish the possibility of knowledge, is that this interpretation highlights that, for Descartes, knowledge questions are part and parcel of the more general project of comprehending the human being through the analysis of two interrelated facts: first, that humans are part of a mechanically organized natural world; and, second, that they have will and reason, so that they can organize themselves freely. Crucially, what matters in this context is not just the question of how knowledge can be acquired, but also the moral question of how to organize one's life in a virtuous way. That this is the project that lies at the heart of many of Descartes' reflections on the human capacity for thought becomes particularly clear if we turn to the *Principles*, a work that recasts major arguments of the *Meditations*, but also synthesizes many of Descartes' earlier natural philosophical works. Originally, he planned to add two separate parts to this work in which he wanted to approach human beings, animals, and plants by analysing their functions in relation to the 'visible universe' that he understands 'as if it were a machine' (1964–76: viiiA. 315; 1984: i, 279). Although these parts were never written, Descartes' intention nonetheless shows that he was convinced that a philosophical treatment of the human being requires a comparative analysis that takes seriously the fact that humans have bodies and, because of this, are organized upon the same mechanistic principles as are all other parts of the material world.

Although within Descartes' framework humans find their place within the greater machine of the universe through their existence as bodies, what renders humans special is that they have a soul (cf. Almog 2008), which brings with it the chance to lead a life that is fundamentally different from the life of ordinary animal machines. In the *Preface* to the French edition of the *Principles* (1647), Descartes makes precisely this point, when writing that 'brute beasts ... have only their bodies to preserve' (1964–76: ixB. 4; 1984: i, 180) while humans can attain 'wisdom', by which he means 'not only prudence in our every day affairs' (1964–76: ixB. 2; 1984: i, 179) but also the kind of knowledge necessary for '*the regulation of our morals and our conduct in this life*' (1964–76: ixB. 4; 1984: i, 180;

emphasis added). So, while the animal simply follows what its bodily impulses dictate, the human being is capable of controlling and regulating its actions, so that a life of wisdom ensues. This control, as Descartes explains in the *Passions*, can be achieved, for instance, by understanding the broader implications of our spontaneously arising action impulses (1964–76: xi, 487; 1984: i, 403) or, as has been discussed in the previous section, by actively creating thoughts that we experience as pleasant when pains and sorrows cause us to suffer.

That it is not merely our capacity for thought that matters to our status as human beings, but also our ability to have a specific kind of life through the active management of our bodily dispositions, is also suggested by Descartes' famous language argument of the *Discourse*. He here states that only humans can make themselves understood, so that the will to communicate one's thoughts becomes an essential feature of human language behaviour (1964–76: vi, 57; 1984: i, 140). Animals, by contrast, are taken to be passive and unable to self-initiate their speech, since it is only through the training they receive that they become capable of making sounds (1964–76: vi, 57; 1984: i, 140). In this context, Descartes also stresses that animals lack reason and thought, which is usually interpreted as his suggesting that animals and humans are different because the latter can think while the former cannot. Yet we need to note that having thoughts is here understood as the mark of an intelligent being that can *act* rather than just *respond*, while the lack of thought that we find in animals denotes a state of being comparable to that of a machine that moves as a mere matter of the unfolding of its internal mechanisms. To emphasize this practical and action-focused aspect of what it means to have thought and intelligence, Descartes writes: 'Even though ... machines might do some things as well as we do them, or perhaps even better, they would inevitably fail in others, which would reveal that they were *acting not through understanding, but only from the disposition of their organs*' (1964–76: vi, 57; 1984: i, 140; emphasis added).

Given that the active-passive distinction plays such a fundamental role in Descartes' comparison between humans and animals, we can now see that the kind of activation of the mind that is at stake in the *Meditations* has a genuinely moral dimension. By stirring up doubt and setting us into action, they help us to overcome our habitual passivity in accepting whatever comes our way. They thereby not only enable us to correct our mistaken beliefs, but, far more fundamentally, also help us to actualize ourselves as humans who are capable of regulating our actions for the purpose of developing a virtuous life.

5. Conclusion

Against this background, it becomes clear that discovering the self as a human self requires more than thinking of it as a thinking thing. Humans, as this chapter has tried to show, are fundamentally different from anything else in the Cartesian universe, precisely because they can act rather than merely passively respond. However, being able to act is something that we have to learn, given that we start our lives as prejudiced and passively responding creatures. The *Meditations* are written as a work that can assist us in achieving this goal, as they provoke active thinking when they challenge our most firmly established opinions, and thus help us to transform our animal-like existence into a truly human life.

All of this suggests that the discovery of the self continues far beyond Meditation II. At this stage, as we have seen in Section 2, the meditator does not yet know that he has a body. He therefore does not yet know what it means to be human, given that, for Descartes, to be human means to be able to actively regulate and manage one's mechanically unfolding sensations, thoughts, passions, and desires. This regulation, as has been argued above, requires that we take care of, and engage with, our bodily dispositions and the way that they affect our thinking. It is therefore not in Meditation II but only in Meditation VI – where the acknowledgement of the body and its sensory apparatus becomes possible – that the meditator can discover that he really is a self that is not only capable of thought, but also able to develop a distinctly human way of life.

Notes

1 See Des Chene (2012) for a study that stresses the importance of the use of the mind.
2 In the *Passions of the Soul*, art. 20, Descartes states that the soul, not the body, is responsible for processes of the imagination when the imagination is concerned with things that we conjure up before our mind or cannot be represented by an image. However, he makes this point in order to clarify that these imaginings involve volitions, and as such constitute a special case of imagining (1964–76: xi, 344; 1984: ii, 336).
3 See Wilson (1999: 495), for an analysis of Cartesian 'ideas' of sense, imagination and memory as physical traces. See Sutton (1998: 100) for an account of mechanistic memory. See Gaukroger (1995: 280–90) for an analysis of Descartes' physiological theory of representation.

4 In articles 34, 43, and 46 of the *Passions of the Soul*, Descartes specifies how it is possible for the will to take an influence on the movements in the brain (1964–76: xi, 354–5, 361–4; 1984: i, 341, 344–5).

5 Leaving aside intellectual love or joy; see Descartes (1964–76: xi, 441; 1984: i, 381). See Brown (2006: 161–2) for a discussion of the intellectual love of God as an emotion that does not involve the imagination, and hence that does not manifest in physiological activity in the material body.

6 In *Passions of the Soul*, art.111, Descartes states a similar point, writing 'when the soul desires anything, the whole body becomes more agile and ready to move than it normally is without any such desire' (1964–76: xi, 411; 1984: i, 367). So here, too, it is a volition that influences how exactly bodily motions manifest themselves and thereby also influences the manner in which a particular passion is generated.

7 See Alanen (forthcoming) for the claim that, for Descartes, 'an attentive grasping, in forming or retrieving and articulating ideas and concepts that structure thinking on which reason operates' is a precondition for having thoughts.

8 See Waldow (forthcoming) for a more detailed account of how activity of mind can become a source of contentment and virtue in addition to being epistemically beneficial.

9 For examples of interpretations that prioritize the epistemic significance of the dream scenario, see Frankfurt (1970), Curley (1978), Williams (1978; 2005), Dicker (1992), and Carriero (2009).

10 See Waldow (forthcoming) for a discussion of the claim that the awakening of the meditator is best conceived as a gradual process.

References

Alanen, L. (2016), 'Self-Awareness and Cognitive Agency in Descartes's Meditations', in M. Gustafsson and E. Minnar (eds), *Philosophical Topics*, 44(1): 3–26.

Almog, J. (2002), *What Am I?* Oxford: Oxford University Press.

Almog, J. (2008), *Cogito? Descartes and Thinking the World*, Oxford: Oxford University Press.

Brown, D. (2006), *Descartes and the Passionate Mind*, Cambridge: Cambridge University Press.

Carriero, J. (2009), *Between Two Worlds: A Reading of Descartes's Meditations*, Princeton: Princeton University Press.

Curley, E. (1978), *Descartes against the Skeptics*, Cambridge: Cambridge University Press.

Des Chene, D. (2012), 'Using the Passions', in M. Pickavé and L. Shapiro (eds), *Emotion and Cognitive Life*, Cambridge: Cambridge University Press.

Descartes, R. (1964–76), *Oeuvres de Descartes*, 12 vols, revised edn, ed. C. Adam and P. Tannery, Paris: Léopold Cerf, 1879–1913.

Descartes, R. (1984), *The Philosophical Writings of Descartes*, 3 vols, ed. and trans. J. Cottingham, R. Stoothoff, D. Murdoch, and A. Kenny, Cambridge: Cambridge University Press.

Descartes, R. (2007), *The Correspondence between Princess Elisabeth of Bohemia and René Descartes*, ed. L. Shapiro, Chicago: University of Chicago Press.

Dicker, G. (1992), *Descartes: An Analytical and Historical Introduction*, Oxford: Oxford University Press.

Frankfurt, H. (1970), *Demons, Dreamers, and Madmen*, Indianapolis: Bobbs-Merrill.

Garber, D. (2001), *Descartes Embodied*, Cambridge: Cambridge University Press.

Gaukroger, S. (1995), *Descartes: An Intellectual Biography*, Oxford: Clarendon Press.

Hatfield, G. (1986), 'The Senses and the Fleshless Eye: The *Meditations* as Cognitive Exercises', in A. O. Rorty (ed.), *Essays on Descartes' Meditations*, Berkeley: University of California Press.

Hoffman, P. (1990), 'Cartesian Passions and Cartesian Dualism', *Pacific Philosophical Quarterly*, 71: 310–33.

Shapiro, L. (2003), 'Descartes' Passions of the Soul and the Union of Mind and Body', *Archiv für Geschichte der Philosophie*, 85: 211–48.

Shapiro, L. (2005), 'What Are the Passions Doing in the Meditations?', in J. Jenkins, J. Whiting, and C. Williams (eds), *Persons and Passions*, Notre Dame, IN: University of Notre Dame Press.

Shapiro, L. (2008), '"Turn My Will Completely in the Opposite Direction": Radical Doubt and Descartes's Account of Free Will', in P. Hoffman, D. Owen, and G. Yaffe (eds), *Contemporary Perspectives on Early Modern Philosophy: Essays in Honour of Vere Chappell*, Boulder, CO: Broadview Press.

Sutton, J. (1998), *Philosophy and Memory Traces*, Cambridge: Cambridge University Press.

Waldow, A. (2017), 'Activating the Mind: Descartes' Dreams and the Awakening of the Human Animal Machine', *Philosophy and Phenomenological Research* 94(2): 299–325.

Williams, B. (1978), *Descartes: The Project of Pure Enquiry*, Harmondsworth: Penguin.

Williams, M. (2005), 'Descartes and the Metaphysics of Doubt', in J. Cottingham (ed.), *Descartes*, Oxford: Oxford University Press.

Wilson, M. (1999), 'Animal Ideas', in her *Ideas and Mechanism: Essays on Early Modern Philosophy*, Princeton: Princeton University Press.

4

Spinoza

Aaron Garrett

1. Introduction

Benedict Spinoza's most ubiquitous concern was the theory of knowledge.[1] From his earliest writings to the last, Spinoza analysed what we know, to what degree and how we know it, and he drew out the consequences of this knowledge for human happiness, morals, and politics. Unsurprisingly, the theory of knowledge was thoroughly connected to his metaphysical views. In fact, one might think of Spinoza as providing a theory of knowledge that was an extension of and (hopefully) consistent with his metaphysics. Indeed, I will suggest that epistemic properties are metaphysical properties for Spinoza, as expressed in thought.

According to Spinoza, the world is carved into three categories: substance, attributes, and modes. All things are either substance, attributes of substance, or modes that inhere in substance – that is, are in and through it. The one and only substance – God – has infinite attributes that express its essence. All finite and infinite minds and bodies are in and through these attributes: each idea in each mind and each part of each body is in turn part of more and more complete wholes, at the limit of which are infinite modes. Examples of the infinite modes are God's infinite intellect in the attribute of thought – in which all ideas are true and adequate – and the infinite mode of motion and rest in the attribute of extension. So we can think of each body or each mind as part of more and more inclusive and even infinite systems of bodies and minds that are in turn modes within the attributes of thought and extension as well as modes of substance.[2]

Giving the systematic character of Spinoza's thought, and given the foundational character of his metaphysics for the rest of his philosophy, it would be surprising if Spinoza's theory of knowledge failed to reflect this picture. More particularly, since ideas are modes in the attribute of thought, and Spinoza presents his theory of knowledge in connection with types of ideas, we might expect the account of ideas to reflect more general metaphysical properties. Don Garrett has argued that the *conatus* has properties of substance to a degree, insofar as it inheres in substance.[3] To put it crudely, beings strive and persist in their existence – humans, puppies, and space dust all strive to continue to persist as the humans, puppies, and space dust that they are – by virtue of the fact that they all are modes that inhere in substance and they share properties of substance to some degree.

Self sufficiency or autarchy is an example of a property that holds maximally of substance but also holds to some degree of modes. In the first Part of the *Ethics* Spinoza argues that there is one substance which he defines as maximally self-sufficient – 'that which is in itself and conceived through itself' – and he equates this substance with causal autarchy or *causa sui*.[4] Self-sufficiency – independence from external causes and the capacity to cause via one's own essence – is desirable for human beings and for groups of human beings. For example, Spinoza argues that men who are guided by reason are freer in a State than in solitude (where freedom is understood in part as a kind of self-sufficiency).[5] Autarchy was, of course, one of the ideals of many types of ancient philosophy ranging from the Platonic forms and *kallipolis* to Aristotle's unmoved mover to the Stoic gods (and more).[6] For Spinoza, just as for Plato and Aristotle, we are only capable of self-sufficiency to a degree. Since we are modes, we are by definition in, through, and dependent.

I would like to suggest that centrality of self-sufficiency extends to Spinoza's theory of knowledge. For Spinoza, to know better is to know in a more self-sufficient way. This is because it is to know more in the way that the divine intellect knows and to be more substance-like.[7] The knowledge we acquire in a more epistemically self-sufficient way helps to make us more self-sufficient. To this end, I will first briefly situate Spinoza's views on knowledge against the views of his predecessors and then give a synoptic general overview of the basic types of knowledge and concepts on which Spinoza draws in his theory.[8]

2. Predecessors

Like many other early modern philosophers, Spinoza was deeply influenced by Descartes. His first publication under his own name was a geometric presentation of the opening sections of Descartes' *Principles*. The influence of Descartes was particularly notable in Holland,[9] so it is not surprising that his writings were an important background for Spinoza. Spinoza often used Descartes' phrase 'clarity and distinctness' to characterize types of knowledge. Like Descartes, he took the ideal sort of knowledge to be self-justifying and certain. Like Descartes, he distinguished these self-certifying kinds of knowledge from sense perception and imagination that were intrinsically uncertain and consequently could not serve as foundational knowledge. Unlike Descartes – and like many other post-Cartesian early modern philosophers, including Locke – refuting scepticism was, for Spinoza, not the central motivation for acquiring certain knowledge.

This is perhaps due to the fact that certitude was also focal for another equally important influence on Spinoza who was not particularly motivated by scepticism: Thomas Hobbes. In the Preface to *De Cive*, the work by which he was primarily known on the Continent, Hobbes sketched an ideal of universal geometrical knowledge that informed Spinoza's geometrical method in the *Ethics*. This account was developed in Hobbes' methodological writings and in *Leviathan*. The highest grade of knowledge for Hobbes was the consequence of a deduction from secure premises. The premises were secured either through introspective knowledge or through stipulated definitions and premises. Either way, the conclusions of the deduction could be as certain as the premises, given the secure manner of deduction.

Many seventeenth-century philosophers were influenced by both Hobbes and Descartes. Spinoza's slightly older contemporary and correspondent Lambertus Velthuysen (2013) wrote both the first major defence of Hobbes in the Netherlands in 1651 and works that advocated for Cartesianism. Samuel Pufendorf, John Locke, and many others drew together epistemic insights from both philosophers. One can see how it would be attractive to combine Hobbes and Descartes. Descartes provided a program for acquiring well-justified premises, and Hobbes for using them as the basis of deductions that provided necessary and causally efficacious knowledge of the natural and civil world. It would not be too strong to say that the synthesis of Hobbes and Descartes was a central preoccupation of philosophers of many stripes writing in the second half of the seventeenth century. Consequently, it is not surprising that Spinoza wished to unite insights from both philosophers.

A third important influence was the widespread belief that religious revelation provided access to infallible and certain knowledge that could not be undermined by reason. Spinoza's *Tractatus Theologico-Politicus* opens with a discussion of prophecy, which explicitly refers to Maimonides' well-known discussion of prophecy in the *Guide for the Perplexed*. Maimonides distinguished levels of prophecy on the basis of their distance from or proximity to the Active

Intellect or the deity, and argued for a philosophical account of prophecy on which the prophet must have a perfected intellect in order to be a prophet, in distinction from the vulgar account of prophecy on which God can and does choose anyone, however intellectually imperfect, for prophecy. Spinoza's clever rhetorical strategy in the opening of the *Tractatus Theologico-Politicus* was to argue for the vulgar account of prophecy against Maimonides' philosophical account of prophecy and to identify prophecy with an unusually developed imagination. Since imagination was for Spinoza the lowest grade of knowledge, this meant that revealed knowledge was identified with uncertain and lower grades of knowledge and consequently was neither infallible nor independent of reason.

This is not to suggest that Spinoza's primary target was Maimonides. He was at least as interested in criticizing the Gomarist or Orthodox Calvinist position within the Dutch Reformed Church that was opposed to the Arminian or Remonstrant position associated with Grotius.[10] The former stressed submission and revelation, and the latter the importance of reason in religion. Spinoza was closely connected with a branch of Cartesian Collegiants centred in Rijnsburg and associated with Pieter Balling.[11] The Collegiants advocated for a Cartesian, inner, rational religion centred on the Sermon on the Mount, and against the external authority of a church. Spinoza himself distinguished Jesus from the prophets and presented him as an ultimate philosopher whose thoughts were adequate and internally justified. Like the Collegiants, he argued for a moral religion of reason that gave rise to a contented and virtuous life. In the fifth and final Part of the *Ethics*, in particular, Spinoza argued that the more we know by the second and the third kind of knowledge, generally the more powerful and contented we are. The third kind of knowledge, in particular, resulted in the highest virtue and contentment.

Taken together, Spinoza's predecessor's theories point to the desideratum of certain, internally justified, rational, general, and powerful knowledge that gives rise to a content and virtuous life.

3. Adequacy, truth, and clarity and distinctness

Spinoza made great use of a cluster of technical terms in his theory of knowledge: adequacy, truth, and clarity and distinctness (and their correlates). Unfortunately, they often seem (and sometimes are) maddeningly interchangeable in his philosophical practice. As noted above, Spinoza took the distinction between clarity and distinctness and confusion from Descartes. He put his own spin on the traditional distinction between truth and falsity. And he added a further distinction between adequate and inadequate knowledge that was central for his account.

An initial puzzle in trying to make sense of Spinoza's theory of knowledge is making sense of the relations between these technical terms. All of these terms were used to characterize ideas. Spinoza defined 'idea' as 'a conception of the Mind which the Mind forms because it is a thinking thing'. He followed this with an axiom that invoked and described the nature of a true idea: 'a true idea must agree with that of which it is the idea'. He then further defined an adequate idea as 'an idea which, insofar as it is considered without relation to its object, has all the properties, that is intrinsic characteristics, of a true idea'. Spinoza also added a gloss – 'I say intrinsic so as to exclude the extrinsic characteristic – to wit the agreement of the idea with that of which it is an idea.'

What is at stake in the differences between these terms and between the respective correlative terms: false, inadequate, and confused? It is tempting to characterize the distinctions between adequacy and truth, and inadequacy and falsity, as between logical notions (truth/falsity) and epistemic notions (adequacy and inadequacy). But it would be anachronistic to impute an understanding of logic to Spinoza on which truth/falsity is a property of propositions. Furthermore, truth and adequacy, and clarity and distinctness as well, all capture different aspects of knowledge and all are properties of ideas. Consequently, it is more helpful to think of these pairs of properties as highlighting different aspects of knowledge – with the caveat that Spinoza is not consistent in his use.[12]

Truth is a relation – the agreement of an idea with that of which it is an idea or its *ideatum*. Consequently, a true idea is one that satisfies this relation. This can be construed in many ways but the most obvious way is to take truth as the agreement between an idea and the *ideatum* that it represents.[13] If my idea of my dog (hence, *Creampuff*) has Creampuff as its *ideatum*, and if *Creampuff* agrees with Creampuff, then it is true.[14] Falsity is correspondingly a lack of agreement between an idea and its *ideatum*. If *Creampuff* is taken to represent another dog – say, Archie – then *Creampuff* is false insofar as it does not agree with what it is an idea of or represents – that is, Creampuff.

An adequate idea has the same 'intrinsic characteristic' as does a true idea but without external correspondence or agreement. If, for example, I form an idea of substance, and in conceiving the idea I conceive all of the very same properties that I would have conceived by checking that my substance idea represented substance, the idea would be adequate. It is forced to discuss this via examples – Spinoza notoriously avoided examples in *The Ethics* – but the general point seems clear. Adequate ideas are conceived in such a manner that they give complete access to all knowledge relevant to that particular idea (Bennett 1984: 177f, 365f.).

Spinoza further used adequacy as a way of describing causation and as a manner of conception. 'What is common to all things can only be conceived adequately': it is the basis for much technical vocabulary. Adequate ideas, adequate conception, and adequate causation all share the sense of complete and self-sufficient – they do not need to rely on anything external.

One can see this further in the distinction between inadequate ideas and false ideas, and a comparison with Descartes. What makes an idea inadequate, as opposed to false? Spinoza suggests that false ideas are false because they are inadequate – 'Falsity consists in the privation of knowledge which inadequate ideas, that is, fragmentary[15] and confused ideas involve': that is, falsity is a consequence of the way in which inadequate ideas are intrinsically confused and fragmentary. This might be because the false idea lacks something that results in a failure of the idea to agree with its object and the way that we conceive them gives rise to representative information that lacks the capacity to correspond with its object.

In the *Meditations* Descartes argues that falsity arises either from human beings wilfully misapplying their understanding to objects or from humans possessing intrinsically confused or materially false ideas. Spinoza cannot hold the former, due to his criticisms of Descartes' voluntarism. Nor can he hold that there are intrinsically confused ideas, where confusion is some sort of positive feature of these ideas. So Spinoza needs to hold that some ideas in perceivers like us are always necessarily confused and incomplete – we always necessarily grasp some features of the world in a fragmentary manner.[16] Adequate ideas always give all of the relevant information.

So, why did Spinoza develop the concept of adequacy in addition to truth?[17] First, since adequate ideas are necessarily true, through them we have a priori access to genuine features of the world in the absence of extrinsic marks. This allows us to have direct access to general true metaphysical features of the world.[18] A more local reason is that adequacy allows Spinoza to avoid the Cartesian Circle insofar as adequacy is a real property of ideas – not a phenomenal property, like clarity and distinctness – such that all of the ideas possessing the property are true (Radner 1971: 351). That adequacy is an unabashedly real property suggests the most important reason. The epistemic standard of adequacy is a reflection of metaphysical properties of ideas (as are the phenomenal properties of experiencing ideas clearly and distinctly). Spinoza was committed to adequate knowledge as being complete, self-sufficient, and self-certifying. Completeness, self-sufficiency, and self-certification ultimately hold to the highest degree of the most real thing: substance. Insofar as adequate ideas are in the divine intellect, and insofar as the divine intellect reflects substance in the attribute of thought, the metaphysical properties of substance as expressed in thought are real and foundational epistemic properties.

Put in slogan form: What ideas are, and how we know them, literally reflects what there is as such. What there is as such is self-sufficient. What we know best is self-sufficient. In the next section I will discuss Spinoza's commitment not just to the thesis that what we know is self-sufficient – adequate ideas – but to the thesis that we know it self-sufficiently and that it gives rise to knowledge that aids us in becoming more self-sufficient human beings.

4. Kinds of knowledge

Spinoza's *Short Treatise* includes the earliest version of his metaphysics, followed by an early version of his theory of knowledge. I will first consider each kind of knowledge as treated there, and then turn to the corresponding kind of knowledge in the *Ethics*.

In the discussion of knowledge in the second part of the *Short Treatise*, Spinoza distinguished between three ways of acquiring ideas – (1) via beliefs, (2) via true belief, and (3) via clear and distinct conceptions. To illustrate the distinctions, he gave the example of the rule of three. Given a pair of finite natural numbers A and B, and a third finite natural number C, one can generate a fourth number that has the same proportion to C as A does to B. The 'rule of three' dictates multiplying B and C and dividing their product by A. For example, if $A=3$, $B=6$, and $C=8$, one can generate $D=16$ by multiplying 6 by 8 and dividing the resultant product – 48 – by 3. The result is 16:8::6:3.

If we follow the rule of three because an authority has told us that it works, our confidence in the rule derives from our confidence in the authority. External dependence on an authority is no more knowledge of the rule, according to Spinoza, than the knowledge that a blind person has of colour or that a parrot has of a proposition which it repeats. These two analogies suggest that confidence in testimony and the actions that follow from this testimony – applying the rule of three – are insufficient for knowledge insofar as they miss something necessary to knowledge. The blind person can't access colour qualia; so, although an authority can tell him that an object is red, he can't know it. A parrot can't generate the content of proposition, and so merely repeats it as given by someone else.

A better sort of knowledge – true belief – involves our own empirical confirmation and consequently a warrant from experience. When we apply the rule of three and see that it works in a number of cases, this provides a further warrant beyond testimony. We now have a true belief. But our true belief is still insufficient insofar as it is partial, depends on empirical confirmation, and cannot be certainly generalized beyond the few cases that provide the warrant. At best, we have a rule of three for a set of numbers and the unwarranted confidence that it is generalizable. This suggests that the right sort of knowledge will be general in addition to accessing the right types of ideas.

These two types of knowledge are impoverished because they depend on external sources. They are bundled together in the *Ethics* with sense perception in one category: imagination or knowledge of the first kind. Imagination is defined as arising from *experienta vaga* or happenstance experience where we are acted upon by external causes. Imagination is the cause of all falsity. Spinoza recognizes throughout the *Ethics*, but particularly in Part IV, that we finite beings are continuously acted upon – 'The force whereby a man persists is limited, and infinitely surpassed by the power of external causes.' Since Spinoza thought that imagination was intrinsically untrustworthy and that it was the cause of all falsity, we might think that we ought to dispose of all inadequate beliefs and confused perceptual experiences and entirely avoid imagination.

In the first part of Part V (1–23), Spinoza suggests that organizing the imagination rationally is a more effective strategy than attempting to bracket it off. First, one needs the imagination to get around the world. And even if one thinks one can avoid getting around the world, the world has a way of affecting one all the same. This is because our minds necessarily involve inadequate ideas, and we are necessarily overcome by external causes and passions, whether we like it or not. The best strategy is thus to harness these forces in such a way that they educe to our rationality and self-sufficiency (Bove 1996). This is what a successful State does as well, by providing citizens a means to be more self-sufficient through security.

What, then, are the conditions sufficient for full-fledged knowledge?[19] In KV Spinoza thinks that we have acquired real knowledge when reason tells us 'on account of the nature of the proportion in these numbers it had to be so, and could not happen otherwise'. This suggests that reason provides necessary justification via a general property – 'the nature of the proportion in these numbers' as opposed to the numbers themselves. If a proportion is in 3 and 6 then, given 8, the same proportion necessarily must generate 16.

Spinoza adds to this a further kind of knowledge where the knower has 'no need of hearsay, or experience, or the art of reasoning, because by his penetration he sees the proportion in all such calculations immediately'. Like the previous kind of knowledge, it is analogous to knowledge of the proportion. But it is distinct insofar as it is wholly self-sufficient and involves immediate knowledge of the proportions in the numbers themselves, as opposed to reasoning about the nature of proportions and then discovering them in the numbers. Consequently, in Spinoza's earliest writings we see a hierarchy of knowledge in terms of the dependency intrinsic to, and/or self-sufficiency of, ways of knowing. And, notably, the more self-sufficient, the more justified. These types of knowledge are referred to in the *Ethics* as the second kind of knowledge, or Reason, and the third kind of knowledge, or *scientia intuitiva*. Spinoza defined Reason as knowledge of what is common to both part and whole, as opposed to knowledge of the essence of a particular thing. So, for example, when we understand the first axiom of Part 1 of the *Ethics* ('all things are either in themselves or in another'), we don't have knowledge of any particular thing or group of particular things; instead, we have knowledge of an axiom common to the parts and wholes of all things. It is true of any thing that it is either in itself or in another. The general mathematical knowledge we have that explains the fourth proportional illustrates this by holding of any and all finite numbers, not of any particular numbers.

Unlike imagination, Reason is adequate and thus self-sufficient. Knowers can access Reason independently of contingent facts about modes and their interdependences.[20] Spinoza notoriously claimed that we all have adequate knowledge of the infinite and eternal essence of God. One way of cashing out that proposition would be that, by virtue of the fact that we are modes inhering in substance and modes of attributes, we have access to structural divine properties – causation, dependence, unity, power – that all modes including ideas (i.e. modes of thought) are necessarily (not contingently) interconnected by and share. This is because all modes, whether of thought or of extension, are in attributes and in and through substance. It also has access to properties that are ubiquitous in particular attributes – properties of motion and rest, and properties that hold of all ideas. From these, we can derive further laws and properties that are also adequate and true.

This also explains why Spinoza conceives of adequate knowledge as self-sufficient. To know adequately is to have adequate ideas that are in the infinite intellect – and all true and adequate ideas are in the infinite intellect. The infinite intellect is an infinite mode in the attribute of thought. Infinite modes share the properties of the attributes. Adequate ideas will also share in these substantial properties – self-sufficiency, causal efficacy, explanatory power – insofar as they inhere in the infinite intellect.[21]

Spinoza contrasted this sort of knowledge with knowledge of universals. We form a universal – like 'Dog' – from perceptions of particular dogs such as Creampuff. The universal, when formed, depends on particular perceptions of dogs for its content, and its truth-value varies according to the particular perceptions of perceiver. As such, it is highly dependent on circumstances and paradigmatic *experientia vaga*. Reason, however, is wholly independent of contingent facts about perceivers because it is ubiquitous and everywhere the same.

Yet even if Reason has all of the virtues that Spinoza suggests, it doesn't seem to give us any purchase at all on what it is to know anything particular. Indeed, it seems to widen the Cartesian gap between imagination and reason. The third kind of knowledge seems meant to fill this gap: 'this kind of knowledge proceeds from an adequate idea of the formal essence of certain attributes of God to an adequate knowledge of the essence of things'. The third kind of knowledge has been very puzzling to many of Spinoza's readers. At the outset, it seems there is a glaring problem. In order to have knowledge of the essences of things, we must be acquainted with things. We are acquainted with things via the imagination. But adequate knowledge can't arise from the imagination. Therefore, we cannot have adequate knowledge of the essences of things.

There have been many attempts at getting around this problem, and many different candidates for the third kind of knowledge have been suggested.[22] Here is one candidate for this kind of knowledge. Directly before Spinoza's presentation of the three kinds of knowledge in the *Ethics*, he demonstrated that we could have adequate knowledge of properties less ubiquitous than motion and rest: 'Of that which is common and proper to the human body and to any external bodies by which the human body is customarily affected, and which is equally in the part as well as in the whole of any of these bodies, the idea also in the mind will be adequate.'

This might provide a means to explain how we might have adequate *social* knowledge (James 2010: 181–99) via knowledge of what is necessarily shared in interactions between specifically human bodies (and, correspondingly, human minds). This would include knowledge of human psychology and political life – what Spinoza treats in Parts III and IV of the *Ethics* and in his political writings. If this knowledge involves essences of social entities or social kinds and 'proceeds from an adequate idea of the formal essence of certain attributes of God', it would then be an example of the third kind of knowledge (Garrett 2012: 50–73).

Unfortunately, Spinoza says very little about this kind of knowledge. What he does say, though, is that it is maximally self-sufficient knowledge. As Spinoza makes clear in his example of the fourth proportional in both the *KV* and the *Ethics*, the third kind of knowledge is grasped immediately and depends on nothing beyond the grasp of the essence of things for its justification. Once again we appear to have a distinction between types of knowledge on the basis of their self-sufficiency. And Spinoza claims that this knowledge which is acquired in a self-sufficient manner – immediate and internally justified – and has self-sufficient adequate ideas as its object is also most essential for our freedom or self-sufficiency. Finally, it is quite literally knowledge of how to gain greater autarchy as individual thinkers and as members of communities and States.

5. Conclusion

As I've suggested, this is due to what ideas are – modes – and how they inhere in substance. Philosophers from Plato and Aristotle to Descartes and Spinoza and beyond have understood ideas and minds as 'things' with reality and metaphysical structure. This structure was thought to be closely connected with the distinctive content of ideas from the Forms, to *nous*, to the idea of God. A metaphysics of thought in this sense is deeply foreign to a post-Kantian sensibility, although its attractions are clearer now that metaphysics is once again on the rise in philosophy.

We can see Spinoza as trying to draw out the consequences of his metaphysics in explaining how ideas can have the import for us that they do. I have argued that the metaphysical centrality of the property of self-sufficiency explains Spinoza's preference for adequacy, and explains in part the distinction between types of knowledge. It is clearly, though, not solely descriptive for Spinoza but is normative: one ought to know via the third kind of knowledge, and what one knows ought to be known both intrinsically and due to the ways in which it is beneficial. However one makes sense of what normativity could mean for Spinoza, it seems likely that he thinks that the metaphysical facts have direct bearing on, constitute, or even are identical with normative facts.[23] It is because substance is most real and perfect, and we inhere in substance, that we can be more real and perfect. It is because substance is self-sufficient that adequate knowledge is self-sufficient. And it is through knowing adequately, and via the second and particularly the third kind of knowledge, that we become more self-sufficient in the many areas of life – in particular, political knowledge and knowledge of the passions and affections – that we can know adequately. All reflect the importance of self-sufficiency in their form, content, and reality due to the unity of Spinoza's metaphysics.[24]

Notes

1   For a recent and particularly good overview of Spinoza's epistemology, see Steinberg (2008). I will only discuss a few aspects of Spinoza's theory of knowledge, but the reader is referred to this excellent discussion.
2   For a brief and very clear presentation of Spinoza's metaphysics and some of the (many) issues involved, see Lin (2006). See also the excellent discussion in Curley (1988).
3   According to Spinoza, every mode strives to persevere in its existence. 'Conatus' is the word that Spinoza uses to describe this striving. Conatus provides the basis of a number of crucial features of Spinoza's theory. These strivings are sources for his account of the affects and the conatuses of our minds – that is, of the modes in the attribute of thought that make up our minds – and is what leads us to be rational. Spinoza goes so far as to equate our essence with this conatus of a mode or group of modes and how substance-like they are – that is, the degree to which they instantiate types of properties that we associate with substance – which in turn is a consequence of the way in which modes inhere in substance: see Garrett (2002). It is a controversial position.
4   All translations are from Shirley (2002).
5   It sounds a bit odd that being in a State is a better way of achieving self-sufficiency than being by one's self. But Spinoza's point is that one is not *sufficient* by one's self.
6   Spinoza's way of thinking about self-sufficiency is quite different from that of many ancient philosophers – in particular, the Stoics. Spinoza was more interested in self-sufficient activity than in protecting the self through negatives walls or boundaries. On Spinoza's complex relation to Stoicism, see Miller (2015).
7   Huenemann (2009) discusses Spinoza's focus on 'epistemic autonomy'. I prefer autarchy or self-sufficiency insofar as it is not only about the application of laws to oneself.
8   Due to considerations of length, I will discuss issues in Spinoza's theory of knowledge that are connected with his account of mind as little as possible – for example, representation – and some central ones not at all – for example, panpsychism. The systematic reasons why the metaphysics and epistemology line up for Spinoza are closely connected with representation and panpsychism.

9 See Verbeek (1992). For a different interpretation, see Douglas (2015).
10 Calvinists and other radical Protestants offered an important motivation for Hobbes as well – in particular, in *Leviathan* – and were one of the reasons why Hobbes argued that the sovereign ought to be the sole interpreter of Scripture.
11 See Fix (1990) for an excellent discussion of Collegiantism and of the Collegiant context of Spinoza's philosophy.
12 'Clarity and distinctness' is particularly interchangeable with other terms.
13 There are good reasons to argue that Spinoza distinguishes between object and thing represented (Radner (1971: 350). If the object of the mind is the body – as Spinoza says – then a true idea would have to agree with the bodily state that is its object – which sounds like a violation of Spinoza's strict attribute dualism: that is, we would be positing some sort of likeness between bodies and minds (Bennett 1984: 153–8; Della Rocca 1996: passim; 2012: 118–27). See also the excellent nuanced discussions in LeBuffe (2010: ch. 3) and Garrett (2013).
14 As will become clear shortly, *Creampuff* is a poor candidate for one of our true ideas.
15 Spinoza uses the Latin word 'manca' (mutilated or imperfect) to describe the epistemic status of inadequate ideas. 'Manca' suggests that inadequate ideas are *partial* epistemic representations and ways of conceiving. They are partial in the sense that they fail to represent their object as a whole.
16 For an excellent discussion of Spinoza on falsity and inadequacy, see LeBuffe (2010: chs 3, 4).
17 For more on the relation between truth and adequacy, see Garrett (1986, 1990).
18 A potential worrisome cost is, since Spinoza holds that adequate ideas do not arise from sense perception, that all adequate ideas must be innate. If this is Spinoza's position, then much of its coherence stands or falls with how we understand innateness (Marshall 2008: 51–88).
19 Spinoza uses '*scientia*' ambiguously, to mean all four types and only the last two types.
20 How this works gets into some of the trickier aspects of Spinoza's theory of representation. See note 12 for pointers to some of the main positions.
21 I recognize that this explanation is brief and needs more steps. One worry is that this is akin to saying a red idea must be red. But, since we are discussing properties that ideas have both materially and formally, this objection does not seem serious. It's a problem to say that a red idea is red. It's not a problem to say that the idea of unity is unified. Spinoza wishes further to claim that the idea of unity will be more unified than the idea of red, in each case because of what the particular idea is of. This sounds a lot like Platonic property inheritance. Spinoza's theory of inherence differs on important points. See Garrett (2002) and Melamed (2009).
22 For an excellent survey of the many positions and many problems involved, as well as an insightful interpretation of the third kind of knowledge, see Primus (2017).

23 Spinoza doesn't make a clear distinction between normative and descriptive, as far as I can tell, which is unsurprising since he is writing before Hume, Moore, and so on. And this sounds like a paradigmatic example of deriving 'ought' from 'is'. Why would one want to be more, unless being more is better? But then we want to be more because it is better, not because it is more. I tend to think there's an underlying premise that it is intrinsically rationally desirable to be more, which is cashed out as expressing one's essence to a greater degree.

24 Thanks to Don Garrett for helpful comments on this chapter.

References

Bennett, J. (1984), *A Study of Spinoza's Ethics*, Indianapolis: Hackett.
Bove, L. (1996), *La stratégie du conatus, affirmation et résistance chez Spinoza*, Paris: Vrin.
Curley, E. (1988), *Behind the Geometrical Method*, Princeton: Princeton University Press.
Della Rocca, M. (1996), *Representation and the Mind Body Problem in Spinoza*, Oxford: Oxford University Press.
Della Rocca, M. (2012), *Spinoza*, London: Routledge.
Douglas, A. (2015), *Spinoza and Dutch Cartesianism*, Oxford: Oxford University Press.
Fix, A. (1990), *Prophecy and Reason: The Dutch Collegiants in the Early Enlightenment*, Princeton: Princeton University Press.
Garrett, A. (2012), 'Knowing the Essence of the State in Spinoza's Tractatus-Theologico Politicus', *European Journal of Philosophy*, 20: 50–73.
Garrett, D. (1986), 'Truth and Ideas of Imagination in the Tractatus de Intellectus Emendatione', *Studia Spinozana*, 2: 56–86.
Garrett, D. (1990), 'Truth, Method, and Correspondence in Spinoza and Leibniz', *Studia Spinozana*, 6: 13–43.
Garrett, D. (2002), 'Spinoza's Conatus Argument', in O. Koistinen and J. I. Biro (eds), *Spinoza: Metaphysical Themes*, Oxford: Oxford University Press.
Garrett, D. (2013), 'Representation and Misrepresentation in Spinoza's Philosophy of Mind', in M. Della Rocca (ed.), *The Oxford Handbook of Spinoza*, New York: Oxford University Press.
Huenemann, C. (2009), 'Epistemic Autonomy in Spinoza', in C. Huenemann (ed.), *Interpreting Spinoza*, Cambridge: Cambridge University Press.
James, S. (2010), 'Creating Rational Understanding: Spinoza as a Social Epistemologist', *Proceedings of the Aristotelian Society, Supp.*, 85: 181–99.
LeBuffe, M. (2010), *From Bondage to Freedom: Spinoza on Human Excellence*, Oxford: Oxford University Press.

Lin, M. (2006), 'Substance, Attribute, and Mode in Spinoza', *Philosophy Compass*, 1: 144–53.
Marshall, E. (2008), 'Adequacy and Innateness in Spinoza', *Oxford Studies in Early Modern Philosophy*, 4: 51–88.
Melamed, Y. (2009), 'Spinoza's Metaphysics of Substance', *Philosophy and Phenomenological Research*, 78: 17–82.
Miller, J. (2015), *Spinoza and the Stoics*, Cambridge: Cambridge University Press.
Primus, K. (2017), 'Scientia Intuitiva in the *Ethics*', in Y. Melamed (ed.), *Spinoza's Ethics: A Critical Guide*, Cambridge: Cambridge University Press.
Radner, D. (1971), 'Spinoza's Theory of Ideas', *The Philosophical Review*, 80: 338–59.
Shirley, S. (ed.) (2002), *Spinoza: Complete Works*, Indianapolis: Hackett.
Steinberg, D. (2008), 'Knowledge in Spinoza's *Ethics*', in O. Koistinen (ed.), *The Cambridge Companion to Spinoza's* Ethics, Cambridge: Cambridge University Press.
Velthuysen, L. van (2013), *A Letter on the Principal of Justness and Decency, Containing a Defence of the Treatise De Cive of the Learned Mr. Hobbes* [1651], ed. and trans. M. de Mobray, intro. C. Secretan. Leiden: Brill.
Verbeek, T. (1992), *Descartes and the Dutch: Early Reactions to Cartesian Philosophy, 1637–1650*, Carbondale: Southern Illinois University Press.

5

Malebranche

Andrew Pyle

1. Introduction: was Malebranche a rationalist metaphysician?

In our histories of philosophy, Nicolas Malebranche (1638–1715) is usually characterized as one of the great rationalist metaphysicians of his age. The rationalist metaphysician, we are told, thinks of the human mind as possessed of a distinctive power of Pure Reason, enabling it to discern important truths about, for example, God and the soul without any reliance on the troublesome and untrustworthy deliverances of the senses. This body of a priori truths can, in principle, be organized into a system of metaphysical knowledge.

This picture of Malebranche the rationalist metaphysician is deeply problematic, for at least three reasons. In the first place, Malebranche insists over and over again that the human mind does *not* possess any autonomous power of Pure Reason. The most fundamental article in his entire epistemology is his insistence that all human knowledge is, at bottom, revelation. The human mind is passive and receptive in its relation to the source and ground of all truth: namely, of course, God. Revealed knowledge divides into three distinct types. There is (1) revelation in its everyday sense, as delivered to us through the Scriptures. There is (2) the revelation of God's Ideas to our intellects, which we rely on in the various branches of mathematics. And there is (3) the revelation of God's will, which comes to us through our experience of the natural world and of our own minds. Although only category (1) is called 'revelation' in ordinary language, Malebranche is perfectly clear and insistent that categories (2) and (3) are also, strictly speaking, types of revelation.

But let us set aside this first scruple, and focus our attention on category (2) – namely, the revelation to our finite intellects of the divine Ideas, which are the archetypes according to which all things were (and are) created. If Malebranche believes that we have sufficient access to these Ideas to develop a body of metaphysical knowledge comparable in its clarity and rigour to the mathematical sciences, then the traditional picture of him as a rationalist metaphysician can be sustained without too much reworking, and with only the non-trivial addition of a layer of theological gloss. But at this point two further difficulties arise. Do we have access to all of the Ideas we would need in order to articulate a body of metaphysical knowledge? And will such access as we have to the realm of Ideas enable us to advance from propositions about Ideas to propositions about things? These are the topics of our present enquiry.

That Malebranche denies that we have a clear Idea of our own souls is well known. Doubtless, there is such an archetype or blueprint of the human soul, contained in the infinite intellect of its Creator, but He has not chosen to reveal it to us. As Malebranche says in one of his most memorable one-liners, 'I am but darkness to myself' (*Meditations Chrétiennes* 9: 1958–78: xi, 102). I know the states of my soul only from experience, not as intelligible modifications of the (unknown) substance of my soul. I have the Idea of body as intelligible extension, *étendue intelligible*, and this enables me, Malebranche argues, to prove that my soul cannot be a mere modification of matter. Whether a body of rational psychology can be built by such a *via negativa* (arguing entirely from the idea of matter) is a subject that divides the commentators.

But even where we find ourselves in possession of an adequate stock of Ideas, a further and deeper difficulty looms before us. Acquaintance with the realm of Ideas allows us only to discover the properties of *possible* creatures. But which of these possible creatures God has chosen to actualize depends not on His intellect (in which we participate) but on His will (in which we do not).[1] The gap between the Ideal (the archetypes of all possible creatures timelessly present in the divine intellect) and the actual (the creatures that God has chosen to actualize from among the legions of mere possibilia) remains unbridged. And it looks as if only the testimony of experience can help us to bridge this gulf.

2. Malebranche and Hume

That Hume owes significant intellectual debts to Malebranche is by now an old story. Hume himself lists the *Recherche* as recommended reading for anyone wanting to understand the *Treatise*,[2] and possible links have been discussed in some detail in McCracken's *Malebranche and British Philosophy* (1993: 254–90).

On the topics of causation, the soul, and natural judgement (see Pyle 2011), it is easy to document the lines of influence. I want to examine a more puzzling and problematic connection between Malebranche and Hume. I think that Malebranche anticipates Hume's famous distinction between 'relations of ideas' and 'matters of fact', clearly sees that only 'relations of ideas' can be known a priori, and then blithely proceeds to make some fairly orthodox metaphysical claims, such as about God and the soul. But how can this be? Is Malebranche simply confused? *Should* he have seen the subversive implications of Hume's Fork for metaphysics? Or can he, by means of some sophisticated manoeuvres, avoid running into flat contradictions?

Let us begin with a famous passage from section 4 of Hume's (1999: 108) *Enquiry*:

> All the objects of human reason or enquiry may naturally be divided into two kinds, to wit, *Relations of Ideas* and *Matters of Fact*. Of the first kind are the sciences of Geometry, Algebra, and Arithmetic; and in short, every affirmation, which is either intuitively or demonstratively certain. *That the square of the hypothenuse is equal to the square of the two sides*, is a proposition, which expresses a relation between these figures. *That three times five is equal to half of thirty*, expresses a relation between these numbers. Propositions of this kind are discoverable by the mere operation of thought, without dependence on what is any where existent in the universe. Though there never were a circle or triangle in nature, the truths, demonstrated by EUCLID, would for ever retain their certainty and evidence.
>
> Matters of fact, which are the second objects of human reason, are not ascertained in the same manner, nor is our evidence of their truth, however great, of a like nature with the foregoing. The contrary of every matter of fact is still possible; because it can never imply a contradiction, and is conceived by the mind with the same facility and distinctness, as if ever so conformable to reality. *That the sun will not rise tomorrow* is no less intelligible a proposition, and implies no more contradiction, than the affirmation, *that it will rise*. We should in vain, therefore, attempt to demonstrate its falsehood. Were it demonstratively false, it would imply a contradiction, and could never be distinctly conceived by the mind. (Emphases in the original)

This all-too-familiar passage is the classic statement of what has come to be known as 'Hume's Fork', and is standardly seen as a powerful weapon in the hands of the empiricist against the pretensions of rationalist metaphysics. We all know how the familiar story is told.[3] But wait just one moment. Here is

Malebranche in Book Six of the *Recherche* (1958–78: ii, 286–7; 1997a: 433–4), discussing the nature of truth as a relation:

> There are three kinds of relations or truths. There are those between ideas, between things and their ideas, and between things only. It is true that twice two is four – here is a truth between ideas. It is true that the sun exists – this is a truth between a thing and its idea. It is true that the earth is larger than the moon – here is a truth that is only between things.
>
> Of these three sorts of truths, those between ideas are eternal and immutable, and because of their immutability they are the standards for all other truths, for every standard must be invariable. This is why only these sorts of truths are considered in arithmetic, algebra, and geometry, because these universal sciences both determine and contain all the particular sciences. All the relations or truths between created things, or between ideas and created things, are subject to change to which every creature is liable. Only the truths between ideas are immutable, because God is not subject to change, nor, consequently, are the ideas He contains.
>
> Thus, we use the mind alone to try to discover only truths between ideas, for we almost always use the senses to discover the other sorts of truths. We use our eyes and our hands to assure ourselves of the existence of things, and to recognize the relations of equality and inequality between them. Relations of ideas are the only ones the mind can know infallibly and by itself without the use of the senses.

There are, of course, significant differences between the two passages. Malebranche's emphasis is on the distinction between the immutable realm of God's ideas and the mutable realm of created things – his epistemological points follow from this central ontological divide. And Malebranche vacillates at an absolutely crucial point. He first says that we '*almost always*' rely on the senses for knowledge of things. But in the final sentence of the passage, he affirms clearly – as it seems he must – that *only* relations of ideas can be known a priori. And his examples of genuine a priori knowledge are precisely the same as Hume's – algebra, arithmetic, and geometry.

Now Hume (1999: 211), we know, saw his famous distinction between relations of ideas and matters of fact as utterly destructive of metaphysics, at least as traditionally conceived:

> When we run over libraries, persuaded of these principles, what havoc must we make? If we take in our hand any volume; of divinity or school metaphysics, for instance; let us ask, Does it contain any abstract reasoning concerning quantity or number? No. Does it contain any experimental reasoning concerning matter

of fact and existence? No. Commit it then to the flames: For it can contain nothing but sophistry and illusion.[4]

If Hume were challenged about the *Enquiry* itself, he would presumably say that it is a contribution to the experimental science of human nature, and thus falls on the 'matters of fact' side of the divide rather than the 'relations of ideas' side.[5] But what does Malebranche think about the possibility of a science of metaphysics, a body of demonstrative knowledge derived a priori from self-evident first principles but dealing with concrete things and their properties? The examples that he gives in the *Recherche* of sciences based on relations of ideas are all drawn from mathematics – arithmetic, geometry, and algebra. But when he comes to write the *Entretiens* (1686) he seems remarkably sanguine about the prospects for metaphysics, as his letter to Berrand shows: 'I am asked to construct a metaphysics. I believe that this is very necessary, and that I would find this easier than most people. It is good metaphysics that must rule everything, and I shall try to establish the principal truths that are the foundation of religion and morality' (1958–78: xvii, 427). There is no sense here of a fundamental problem threatening the very possibility of the discipline of metaphysics. Malebranche, it seems, has all the premises in place for Hume's argument, but shies away from the conclusion. Here is how the argument would go:

- Metaphysics must be an a priori discipline delivering a priori knowledge;
- a priori knowledge is only possible for relations of ideas;
- knowledge of relations of ideas has no implications for real existence;
- metaphysics must produce knowledge of real existence;
- therefore, metaphysics is impossible.

In the next section we shall take a closer look at Malebranche's own list of 'axioms' of metaphysics to see whether they can plausibly be read as affirming only relations of ideas or whether they involve empirical claims about the created world.

3. The axioms of metaphysics

In chapter 11 of Book Four of the *Recherche*, Malebranche finds himself discussing the distractions posed by the pleasures of the senses, and the difficulty that the human mind feels in concentrating on abstract questions.

We humans, Malebranche (1958–78: ii, 90; 1997a: 315) tells us, are not natural metaphysicians:

> Metaphysics is a similarly abstract science that does not flatter the senses, and to whose study the soul is not drawn by any prevenient pleasure; for the same reason this science is very much neglected, and one often finds people foolish enough to boldly deny common notions. There are even some who deny that we can and should assert of a thing what is included in the clear and distinct idea we have of it; that nothingness has no properties; that a thing cannot be reduced to nothing without a miracle; that no body can move itself by its own forces; that an agitated body cannot communicate to bodies with which it collides more motion than it possesses, and other such things. They have never considered these axioms from a viewpoint clear and focused enough to discover their truth clearly. And they have sometimes performed experiments that convinced them falsely that some of these axioms were not true.

In my discussion of these axioms in my *Malebranche*, I let the first four of these five so-called axioms pass, challenging Malebranche's title only to the last of the five, which was there described as 'an act of trespass on the empirical domain' (Pyle 2003: 237). But let us scrutinize these axioms more closely, to see if (and how) they might be construed in terms of relations of ideas.

> M1. 'We can and should assert of a thing what is included in the clear and distinct idea we have of it.'

At first sight, this may seem to affirm a relation between a thing and its idea, and thus not to be the sort of claim that could be established a priori. But this is not a proposition in which we *use* a clear and distinct idea to think about possible things (e.g. 'all triangles have internal angles equal to two right angles'); rather, we are here thinking *about* ideas and their relation to things. This axiom might plausibly be interpreted as *metamental*, as a second-order thought about what it is to be a clear and distinct idea. It is part of our idea of a clear and distinct idea that it presents to the attentive mind the properties of the things (if any) of which the idea is an idea. So Malebranche can plausibly defend M1 as a true axiom of metaphysics, involving a hierarchic relation between ideas. How many such clear and distinct ideas we have access to is a further question. The existing a priori disciplines of the mathematical sciences show (to all but the most obdurate sceptic) that we have access to at least one such idea, that of *étendue intelligible*. Whether we have similar access to any other clear and distinct ideas remains an open question.

M2. 'Nothingness has no properties.'

This cannot be a proposition *about* nothingness, affirmed on the basis of a clear and distinct idea of nothingness, for the elementary reason that there is no such clear and distinct idea. There is no content to represent. If we are to make sense of M2, it must be construed as an assertion about *properties*. We could say that it belongs to our concept of a property that a property inheres in some substance or other. Translated into Cartesian terms, this seems more obviously self-evident: a *mode* is only conceivable as a *modification* of some substance. There is a relation of ideas (a logical connection of concepts) linking mode to substance. The 'axiom' will be employed in Malebranche's reconstruction of the Cartesian argument from the *cogito* to the real distinction. There are thoughts and feelings; but these are modes; modes must be modifications of substance; therefore there is a thinking substance. But this thinking substance cannot be material (we have a clear and distinct idea of matter, and a clear and distinct idea excludes whatever it does not include); so there is an *immaterial* thinking substance of which thoughts and feelings are modifications. The argument will turn, of course, on the identification of something *given* in experience with something *conceptualized* under a category of metaphysics – many will baulk at just this point. But we can at least see how Malebranche might plausibly claim to defend M2 as an axiom of metaphysics.

M3. 'A thing cannot be reduced to nothing without a miracle.'

This 'axiom' is going to be required if Malebranche is ever to establish the immortality of the soul. Even without a clear idea of the soul, he claims in Book Four of the *Recherche* (1958–78: ii, 22, 1997a: 273), its immortality can be clearly established, once its status as an immaterial substance is secured. For a substance to cease to be, he writes to Arnauld, is 'impossible by the ordinary forces of nature', for 'it is only modes which perish' (vi, 163). But this looks deeply problematic on at least two counts. In the first place, there is the problem of identification already noted: to construe my thoughts, feelings, and sensations as modes is already to buy into the substance-modification metaphysic. Worse still, the endurance of some non-material substance when my body is decomposing in its grave does little to secure *my* survival – difficult questions about personal identity are being overlooked here.

If we construe the generic 'thing' in M3 as the more specific 'substance', can we plausibly defend M3 as implicitly analytic, as part of what we mean by calling something a substance? Even this looks problematic: for the Aristotelians, many substances perish in the course of nature. Does the term 'substance' have completely different meanings in the work of peripatetic and Cartesian metaphysicians? Or have the Aristotelians failed to meditate sufficiently? And, of course, Malebranche himself thinks that all created things would lapse immediately into nothingness without God's action of continuous creation. To spell out the grounds for M3 in more detail would require Malebranche to explain how God sustains His creatures (by means of *volontés générales* rather than *volontés particulières*), and how this in turn requires the continued existence of all created substances unless God exerts a particular volition to annihilate them. It is hard to see how M3 could be interpreted simply as asserting a relation of ideas.

M4. 'No body can move itself by its own forces.'

This is the easiest of the five axioms for Malebranche to explain and defend.[6] We have one clear and distinct idea of material substance, *étendue intelligible*, which is the eternal and immutable archetype that God employed in creating the material universe. We can pay close attention to this idea, and discover that every body must have some determinate size and shape, be infinitely divisible, and be capable of local motion (i.e. of entering into different spatial relations with other bodies at different times). But this capacity for local motion is a mere passive power, a capacity to be moved, not to move itself. The idea of a body does not contain any dynamic power, either to move itself or to impel another body by impact. But a clear and distinct idea excludes whatever it does not include (vi, 161). So, we are entitled to conclude, by applying M1 in this context, that no body has the power to move itself. This axiom can clearly be established on the basis of reflections on relations of ideas.

M5. 'An agitated body cannot communicate to bodies with which it collides more motion than it possesses.'

This axiom needs disambiguation. If construed in strict metaphysical terms, its proof is easy, and is an exact parallel to that for M4. Bodies, strictly speaking, have no power to 'communicate' motion at all. But it is clear from the context that Malebranche has occasional causation in mind – he speaks, after all, of this rule seeming (mistakenly) to conflict with experiments. Construed as an axiom about occasional causation, it amounts to the claim that we could know a priori that God couldn't create super-elastic bodies (i.e. bodies whose coefficient of elasticity is greater than 100 per cent). Now, in his later discussions of these issues Malebranche derives one set of laws for the collision of soft bodies (in which momentum is conserved but *vis viva* is lost), and a different set of laws for the conservation of perfectly elastic bodies (for which Leibniz's principle of conservation of *vis viva* holds). But which laws *actual* bodies observe depends on God's will rather than His intellect, and such questions can only be settled by experience: 'For, since we cannot grasp the Creator's designs, nor understand all the relations which they have to His attributes, whether to conserve an equal quantity of movement seems to depend on a purely arbitrary volition of God, of which in consequence one could only be assured by a type of revelation such as experience provides' (xvii–1, 55). If zero elasticity is logically possible, and 100 per cent elasticity is logically possible, why not 200 per cent elasticity? We could write out the laws for such collisions as an amusing intellectual exercise. There seem to be no internal contradictions in such a system of laws, although any universe that embodied them would be very different from our own. On what basis could we therefore claim to know a priori that God has not created such super-elastic bodies? From our point of view, the laws of impact appear arbitrarily chosen rather than rationally necessary.

In thus calling the will of God 'purely arbitrary', Malebranche is not lapsing into the hated doctrine of voluntarism, which he consistently opposed.[7] God's actions always express His attributes, and His creation of this physical universe is in accordance with Order, which requires a sort of optimum weighted sum of this expression. Malebranche's point is epistemological rather than metaphysical: we humans cannot expect rational insight into why the laws of motion are as they are rather than otherwise, but must turn humbly to the revelation of the divine will that is experience. As the Word explains in the *Meditations Chrétiennes*, I will always answer your questions, so long as you ask me for what I contain in my capacity of Universal Reason, not for what belongs to the Will of God as expressed in His creation (x, 30). You can expect help with your geometry but not with your dynamics.

The inclusion of M5 in the list of axioms in the *Recherche* looks like a piece of simple inadvertence on Malebranche's part. Thanks to the labours of André Robinet,[8] we know that the *Recherche* is a stratified text involving 'layers' from different periods of Malebranche's intellectual career. M5 belongs to an older period when the young Malebranche had more confidence in Cartesian physics; when he came to revise the *Recherche* for the later editions, he should have excised it from the list of axioms of metaphysics. Since it is not simply a matter of the relations of ideas, and since we cannot work out for ourselves how God's attributes are to be expressed in His creation, it is not something that could be known a priori.

4. Malebranche's positive metaphysics 1: God and the soul

Malebranche's various discussions of the proofs of the existence of God are scattered around his *oeuvre*, and continue to puzzle commentators. In Book Four of the *Recherche*, for example, he continues his discussion of the axioms of metaphysics with an analysis and defence of Descartes' ontological argument from *Meditation Five*. Here Malebranche (1958–78: ii, 92–3; 1997a: 318) cheerfully talks about the *idea* of God, or of 'being in general', 'being without limit', or 'infinite being', and argues that this idea includes that of necessary existence. If we take this at face value, we must interpret Malebranche as committed to a textbook version of the ontological argument as resting on a relation of ideas.

This, however, is not Malebranche's considered view. In his 'elucidation' of Descartes' argument he insists that we know God in a quite different manner from our knowledge of creatures. Creatures we know through their ideas; God can only be known in Himself – that is, immediately and without idea. In knowing anything at all, Malebranche explains, I come into contact with whatever divine perfections it participates in (however imperfectly). So, any awareness of anything at all is, strictly speaking, a proof of God, not by way of any idea but immediately. If this is correct, we can be as certain of God's existence as we are of our own existence, since any act of thought or awareness must have an object – to see nothing is not to see at all. But this is no longer an argument that rests on a perception of a relation between ideas; it is an argument of an entirely different sort, a 'preuve de simple vue'.

In the second of the *Entretiens*, Theodore explicitly warns Ariste against the mistaken supposition that God could be known by means of any idea:

> But above all take note that God or the infinite is not visible by any idea that represents Him. The infinite is its own idea. It has no archetype. It can be known, but it cannot be made. It is only creatures, only particular things which can be created, which are visible by the ideas representing them even before they are produced. We can see a circle, a house, a sun, without there being any such thing. For everything finite can be seen in the infinite which contains their intelligible ideas. But the infinite can only be seen it itself. For nothing finite can represent the infinite. If we think of God, He must exist. (1958–78: xii, 53; 1997b: 23)

If we can make sense of this, Malebranche's metaphysical theology offers us the prospect of a body of knowledge that is a priori in one sense (because not dependent on particular information from the senses, and thus immune against sceptical doubts), but not derived from analysis of ideas and their relations. Phenomenology – that is, the awareness of *anything at all* – necessarily involves some cognitive contact with Being, and thus (for Malebranche) with God.[9] If this is possible, we have a principled way of avoiding the disastrous implications of Hume's Fork.

As regards our knowledge of the soul, the position is much clearer. We have direct and incorrigible awareness of our sensations, passions, and current inclinations. We spontaneously take these to be *modes* or modifications of some substance or other. Although we have no idea of the substance of the soul, we can know by way of a *via negativa* proof that it is *not* material. How does this argument work? Malebranche's clearest account is in one of his replies to Arnauld. One has an idea of X, he there explains, when one can tell, by inspecting one's idea, which properties X must possess and which it must lack. I know extension, and hence body, by means of such an idea (*étendue intelligible*). Consulting this idea, I perceive that every body is divisible, mobile, and capable of assuming many different figures, like Descartes' wax:

> I see moreover that it is capable only of this: because the idea of extension – I do not say of an extended thing to avoid any misunderstanding – excludes every thought, every feeling, pain, colour, flavour, etc. Thus, in considering the idea of extension, I see, or can see in a simple glance, its general properties. I see what it contains and what it excludes, because it excludes everything that it does not contain. (1958–78: vi, 161)

Even without an idea of the soul, there is still the possibility of some metaphysical knowledge of its nature, and derived in the standard way by means of relations of ideas. If Malebranche is right and a (clear) idea excludes everything it doesn't include, we have a way of 'rescuing' Descartes' proof of the real distinction simply by reasoning from the clear idea we *do* possess – that of body. We can then talk justifiably of the soul as an *immaterial substance* in this purely negative sense, although of course we are still far from being in a position to provide proofs of its immortality, freedom, and spirituality.[10] We can also develop a series of analogies that enable us to say rather more about the soul than we would otherwise be able to do. We can distinguish dispositional from occurrent states, and speculate that inclinations are to souls as motions to bodies.[11] As Jean-Christophe Bardout (1999) explains in his study of Malebranche's metaphysics, the absence of a clear idea of the soul doesn't entail that we can have no knowledge of it. Metaphysics, he explains, can thus reappropriate an entity that seemed to be slipping beyond its grasp (280).

5. Malebranche's positive metaphysics 2: the world of bodies

The creation of the physical universe, Malebranche tells us, is a free action on God's part, not any sort of metaphysically necessary 'emanation', as some Platonists had imagined. But, given that God decides to create a universe,[12] Order requires that it be a creation worthy of God, which means an optimum expression of the divine attributes, a sort of ideal weighted sum expressing His omnipotence, omniscience, wisdom, immutability, benevolence, justice, and so on. We cannot list all of the attributes contained in the notion of a maximally perfect Being, nor can we assign their respective weights in the sum, so we cannot take it upon ourselves to determine God's plans a priori. We remain confident *that* the creation is a worthy expression of the divine attributes, although we cannot hope to establish in detail *how* it is so.

But can we say nothing a priori about God's designs for the physical universe? Within the Cartesian tradition, metaphysics was meant to impose significant constraints on theorizing in physics. No Cartesian imagined that all of the details could be spelled out from first principles, but the principle of clear and distinct ideas was supposed to provide grounds for confidence that Nature would conform to certain basic principles of intelligibility. Causes should precede (or be simultaneous with) their effects; bodies should move in continuous paths; motion should be conserved; bodies should be moved only by impulse and not by any unintelligible action at a distance; and so on.

Malebranche's early work shares this Cartesian confidence in our ability to establish a priori at least the most general principles of Natural Philosophy. But this confidence did not last. Nowhere is this more evident than in his successive discussions of the rules of impact.[13] Malebranche starts with Descartes' rules, but modifies them at least three times during the next forty years, responding to the twin pressures of experimental evidence (Mariotte, Huygens) and rational critique (Huygens, Leibniz). In his final discussion of the topic he lays down one set of rules for soft bodies, another for elastic bodies, and admits that which type of body God has chosen to create is left to the 'arbitrary' will of God, and hence is something that we can learn only from experience.

But if Descartes' scalar conservation principle is simply false and only the vector conservation principle (our conservation of momentum) is true, it follows that the physical universe may be winding down. Leibniz's principle of the conservation of *vis viva* would prevent this, but the Newtonians deny this principle, and, as far as experience goes, they may be right. Descartes had, of course, tried to derive his (scalar) conservation principle from God's immutability. Now, the principle that God's creation must bear the mark of His attributes is, says the older Malebranche, 'incontestable'. But Descartes' rules are erroneous. It follows that his inference, although plausible (*vraisemblable*) was not valid (Malebranche 1958–78: vii-1, 71–3). The true conservation principle still, Malebranche insists (vii-1, 75), bears the mark of the divine attributes, since it involves a sort of balance or equilibrium, a fitting expression of the divine wisdom. But our grounds for believing the vector conservation principle are now purely empirical: although Malebranche says that it is a fitting expression of God's wisdom, there is no attempt at an inference from 'God is infinitely wise' to 'He will conserve the vector quantity momentum in His continuous creation of the physical universe'. The theological gloss is a post hoc rationalization of an independently delivered empirical finding.

If conservation laws are problematic, what about continuity? It belongs to our clear and distinct idea of body that any body is capable of local motion. It equally belongs to our concept of local motion that it is continuous – that is, that a body cannot move from A to C without passing through B. Could we claim, on this basis, to know a priori (on the basis of these relations of ideas) that the law of continuity holds in nature? The answer, unfortunately, must be 'no'. Why not? Because even if it is an analytic truth, in modern terms, that bodies can move only continuously, it is not an analytic truth that bodies can only get from one place to another by local motion. In his polemic over Cartesianism and the Eucharist with the Jesuit Louis La Ville, Malebranche insists that God can create body at A at an instant t_1, and then re-create *that numerically identical body* at C at t_3, without any implication that it was ever present at B (vii-1, 491). The senses and the imagination may revolt at this picture, and may clamour that spatiotemporal continuity is essential to the identity-conditions of bodies, but the senses and the imagination are no guides to truth and must simply be overruled (vii-1, 492). The existence of 'gappy' objects (in terms of both space and of time) is self-consistent, and so is permitted by reason. God could choose to create such objects.

As for reverse causation, Malebranche explicitly accepts this in another theological context. The prayers of the human soul of Jesus Christ are, he argues in his *Traité de la Nature et de la Grace*, the occasional causes of God's distribution of gifts of grace to human souls. But, respond the critics, what of the gifts of grace to the patriarchs? On occasionalist principles, Malebranche replies (vi, 158), this objection is deprived of all its force. Since God is omniscient, He knows timelessly the contents of Jesus' prayers. Since the cause (occasion) has no efficacy of its own, and no necessary connection with the effect, why should it not be the case that Abraham receives the gift of grace in 1000 BC because Christ prays for him in 30 AD? Such backwards causation, Malebranche admits, seems 'contrary to order', but on his principles it remains perfectly possible. Since it can be described without self-contradiction, we cannot know a priori that grace is not distributed according to such principles. It may be only prejudice that leads us to regard it as contrary to order.

Occasionalism, it seems, lays down no clear rules regarding what can cause (i.e. provide the occasion for) what, and thus permits a slide into something like Humean empiricism, with its insistence that, as far as a priori reasoning is concerned, anything can cause anything. In his *doutes sur le système physique des causes occasionelles*, Fontenelle (1818: i, 615–38) challenges Malebranche to defend, on his occasionalist principles, the Cartesian insistence that bodies are moved only by impact and never by action at a distance. If there is nothing in the impacting body that qualifies it to be the *true cause* (as opposed to the mere occasion) of the ensuing motion of the struck body, why, he asks, should contact be required at all?

> I shall suppose therefore that God, instead of establishing collision as the occasional cause of the communication of motions, has established as the occasional cause the passage of two bodies to a certain distance from one another, for example to a line which is the mean proportional between their diameters. The entire order of the material universe would then depend on this new principle. (Malebranche 1958–78: xvii–1, 588)

If we are to defend Malebranche against this objection, we cannot say that God *could* not have chosen such a rule. We must argue instead that He *would* not choose such a rule.[14] Why not? It is stated in terms of clear and distinct ideas, without any reference to occult qualities or mysterious powers of repulsion. And it gives perfectly determinate solutions to collision problems. If Order prohibits it, it must be because it involves an element of arbitrariness. The bodies rebound, according to this rule, when their separation is the harmonic mean of their diameters, a distance $\sqrt{nm}$ (where n and m are the diameters of the colliding bodies). But why not the arithmetic mean, $n+m/2$? Or why not the sum, $n+m$? Or the product nm? There are, it seems, any number of possible rules, and no obvious ground for choosing one over another. But a distance of zero for rebound is non-arbitrary, because interpenetration would involve annihilation.

We can 'save' Malebranche, it seems, only at the cost of shifting his position towards that of Leibniz. When Malebranche says that the choice of one type of body rather than another is 'purely arbitrary', dependent merely on the (for us) inscrutable will of God, we have to decide whether we are to take him at his word or to regard this as a regrettable piece of exaggeration. If we take him at his word, we have to conclude that there are no a priori constraints over and above bare logical consistency governing occasional causation – anything can be the occasion for anything. If we reject the language of arbitrary choices as a regrettable lapse, we can try to say something more positive. Our own glimpses of Order, we might hope, allow us some glimmerings of rational insight into God's reasons for choosing a physical universe in which motion is conserved (albeit only the vector quantity momentum), bodies generally *move* rather than 'hop' from one place to another, and bodies impart motion to other bodies only by impulse. We cannot be certain a priori that these principles hold in Nature, because their negations involve no self-contradiction. But through our (partial and limited) participation in Universal Reason, we can obtain a modest degree of confidence that our sense of what is 'fitting' or 'appropriate' is also God's sense. The problem, of course, is that we have no decisive criterion of correctness, no way of distinguishing something merely *vraisemblable* (e.g. Descartes' derivation of his scalar conservation principle) from something genuinely based on a rational perception of Order.

6. Conclusion

We have now sketched at least the outlines of Malebranche's possible response to our original problem – that he ought to have concluded, on the basis of his own principles, that metaphysics is an impossible discipline promising more than it could ever deliver. If the 'preuve de simple vue' of God's existence can be made to work, there is a type of knowledge that can reasonably be labelled a priori but that does not rest on relations of ideas. If the *via negativa* argument for dualism can be made to work, we have at least some knowledge of the soul that belongs to the class of relations of ideas. And if we reject as a regrettable exaggeration the notion that God's will must seem to us 'purely arbitrary', we can allow our own glimmerings of what is, or is not, required by Order to have some sort of epistemological status. We cannot, of course, achieve certainty in this regard (if Descartes can go wrong, despite all his care and his efforts to avoid errors, anyone can go wrong). Experience can always force us to rethink, as it forced Malebranche to rethink several times his laws of motion. We know that God is wise and immutable, but we don't know precisely how these attributes are to be expressed in His creation. Only experience can tell us that.

Throughout the positive part of this chapter, I have deliberately avoided using the textbook terms 'rationalist' and 'empiricist'. On the standard story, Malebranche is a committed rationalist who finds himself obliged to make a series of concessions to empiricism. But this story may be merely anachronistic. Malebranche himself would say that all of our knowledge is *revelation*, and that his philosophy is best regarded as a search for reflective equilibrium incorporating and synthesizing elements drawn from the three key types of revelation available to humans: the revelation of Universal Reason through the Word, the revelation of God's Will through Experience, and the revelation of God's purposes for man through Scripture. Since all three are sources of Truth, and all stem from the same source, there can be – in the final analysis – no contradictions between them and hence no need to oppose one to another. We just need to meditate harder to still our own passions and prejudices and thus to discern their true voices.

Notes

1 For a beautifully lucid and thought-provoking account of the thesis that in our intellectual activity we participate in the mind of God, see Craig (1987).
2 Hume, Letter to Ramsay, Orleans, 31 August 1737. Quoted from Mossner (1980: 104).
3 I am not for one moment endorsing the old interpretation of Hume as a proto-positivist. The impossibility of metaphysics will follow equally – albeit for different reasons – for both the 'old' and the 'new' Hume.
4 The allusion to school metaphysics as 'sophistry and illusion' could fit either the proto-positivist 'old Hume' or the sceptical realist 'new Hume'. For the former, the would-be metaphysician is not even succeeding in advancing propositions; for the latter, he advances propositions that we could never know to be true. The impossibility of metaphysics follows in either case. For a good collection of literature on the 'New Hume debate', see Read and Richman (2000).
5 Hume might say the same of those aspects of the *Recherche* that he valued. Much of it is, of course, a close study of the human mind and its propensities to errors of various kinds.
6 See the discussions in the *Méditations Chrétiennes* – (Malebranche 1958–78: x, 47) – and the *Entretiens sur la metaphysique et sur la religion* – (xii, 154–5; 1997b: 110).

7 For a lively recent treatment of the three-cornered debate between Malebranche, Arnauld, and Leibniz on this subject, see Nadler (2010).
8 For more detail on the tortuous story of the various editions of the *Recherche*, see Robinet (1965).
9 Of all the commentators on Malebranche, the only one who comes close to grasping this point is Rome (1963). Of course, if Rome is right, Malebranche is closer to the scholastics than he might want to be.
10 I argue in Pyle (2003: 197ff) that Malebranche finds himself unable to fulfil his promises on this score. A more positive reading is provided by Schmaltz (1996), who argues that Malebranche can still provide reconstructions of the Cartesian arguments for the soul's liberty, spirituality, and immortality.
11 For helpful commentary, see Bardout (1999: 279–80).
12 We might wonder why Malebranche doesn't simply consider the null universe (no creation at all) as one possible world among many, and then ask if Order would permit God to choose it.
13 For more detail, see Pyle (2003: 131–57).
14 For this rather Leibnizian line of defence of Malebranche, see Schmaltz (2008).

References

Bardout, J.-C. (1999), *Malebranche et la Metaphysique*, Paris: Presses Universitaires de France.
Craig, E. (1987), *The Mind of God and the Works of Man*, Oxford: Clarendon Press.
Fontenelle, B. (1818), *Oeuvres*, 4 vols, Paris: Belin.
Hume, D. (1978), *A Treatise of Human Nature*, ed. L. A. Selby-Bigge, 2nd edn, ed. P. H. Nidditch, Oxford: Oxford University Press.
Hume, D. (1999), *An Enquiry Concerning Human Understanding*, ed. T. L. Beauchamp, Oxford: Oxford University Press.
Malebranche, N. (1958–78), *Oeuvres Complètes de Malebranche*, ed. A. Robinet, 20 vols, Paris: Vrin.
Malebranche, N. (1997a), *The Search after Truth*, ed. and trans. T. Lennon and P. Olscamp, Cambridge: Cambridge University Press.
Malebranche, N. (1997b), *Dialogues on Metaphysics and on Religion*, ed. Nicholas Jolley, trans. D. Scott, Cambridge: Cambridge University Press.
McCracken, C. J. (1993), *Malebranche and British Philosophy*, Oxford: Oxford University Press.
Mossner, E. (1980), *The Life of David Hume*, 2nd edn, Oxford: Oxford University Press.
Nadler, S. (2010), *The Best of All Possible Worlds: A Story of Philosophers, God, and Evil in the Age of Reason*, Princeton: Princeton University Press.

Popkin, R. H. (1979), *The History of Scepticism from Erasmus to Spinoza*, Berkeley: University of California Press.

Pyle, A. (2003), *Malebranche*, London: Routledge.

Pyle, A. (2011), 'Malebranche and Hume on Natural Belief', in P. Dessi and B. Lotti (eds), *Eredita Cartesiane Nella Cultura Britannica*, Florence: Le Lettere.

Read, R. and Richman, K. (eds) (2000), *The New Hume Debate*, London: Routledge.

Robinet, A. (1965), *Système et existence dans l'oeuvre de Malebranche*, Paris: Vrin.

Rome, B. (1963), *The Philosophy of Malebranche*, Chicago: Henry Regnery.

Schmaltz, T. (1996), *Malebranche's Theory of the Soul: A Cartesian Interpretation*, New York: Oxford University Press.

Schmaltz, T. (2008), 'Occasionalism and Mechanism: Fontenelle's Objections to Malebranche', *British Journal for the History of Philosophy*, 16: 293–313.

6

Leibniz

Justin E. H. Smith

1. Introduction

The philosophical system of Gottfried Wilhelm Leibniz (1646–1716) has something of the character of a carrousel: you can get on at any point, you can begin with any claim, and by following the natural track of the claim you will eventually arrive at every other claim. This is the sense of one of Leibniz's best-known mottos: *tout est lié*, everything is connected.

Where, then, to get on? If we are interested in Leibniz's metaphysics of nature, we will naturally begin with those passages of his late philosophy in which he describes natural bodies as infinitely structured 'divine machines'. If it is the logic that interests us, we will probably wish to begin with a text such as the *Primary Truths* of 1689 that sets out from the Principle of Sufficient Reason and the Principle of the Identity of Indiscernibles to deliver us, soon enough, more or less everything else we are familiar with from Leibniz's philosophy – including the structure and nature of natural bodies.[1]

But where are we to get on if what interests us is, say, knowledge? The truth is, again, here as elsewhere, any point will do. We can start with the foundational truth of the logical principles, or we can start with bodies. In fact, because any truth will quickly bring us around to any other, we may rightly ask in what sense the logical principles such as the Principle of Sufficient Reason are 'foundational' at all. But let us hold that question, for now, in order to discover, first of all, what knowledge is for Leibniz, and, second, how it connects with the other elements of his philosophy, how it comes around to all the other points on the carrousel.

2. Leibniz's theory of knowledge: the basics

There are two principal and interrelated elements of Leibniz's theory of knowledge. The first is that knowledge is a matter of degree: there is no firm boundary between unconscious or confused representation of the order of things and of facts on the one hand, and clear, conscious, awareness of this order on the other. Sometimes these two states are described as 'perception' and 'apperception' – knowing, however dimly, and knowing that one knows. The key thing for us to appreciate at the outset is that these are not two different and opposed states, but rather points on a continuum, blending into one another like black and white on a greyscale. The second key point is that all knowledge is in the end omniscient knowledge, even if the knower is not fully aware of this, is not able to consciously discern the chains of implication that lead out from all the infinitely many other truths. These two features of the theory are, again, connected: in order to be omniscient, any knower, or at least any knower other than God, must have only confused knowledge of the vast majority of truths. Otherwise, that knower would in fact *be* God, or at least attain to a state of knowledge reserved for the Divine: a state of direct, immediate, conscious apprehension of all truths.

3. Leibniz on substance

But in order to understand Leibniz's theory of knowledge, we must ask not only what knowledge is for him, but also what sort of thing he knows. What are these other knowers besides God, which perceive all things, and occasionally apperceive at least some things? The answer, in short, is substances, which are also, after the mid-1690s, frequently identified as 'monads'. For Leibniz, a substance is the same thing as a monad since, by definition, whatever truly exists must have true unity, must be 'one'. As Leibniz (1849–60: vi, 598) writes in the *Principles of Nature and Grace* (*Principes de la nature et de la grâce*) of 1714: '*Monas* is a Greek word that signifies unity or that which is one. Composites or bodies are multitudes, and simple substances, lives, souls, spirits, are unities.'

Why divide things up in this way? Why is being equated with unity? Part of the answer is that, for Leibniz, whatever exists only through the arrangement of its parts can be just as easily taken out of existence by a process of disassembly. But what sort of entity worthy of being called a *being* would be so dependent on the current conformation of its parts, so fragile as to be unable to survive the removal of half, or indeed of nearly all, of its current bodily parts? How could any such entity ever pass from being on an ontological par with a mere machine or any other such 'entity by aggregation', to being on a par with a human being, a horse, or any other such 'entity in itself'?

This does not mean that a human being, considered not just as a human soul, but as a human soul together with an organic body, is not a unity. Although in some sense it can be divided, as, for example, when my arm is amputated, it cannot really be divided, in the sense that I do not in any way become less a person, or indeed less *the* person I already was, when I lose my arm. In this, I, as a corporeal substance, am very different from an entity by aggregation, such as a pile of sawdust, which is exactly 10 per cent less the pile it was when 10 per cent of the sawdust constituting it is taken away. In this respect, a human being is not so much divisible, as it is – to use R. C. Sleigh's (1990: 126) helpful term – 'deconstructible component-wise', where the component in question is, namely, the body. Although Sleigh might have done better to say 'reducible' rather than 'deconstructible', for the key point is that you cannot really get rid of a corporeal substance (again, understood as the organic body taken together with the soul or dominant monad), you can only cause it to retreat, as Leibniz sometimes says, 'to the smaller theatre'. This is the case even if you cut off not its arm, but indeed its head, whereupon some small organic kernel of the organic body begins its 'afterlife' as a microorganism. This afterlife, however, unlike those of souls that ascend to heaven, is perfectly natural: the being stays within the empirical world, floats around in the air, or drifts in the scum of the pond, until the end of time.

We may seem to have drifted ourselves, far from the topic of knowledge. But, again, one cannot drift, so long as one stays attached to actual commitments in Leibniz's philosophy; one can only move in a circle. We have just arrived at yet another respect in which created substances are like God: they are not only omniscient (if dimly so); they are also immortal. These two features of substances are, not surprisingly, connected. An organic body – and all bodies are organic for Leibniz, in the end – is infinitely structured, which is to say that there is no way to break it down to a point where one has no organic structure, but only an undifferentiated mass. But what this organic body is, in the end – 'in metaphysical rigor', as Leibniz likes to say – is the phenomenal result of the mutual perceptions, at varying degrees of confusion and clarity, of an infinite ensemble of immaterial monads. We do not need to enter into the technical details of how this result occurs, or into the historical development of Leibniz's account over the several decades in which he sought to work it out. It will be enough for us here to note that in this infinite ensemble there is also an infinite hierarchy of relations of domination and subordination, where a monad that perceives another set of monads more clearly than they perceive it, or perhaps even than they perceive themselves, will for that same reason dominate that set of monads.

Phenomenally, this domination that is grounded in immaterial perception will manifest itself in bodiliness. For example, my soul perceives more clearly the monads from which my left big toe results than any of these monads perceive my soul. For this same reason, my toe manifests itself phenomenally as part of my body, or, in other words, my toe belongs to me, where 'I' am both a corporeal substance and the monad dominating the organic body of this corporeal substance, and not to someone else. How bodies are individuated, then, to which corporeal substance a given toe is to be ascribed, for example, is in the end a result of the degrees of clarity of perception of immaterial monads. This is also how what we think of as mind-body causation is to be explained. Thus, Leibniz (1849–60: ii, 71) writes to Antoine Arnauld in 1686 that one is 'quite right to say that my will is the cause of this movement of my arm ...; for the one expresses distinctly what the other expresses more confusedly, and one must ascribe the action to the substance whose expression is more distinct'. The same year, he further explains in section 33 of the *Discourse on Metaphysics* of 1686 that

> the essence of the soul brings it about that all of its appearances or perceptions should be born of out of its nature and precisely in such a way that they correspond of themselves to that which happens in the universe at large, but more particularly and more perfectly to that which happens in the body associated with it, because it is in a particular way and only for a certain time according to the relation of other bodies to its own body that the soul expresses the state of the universe. This last fact enables us to see how our body belongs to us, without, however, being attached to our essence. (iv, 458–9)

There is in the end no definite boundary between 'my' body and the entirety of the bodily world. In fact, my soul perceives all of the bodies in the universe, and, just as in its relation to my own body, it stands to them in a relation of what Leibniz in 1686 calls 'sympathy', and of what he will later call 'harmony'.

What will soon enough become the doctrine of pre-established harmony will amount to a further elaboration of the curious claim about the soul at the beginning of the quoted passage, so subtle as to easily pass unnoticed: namely, that all perceptions 'should be born out of its [the soul's] own nature'. Could Leibniz really be saying that perceptions are *not* born from the encounter of the soul with the external world? Indeed, he is. One way that this point is sometimes put is to say that for Leibniz there can be for a substance 'no purely extrinsic denominations'[2]: that is, nothing outside of it can play a causal role in the succession of its states. It is causally self-sufficient; or, as Leibniz will come to put it when he starts speaking of substances as monads, it is 'windowless'. It is also, one might add, doorless: there is no way for anything to get into it from outside, no new perceptions, and certainly no new knowledge.

4. Determinism

It is by now not hard to see why Leibniz is considered a 'rationalist' philosopher. Indeed, we might justly describe him as a radical rationalist, or at least as a thoroughgoing one. For a philosopher such as Plato, there might be a number of things that we come to know, at least in a certain qualified sense, through our encounter with the empirical world, even if this knowledge is in fact mere 'opinion' (*doxa*). For Leibniz, by contrast, absolutely everything that we learn in fact merely surfaces, or rises to consciousness, from among the infinitely many truths about the world that have always been packed into our souls, into what Leibniz calls in the period of the *Discourse on Metaphysics* our 'complete concept'. Everything that has ever been true, or will ever be true, of Julius Caesar (and recall that Julius Caesar is immortal, like all other substances) can be known if one simply has adequate knowledge of his complete concept, and can in principle be derived logically from any other truth about him. Thus, if you have full knowledge of the meaning of the name 'Julius Caesar', then you will know, as a sort of logical truth, that he crossed the Rubicon (or that he ate this or that for breakfast the day of the crossing). What is more, because each substance expresses the entire state of the universe, you could in principle derive from *my* complete concept the truth of what Julius Caesar had for breakfast on the day when he crossed the Rubicon. Not only is there no real boundary between necessary and contingent truths; it is also the case that every apparently contingent truth can be logically derived from every other one. To be sure, it would take infinitely many steps to complete the logical derivation, and this is something of which only God is capable, while from our point of view the difference between contingent and necessary truths will continue to appear salient and insurmountable. Nonetheless, the translation of this difference into one between finity and infinity, rather than between two different *kinds* of truth, departs in fundamental ways from the traditional account of the distinction between contingency and necessity.

This departure is of central importance for understanding Leibniz's theory of knowledge. He is committed to the view that we know what Julius Caesar had for breakfast, in the same way that we know, say, the Principle of the Identity of Indiscernibles, even if it is significantly more difficult for us to access the former truth. All knowledge is a priori, and all truths are necessary, written into the deterministic order of the world at the moment of the Creation, which is to say at the moment of God's choice of this world from among infinitely many possible worlds.

5. Leibniz's 'rationalist empiricism'

It would be a mistake to suppose that the ultimate a priori nature of all knowledge led Leibniz to undervalue or downplay the importance of empirical discovery. In fact, we might do well to think of Leibniz as a sort of 'rationalist empiricist', a label that only sounds oxymoronic, somewhat like 'democratic republican', when we are using each of its two terms not with respect to their original meaning, but as the labels for opposed camps. From the early text of 1671 entitled *Directiones ad rem medicam pertinentes* (*Directions Pertaining to the Institution of Medicine*),[3] to the late correspondences with Peter the Great's councillors on the establishment of a scientific academy in Berlin, Leibniz was consistently interested in promoting projects for the discovery and accumulation of particular facts. Even if in metaphysical rigor these facts are already contained within us, Leibniz never thought that it would be expedient or feasible to attempt to draw them out in an armchair fashion, and always maintained that, for our purposes, the best way to advance scientific knowledge is through empirical methods. In fact, even in his own lifetime he seems to have regretted being overly associated with reflection on classical a priori truths, when what interested him most were the 'singular things' of history, understood as the discipline that concerns itself with particular facts. Thus, he writes to the Swedish linguist J. G. Sparwenfeld in 1698 that 'people ... tell me I am wrong to abandon solid and eternal truths in order to study the changing and perishable things that are found in history and its laws' (1873: 38).

Nor, however, does Leibniz think of the study of singular things as a departure from the study of the universal. To put this another way, he does not see empiricism as a distinct project from rationalism. Rather, the accumulation of particular facts yields up, sooner or later, new confirmation of the rational order and the unity of nature. One may thus deploy empirical methods to deepen one's appreciation of the truth of rationalism. A vivid example of this is in Leibniz's longstanding interest in the study of magnetic variation. By the beginning of the seventeenth century, it had become clear that the distance between magnetic north and 'true north' varies from place to place, a fact about the earth that presented no small problem for navigators. Over the next few decades, to make matters worse, it turned out that not only does the measure of 'the two norths' differ from place to place; it differs also, at any given place, from moment to moment. As Henry Gellibrand (1635: 2–3) wrote in his 1635 *Discourse Mathematicall on the variation of the Magneticall Needle*, there is an 'abstruse and admirable variation of the Variation'. Far from being a proof of the fundamentally chaotic nature of the world, however, some decades later Leibniz would see this variation of variation as an ideal instance for the application of his empirical method, in which a massive collaborative effort for the accumulation of what we might call 'big data' would eventually yield a picture of the order behind the apparent chaos, an order that we can know to exist on a priori grounds. Leibniz proposes in a letter to Peter the Great of 1716 that a systematic effort should be made to set up research stations across the Arctic coast of the Russian Empire, with measurements taken at regular intervals, so that eventually 'magnetic maps' (*Magnetische Charten*) could be made that would show the variations within a given time interval, eventually to be replaced by newer ones when these have expired. Leibniz believes that 'there is no doubt that in time a certain order would show itself within the variation itself [*in der veränderung selbst sich eine gewisse ordnung zeigen ... würde*]' (1873: 239). In the end, this order would be a small sliver of the total determined mechanical order of the motions of natural bodies and the various forces governing them, and this mechanical order is in turn the phenomenal, or bodily, manifestation of the infinite order of mutual perception among simple substances or monads. This order is known by all substances a priori, to the extent that each substance is an equal participant in this web of mutual perception, fully expressing everything that occurs in each other substance. Empiricism thus fills out and brings into focus what we already know confusedly.

6. Representation and anti-materialism

We have just spoken of perception as expression, a substitution that might have been unexpected. Perception often functions as something close to a primitive in Leibniz's philosophy, as when he writes to Burchard De Volder in 1704 that 'there is nothing in the world but simple substances, and in them perception and appetite' (where appetite is the tendency to move from one perception to the next). Elsewhere however, as in the *New Method of Learning and Teaching Jurisprudence* of the late 1690s, Leibniz (1923ff: series 6, i, 286) further defines 'perception' as 'the expression of many things in one, or in simple substance'. This is a point to which Leibniz returns frequently in his account of expression: it is the power of the simple substance to hold within it, though it is simple, a multiplicity of things. These things are not actually contained within it, but they are rather represented within it. This representation, again, does not depend on the external things of which they are representations, and would be occurring just as it does even if they did not exist. The capacity for expression of each individual substance is what ensures that, though there are only simple unities in the world, they are nonetheless the bearers of the world's diversity. Seen from the other direction, the diversity of things is in turn underlaid by unity. It is this bidirectional relationship between unity and diversity that Leibniz sometimes describes in terms of 'unity compensated by diversity'.

It is, again, a simple substance that has this power, and not a brain or body or any other physical system. What it is that expresses, in fact, could not possibly be a body for Leibniz (even if the body is a phenomenal result of this expressing activity), since all that we ever find in the body is *partes extra partes* – literally, 'parts beyond parts',[4] but also perhaps 'ever more parts'. And that which consists in parts, again, cannot have true unity, and so cannot be a being, and so, in turn, cannot be the locus of perceptions or thoughts. Rather, in order for there to be a being in the bodily world, there must be, behind or beneath the phenomenal manifestations of body, something, as Leibniz puts it, 'that is analogous to the "I"'. It follows from these considerations that no materialist account of mental activity could ever satisfy Leibniz, not because we lack sufficient knowledge of the workings of the brain, but for fundamental conceptual reasons. It is a basic category mistake to suppose that a bodily organ is the sort of thing that *could* think. In this connection, in the *Monadology* of 1714 Leibniz (1849–60: vi, 609) offers his very well-known 'mill' argument against materialism:

> We are moreover obliged to confess that perception, and that which depends on it, is inexplicable by mechanical reasons, that is to say by figures and by movements. And if we imagine a machine the structure of which causes it to think, to feel, to have perception, we could imagine it blown up in size while keeping the same proportions, so that we could enter inside it, as in a mill. And if this is supposed, we would find on visiting its interior only parts that push

one another, and never that which explains perception. Thus it is in the simple substance, and not in the composite or in the machine that it must be sought.

All that a mill, or a brain, will ever give us is more parts, but mental activity cannot result from an arrangement of parts. Therefore, what thinks is not the brain.

The 'I' that is the locus of thought and perception is a transcendent subject, which means among other things that it endures through any and all changes in its circumstances: it is not dependent on any particular circumstances, or on the preservation of any particular quality of its perceptions, in order to be the subject it is. Thus, for Leibniz, the criterion of identity over time for a subject could not be – as it is for John Locke – the continuity of conscious experience and of memory. A substance could very well have 'blackouts', in which it drops into a deep slumber or stupor, from which it could then wake up without any interruption in its being. In fact, a stupor is never total; it is only a temporary relative decrease in the clarity of perceptions, so that all of these drop below the threshold of consciousness or apperception. With this view, significantly, Leibniz positions himself as a rare philosopher, prior to the era of Freud, who is willing to commit himself to the existence of subconscious mental activity, or mental activity in which the thinker is unaware of the fact that he or she or it is engaging in mental activity. It is this activity that ensures, and that is required by, the perpetual endurance of the metaphysical subject – of that in the substance that is analogous to the 'I'.

So, consciousness and continuity of memory are not necessary for continuity of identity. Nonetheless, Leibniz agrees broadly with Locke that, as he puts in a text of the early 1680s, 'consciousness is memory of our actions' (1923ff: series 6, iv, 1473). We may still ask how, for Leibniz, memory is supposed to work. Clearly, knowing our previous states follows from our knowledge, however confused, of every state of every substance in the world. But we may still ask how it is that memories, or traces of previous perceptions, have the character they do, as traces of our actions in particular. Sometimes, Leibniz seeks to explain memory in the seemingly metaphorical terms of enduring 'vibrations'. Thus, in a letter to Johann Bernoulli of 6 May 1712, Leibniz (1849–63: iii, 884–5) writes:

> In organic beings many things seem to consist in perpetual, imperceptible vibrations, which, when we perceive them to be at rest, are in fact being held back by contrary vibrations. Thus in truth we are led back to an elastic force. I suspect that memory itself consists in the endurance of vibrations. Thus there does not appear to be any use for a fluid that goes by the name of animal spirits, unless it is traced back to the reason itself of the elastic force.

Here one might reasonably ask whether vibration isn't something that would occur in the parts of a composite being rather than within the expressive unity of a simple substance. And, if so, is Leibniz's explanation to Bernoulli not in direct contradiction of the mill argument that he will present in the *Monadology* two years later? It would seem that what Leibniz means to say to his correspondent is that these vibrations are the bodily counterpart of what occurs in the soul as memory – that they accompany memory in the same way that, by pre-established harmony, there is always a particular brain state corresponding to any mental activity – but that he did not wish to enter into the deeper metaphysics of the problem with a correspondent with whom he mostly enjoyed discussing mathematics.

We have principally been treating perception, while the primary concern of this volume is not perception but instead knowledge. The reason for this is, as has been explained, that perception for Leibniz is the basic and generic form of mental activity, while knowledge is a variety of perception, which occurs at one extreme end of a spectrum running from pure confusion to pure clarity. Now, typically we distinguish knowledge from perception on the grounds that the latter may be false, that it might not correctly reflect the actual state of things. Perceptions, we typically suppose, insofar as they are confused, are false. But, for Leibniz, confusion is in no way an epistemic failure; it is only the mode of perception most suited to created beings constrained to represent the world under the aspect of bodiliness or phenomenality. Leibniz understands the word in its etymological sense: that which is *con-fused* is literally fused together. A body is the result of the representation *as* fused-together of what is in reality discrete: namely, an infinite ensemble of simple substances. It is not a mistake or an error to represent the world in this way; it is simply the mode of representation appropriate to a finite mind. God, for his part, always represents the infinite ensemble of the world's monads to himself as they really are, which is to say as discrete and simple unities. This is just another way of saying that God *knows* them fully. But knowing them less fully is not failing to know them, and finite minds will always perceive things in a way that somehow fails to capture them with perfect clarity. Knowledge is therefore not a matter of a threshold for Leibniz; one may 'sort of' know things.

7. Knowledge and truth

If one may 'sort of' know things, does this mean that propositions about these things are 'sort of' true for Leibniz? If knowledge admits of a more and a less, does truth do so as well? In fact, no. 'True' and 'false' is an all-or-nothing affair for him. And yet propositions that aim to capture the truth may still do so with varying degrees of success. One of the more remarkable features of Leibniz's perspectivalist philosophy, according to which every substance represents to itself the same world as every other, but from a different and unique point of view, is that for Leibniz different accounts of the way that the world is can not only simultaneously be true, but can in principle be shown to be saying the very same thing, expressing the very same truths. Leibniz likes to invoke in this connection the analogy of different perspectives on one and the same city. As he writes in the *Discourse on Metaphysics* of 1686 (1849–60: vi, 607):

> Just as the same city viewed from different directions appears entirely different, and, as it were, multiplied perspectively, in just the same way it happens that, because of the infinite multitude of simple substances, there are, as it were, just as many different universes, which are, nevertheless, only perspectives on a single one, corresponding to the different points of view of each monad.

God's perspective, presumably, is something like Thomas Nagel's (1986) 'view from nowhere'. It captures the city itself, rather than the city from this or that angle, with only these or those surfaces on display. To some extent, what we today call 'science' and, more generally, human artifice and ingenuity can enable human beings to approximate that view from nowhere, which is to say that these can enable an increase in the clarity of perception. Leibniz sees crucial technological aid for this increase in the parallel projects of computing and artificial language. In the use of such devices as the stepped reckoner in arithmetic, or the binary calculus, and in the replacement of natural language for many purposes by an ideal formal language or 'universal characteristic', Leibniz believes that we will be able to advance to a state in which the expression of ideas will not be hampered by ambiguities or confusion. In the case of disagreements, translation into a formal language will enable the opposed parties to see whether they are in fact saying the same thing but simply using different terms. Famously, Leibniz hoped that someday soon two parties involved in a diplomatic conflict could simply declare *Calculemus!* – 'Let us calculate!'[5] – and resolve their apparent disagreement by 'calculating', or rendering in formal language, all of the relevant terms.

The belief that disagreements could be resolved in this way is a plain expression of Leibniz's optimism, and of his eirenism. Indeed, one frequently has the impression in reading Leibniz that he is overly disinclined to acknowledge the reality of substantive disagreements between people. He believes that everyone is, in their own way, getting things right. But this is not at all because Leibniz is a relativist for whom each person has their own truth. Rather, there is one truth, and each person reflects that truth from a different point of view.

8. Logic and the question of foundationalism

We have made nearly the whole tour of the Leibnizian carrousel, and yet the experienced rider will have known to expect, before completing the circle, to encounter the basic logical truths that have been thought by some commentators to provide the very fundament of Leibniz's philosophy. These are, most importantly, the Principle of Identity, which says that everything is what it is, and not some other thing; the Principle of the Identity of Indiscernibles, that if two things have all properties in common, then in fact they are not two things at all, but one; and the Principle of Sufficient Reason, that everything that happens has a reason, that there are no gratuitous or ungrounded events. These are important principles for Leibniz, but it is hard to think of them as fundamental in any real sense, as, say, Descartes' *cogito* is fundamental to his epistemology, since in fact we could have seen them coming from what we already saw of Leibniz's metaphysics of substance, his theory of perception, and his account of the bodily world. Every state of a substance unfolds from its complete concept or program, and so cannot arise from nowhere, let alone from the influence of something outside of it. What it is to be a particular thing is to have a particular complete concept or program; this is something that is not determined relationally, as indeed there are no extrinsic denominations for a thing, and from this the Principle of the Identity of Indiscernibles follows of necessity. The Principle of Identity follows, too, from the definition of substance at the heart of Leibniz's metaphysics of individuality.

Are these basic logical truths better known than other truths? They may at least be said to be known consciously by rational, reflective beings. But conscious knowledge of them is not a precondition of knowledge of the rational order of the universe and of the metaphysics of substance that informs this rational order. It is not that these logical principles need first to be grasped in order to make sense of other domains of Leibniz's philosophy, but rather that these principles are mutually implicated along with the claims of these other domains. Leibniz is not a foundationalist philosopher. He is a hyper-rationalist, for whom all truths mutually imply all other truths.

9. Conclusion

Nor is he, first and foremost, an epistemologist. He is a metaphysician, and one of the implications of his metaphysics is that it is part of the nature of a substance to know things, even if most substances do not know things with any degree of clarity that would warrant calling them rational beings. In this respect, while Leibniz has a theory of knowledge, he is not in any significant sense a theorist of knowledge. We are tempted to make him into one largely because he is active in the historical period after Descartes, who is credited with transforming epistemology into 'first philosophy'. But in this respect, as in many others, Leibniz remains immersed in a pre-Cartesian world of concerns. Leibniz sees mental activity akin to knowledge not as a special capacity of a special class of beings, but as a basic condition of existence. He sees every thing that may be said to exist as in some important sense a mirror of God's omniscience. God knows everything with perfect clarity, while created substances know with a mixture of clarity and confusion. It is this mixture that gives rise to the bodily world and its complex hierarchies of action and passion. Leibniz does not need to have an independent, well-bounded theory of knowledge, since for him epistemology – the account of what knowledge is – is entirely interwoven into the metaphysics that continues, for him, to constitute first philosophy.

Notes

1. For approaches to Leibniz's philosophy that begin with the primary truths of logic, see, in particular, Russell (1900) and Rodriguez-Pereyra (2014).
2. See Leibniz (1923ff: series 6, vi, 227; 1849–60: vii, 311).
3. See Smith (2011: Appendix 1).
4. See Duchesneau and Smith (2016: 127).
5. Leibniz, 'La vraie méthode' (1677), in Leibniz (1923ff: series 6, iv, 3).

References

Duchesneau, F. and Smith, J. E. H. (eds and trans.) (2016), *The Leibniz-Stahl Controversy*, New Haven: Yale University Press.

Gellibrand, H. (1635), *Discourse Mathematicall on the Variation of the Magneticall Needle*, London: William Iones.

Leibniz, G. W. (1923ff), *Sämtliche Schriften und Briefe*, Berlin: Preussische Akademie der Wissenschaften.
Leibniz, G. W. (1849–60), *Die philosophischen Schriften von G.W. Leibniz*, ed. C. I. Gerhardt, 7 vols, Berlin: Olms.
Leibniz, G. W. (1849–63), *Leibnizens mathematische Schriften*, ed. C. I. Gerhardt, 7 vols, Berlin and Halle: Olms.
Leibniz, G. W. (1873), *Sbornik pisem i memorialov Leïbnitsa otnosyashchikhsya k Rossii i Petru Velikomu*, ed. V. I. Ger'e, Saint Petersburg: Imperial Akademi.
Nagel, T. (1986), *The View from Nowhere*, New York: Oxford University Press.
Rodriguez Pereyra, G. (2014), *Leibniz's Principle of Identity of Indiscernibles*, Oxford: Oxford University Press.
Russell, B. (1900), *A Critical Exposition of the Philosophy of Leibniz*, Cambridge: Cambridge University Press.
Sleigh, R. C. (1990), *Leibniz and Arnauld: A Commentary on Their Correspondence*, New Haven: Yale University Press.
Smith, J. E. H. (2011), *Divine Machines: Leibniz and the Sciences of Life*, Princeton: Princeton University Press.

7

Locke

Peter R. Anstey

1. Introduction

The leading English philosopher John Locke (1632–1704) had a rich and variegated theory of knowledge. So, while the branch of philosophy that is today called epistemology did not exist in Locke's time, many of the signature doctrines to be found in Locke's famous *An Essay concerning Human Understanding* (hereafter: *Essay*) now find their natural home within that discipline. Indeed, some would say that, from an historical perspective, the *Essay* proved to be an important stimulus to the emergence of epistemology as a subdiscipline within philosophy. This chapter sets out Locke's theory of knowledge. The general contours and central claims of that theory are clear and easily stated. Some of the finer details, however, are more difficult to pin down and in some cases there is no scholarly consensus as to how Locke is to be interpreted. The exposition that follows presents an integrated interpretation of Locke's theory rather than a survey of the different readings that are staked out in the secondary literature.

2. Background

Virtually all attempts to theorize about the nature of knowledge or to formulate a method for the discovery of knowledge in the early modern period begin with the same template. This is the Aristotelian theory of knowledge acquisition, as set out in Aristotle's *Posterior Analytics* (1984: ii) and refined and debated over the centuries. According to this template, a science is a structured body of knowledge claims demonstrated from principles that are known to be certain. The template had three constituents: first, a theory of principles that provide the foundations for the science; second, a theory of demonstration by which one moves from the principles to new knowledge; and third, an account of the sciences which derive from the principles by means of the application of the mechanism of demonstration. The prime exemplar of the first constituent, the principles, was the postulates of Euclidean geometry. As for the second constituent, the predominant theory of demonstration was Aristotle's syllogistic logic. This provided a set of valid argument forms and analyses of argument types and had no serious rival until the nineteenth century. The prime exemplar of the third constituent, the sciences, was Euclidean geometry.

Of course, by Locke's day, all three constituents were widely discussed. There were many different theories of principles and one of the exemplar principles – Euclid's parallels postulate – was being subjected to sustained scrutiny. Aristotle's syllogistic was, in some quarters, under attack, and the understanding of what constitutes a science and how the sciences differ from each other was also a contested matter. Nevertheless, these three features of the Aristotelian template provide the best terms of reference for understanding Locke's theory of knowledge. For Locke was embedded in this tradition, even though in his own way he was straining against it: he had a theory of principles, he had a theory of demonstration, and he had views about the sciences that derive from them.

3. Locke on principles

The *Essay* begins with a frontal assault on principles, or, to be more precise, on the claim that there are innate principles in every human mind. Locke had modestly claimed in the 'Epistle to the Reader' to the *Essay* that, as an under-labourer to the great master-builders, he would remove some of the rubbish 'that lies in the way to Knowledge' and Book One is just such an exercise in epistemic hygiene. He was not attacking a straw man here. The Cambridge mathematician Isaac Barrow (1734: 107), for example, claimed of the Law of Non-contradiction was 'immediately connate with our Minds, and implanted in us by God'. The attack on principles broadens in Book Four when he challenges the claim that the process of knowledge acquisition always starts with principles. This is the central claim of the chapters entitled 'Of Maxims', where maxims are a type of principle, and 'Of the Improvement of our Knowledge' (1975: 4.7, 4.12).[1] Instead of starting with principles, the acquisition of knowledge, according to Locke, commences with the acquisition of simple ideas through the senses and through reflection on the operations of our own minds.

Far from the newborn entering the world with a set of ready-made principles that prime the pump of human reason, each neonate enters the world with a mind that is like a fresh sheet of white paper, a blank slate or *tabula rasa*. Of course, Locke is aware that foetuses can acquire ideas in utero, but the gist of the claim is that there are no preformed propositions in the mind at birth. The process of constructing propositions that might serve as a basis for the acquisition of a body of knowledge is a long and painstaking one, and Locke sets about describing it through what many called his way of ideas.

Ideas, for Locke, are the immediate objects of perception, and perception is the primary faculty or power of the understanding. The two sources of ideas are sensation – that is, the five senses – and reflection. Reflection is the perception of the operations of our minds from which we acquire the ideas of thinking, doubting, remembering, and so on. These two sources provide only simple ideas, ideas that cannot be broken down into further ideas and which cannot be defined, and together these two sources of ideas are called experience. Locke has a sophisticated theory of how complex ideas are constructed from these rudiments acquired via experience, a theory that includes a very interesting typology of ideas. Some features of this theory will be touched on as the exposition of his theory of knowledge unfolds; however, the finer details can be safely ignored here.

What is crucial is that the ideas, whether they are simple or complex, whether they are of qualities, relations, or substances, are the basic constituents of all that we know. In fact, knowledge, for Locke, just is the perception of certain relations between ideas. Thus, if we are to acquire knowledge of any principles at all, they have to be constructed out of ideas that have their origins in sensation and reflection. Locke believed that we can acquire new beliefs through revelation, beliefs such as that there will be a resurrection of the dead. However, such revealed beliefs have as their constituents only ideas acquired through experience.

It may seem, therefore, that Locke was setting himself against the Aristotelian theory of knowledge acquisition – that he was opposed to founding the sciences on principles. Yet nothing could be further from the truth. What Locke criticizes is, first, one widely held view about how we acquire principles (namely, innatism); second, and more importantly, over-reliance on untested, speculative principles that have no basis in experience; and, third, overblown claims about the fertility of a priori principles, such as 'whatever is, is'. Locke, then, was firmly committed to the first constituent of the template. His polemical moves were internal to the template, and pertained to the theory and use of principles rather than to their suitability as foundations for a science.

Locke firmly believed that if we can understand the processes by which we gain epistemic access to principles, then we are far less likely to build our sciences on the wrong ones. For him, the path to knowledge begins not with the principles themselves but rather with the process by which the understanding acquires them. An exposition of that process takes us to the heart of Locke's theory of knowledge. Yet, before examining that process, two more points about Locke on principles are worthy of note.

First, his polemics against various claims in the theory of principles did not appear de novo: they are indicative of a broader intellectual context. For Locke rubbed shoulders with the leading exponents of, and was himself a firm advocate of, the new experimental philosophy that emerged in England in the latter half of the seventeenth century. One thing that characterized the methodology and public rhetoric of the experimental philosophers was their opposition to speculative systems, hypotheses, and principles that were not founded upon observation and experiment. There is copious evidence of this in the writings of experimental philosophers. In fact, it is even reflected in Locke's early medical writings. His critique of various aspects of the theory of principles in the *Essay*, therefore, almost certainly has its origin in this broader opposition to speculation in the period.

Second, there is often a danger in an expository chapter such as this, of presenting a static conception of a philosopher's views, as if they were not subject to change and development. It is pertinent, therefore, to note that there is evidence that Locke's views on principles were challenged and subject to revision after the publication of the first edition of the *Essay* in 1690. For, as the achievement of Newton's *Principia* dawned on Locke throughout the 1690s, he came to see not merely that one determinate principle to which he was committed was false – namely, that all change in nature results from impact – but that a natural philosophy based upon principles acquired independently of the laborious process of natural history was not merely possible but was actual and was generating new knowledge. Thus, by 1693 we find Locke (1989: 248) speaking of 'principles that matter of fact justifie', and in *Of the Conduct of the Understanding*, which he originally intended to graft into the *Essay*, Locke (1823: iii, 282) claims this:

> There are fundamental truths that lie at the bottom, the basis upon which a great many others rest, and in which they have their consistency. These are teeming truths, rich in store, with which they furnish the mind, and, like the lights of heaven, are not only beautiful and entertaining in themselves, but give light and

evidence to other things, that without them could not be seen or known. Such is that admirable discovery of Mr. Newton, that all bodies gravitate to one another.

4. Locke on demonstration

Not only was Locke critical of certain features of the theory of principles in his own day, he was also critical of the predominant theory of demonstration, namely, Aristotle's syllogistic. He famously claimed that 'God has not been so sparing to Men to make them barely two-legged Creatures, and left it to *Aristotle* to make them Rational' (1975: 4.17.4).

It is not that there is anything wrong with the syllogistic per se; it is just that, according to Locke, it provides a post hoc propositional reconstruction of what goes on in the understanding at the level of ideas. Locke believes that the understanding has 'a native Faculty to perceive the Coherence, or Incoherence of its *Ideas*, and can range them right' (ibid.) without the need for the valid argument forms of the syllogistic. Thus, he offers his own theory of demonstration, a theory centred on the way of ideas.

That theory has as its foundation Locke's primitive conception of what constitutes knowledge. And, while not all knowledge involves demonstration, most of it does: 'The greatest part of our Knowledge depends upon Deductions and intermediate *Ideas*' (4.17.2). Moreover, the mechanism underlying demonstration is essential to the formation of opinions or judgements as well. So, Locke's theory of demonstration is central to his theory of knowledge. What, then, is his primitive or basic conception of knowledge?

For Locke, knowledge is the perception of the agreement or disagreement of any of our ideas (4.1.2, 4.7.2, 4.17.2). This is not a casual claim but is the very definition of knowledge itself. Just what Locke means by 'perception' here is a difficult matter to be discussed below. For now, let us consider what he means by 'agreement' and 'disagreement'. Agreement and its contrary disagreement are relations. Knowledge, then, is the perception of the holding of one of these relations between ideas. Locke tells us that there are four different types of agreement or disagreement. They are (1) identity or diversity (e.g. blue is not yellow); (2) relation (e.g. two triangles upon equal basis, between parallels, are equal); (3) coexistence or necessary connection (e.g. iron is susceptible of magnetical impressions); (4) real existence (e.g. God is). These four sorts of agreement contain 'all the Knowledge we have' (4.1.7).

Having set out the four types of agreement and disagreement, Locke proceeds to claim that there are three degrees of knowledge, by which he means degrees of certainty. The first and highest degree of knowledge is intuitive knowledge. This involves the immediate (i.e. unmediated) perception of agreement between two ideas. For example, 'A circle is not a triangle'. This form of knowledge involves intuition and not demonstration (4.2.1). The second degree of knowledge is demonstrative knowledge. This is the perception of the agreement or disagreement of two ideas with the assistance of a third intermediate idea, called a proof. According to Locke, most of our knowledge is of this form, hence the importance of his theory of demonstration. Moreover, each step in the construction of demonstrative knowledge involves an instance of intuitive knowledge, so demonstrations are chains of intuitive knowledge strung together by reason. The third degree of knowledge is sensitive knowledge. This is knowledge of 'the existence of particular external Objects' (4.2.14) and is restricted to those objects that are 'actually present to our Senses' (4.3.5).

So, to summarize, knowledge is the perception of the agreement or disagreement of ideas and the term 'agreement' (ignoring 'disagreement') covers four different relations: identity, relation, coexistence, and real existence. Moreover, this perception of agreement or disagreement comes in three decreasing degrees of certainty: intuitive, demonstrative, and sensitive knowledge. Now, in setting out all of this, Locke never loses sight of his critique of the theory of principles. Thus, when discussing agreement and disagreement as identity or diversity, he says that the mind knows the ideas of White and Round differ from Red and Square and that no 'Maxim or Proposition in the World [can] make him know it clearer or surer than he did before' (4.1.4; see also 4.2.8). And, when discussing ways of improving our knowledge in Book Four, he says that

> the Knowledge of the Certainty of Principles, as well as of other Truths, depends only upon the perception, we have, of the Agreement, or Disagreement of our *Ideas, the way to improve our Knowledge,* is not, I am sure, blindly, and with an implicit Faith, to receive and swallow Principles; but is, I think, *to get and fix in our Minds clear, distinct, and complete* Ideas, as far as they are to be had, *and annex to them proper and constant Names.* (4.12.6; emphases in the original)

We turn now to the tricky term 'perception' in Locke's definition of knowledge. What is involved in perceiving the agreement of two ideas? On this question, proponents of the orthodox interpretation of Locke on knowledge are quick to point out that he claims at least twice that all of our knowledge is knowledge of propositions.[2] There is then a natural inference from both the claim that knowledge is the perception of the agreement of ideas and the claim that all knowledge is of propositions, to the view that to perceive that ideas agree or disagree just is to form a proposition out of those ideas. Thus, the act of perceiving that the ideas White and Black disagree is the forming of the true proposition 'Black is not white.' Moreover, to perceive that the proposition 'Black is not white' is true is just to perceive the agreement of the ideas Black and White. On this interpretation, perceiving and proposition formation are the very same thing. That is, one perceives the agreement or disagreement of ideas *A* and *B* *if and only if* one forms a true proposition containing ideas *A* and *B*. This interpretation of Locke collapses the perception of the agreement of ideas into the formation of propositions. It has the advantage of being consistent with Locke's apparent claim that all knowledge consists in propositions. It also requires that it be consistent with Locke's theory of propositions because to know in its most primitive sense, according to this view, just is to form a proposition. So, let us examine Locke's theory of propositions.

Locke says that there are two kinds of signs – ideas and words. And there are two kinds of propositions corresponding to these signs – mental and verbal. A proposition is formed by the joining or the separating of signs. The formation of propositions by the relation of identity, such as 'Black is black', seems straightforward on this view. What about true contingent propositions whose agreement is real existence? These consist in 'putting together, or separating these Signs, according as the Things, which they stand for, agree or disagree' (4.5.5).

Now, proponents of the orthodox view at this point face a dilemma, for their view works well for conceptual knowledge, such as 'All triangles are closed three-sided figures', where there is no need for things in the world to agree or disagree: no need for truthmakers, so to speak. However, for contingent propositions, such as 'This snow is white', it is required that things *in the world* agree.

In order to deal with contingent propositions, advocates of the propositional interpretation are faced with two options. The first option is to claim that Locke has two senses of the terms 'agreement' and 'disagreement', one for conceptual truths and another for contingent truths.[3] This is the interpretation from Ruth Mattern, who searches hard in the *Essay* for this second sense of 'agreement'. The second option is to claim that, for Locke, we cannot have knowledge of contingent truths.[4] This is the view from Samuel Rickless, who claims that Locke restricts what we can know to necessary truths. Neither of these interpretations is very satisfying. There is little indication in the text of the *Essay* that Locke has two different senses of 'agreement' and 'disagreement', and it seems to be a very odd theory of knowledge that claims that we cannot have demonstrative knowledge of any contingent truths.

There is, however, an alternative interpretation of Locke's definition of knowledge. This approach to Locke's definition does not identify perceiving the agreement of ideas with forming propositions; instead, it keeps apart the act of perceiving and the act of forming propositions. The view begins with the plausible distinction between two different objects of knowledge – namely, ideas and propositions. On this view, for Locke, the basic act of knowing is that of perceiving the agreement of ideas, and this is non-propositional. The objects of knowledge are ideas, and the perceiving is the perception of a fact, not the perception that it is a fact.

If this account of Locke's foundational notion of knowledge is correct, the perception of agreement of ideas is a form of knowledge by acquaintance, not a form of propositional knowledge or knowledge *that*. This interpretation has some advantages over the propositional account. First, unlike Mattern's view, it does not require us to posit two different senses of 'agreement' and 'disagreement'. Second, unlike Rickless' view, it does allow for demonstrative knowledge of contingent facts. And, third, it does seem to capture the primacy of Locke's definition of knowledge as a form of perception of ideas. For nowhere in his definitional statements concerning knowledge does Locke claim that propositions are the objects of perception. For example, in the following passage he seems to contrast non-propositional knowledge with propositional knowledge:

> There are several ways wherein the Mind is possessed of Truth, each of which is called *Knowledge*.
> 1. There is *actual Knowledge*, which is the present view the Mind has of the Agreement or Disagreement of any of its *Ideas*, or of the Relation they have one to another.
> 2. A Man is said to know any Proposition, which having been once laid before his Thoughts, he evidently perceived the Agreement, or Disagreement of the *Ideas* whereof it consists. (4.1.8; emphases in the original)

To be sure, Locke speaks of 'our Knowledge, which all consists in Propositions' (2.33.19) and claims that 'Every thing which we either know or believe, is some proposition' (1823: iv, 357); but these locutions are most naturally taken as references to items of knowledge, where the expression 'consists in' means 'is constituted of'. It is true for Locke that every item of knowledge is some proposition, but this does not entail that knowledge is intrinsically propositional.

The faculty of the mind that carries out demonstrations is reason. Reason is actually the combination of two powers – sagacity and illation. Sagacity is that power by which the mind seeks out and applies appropriate proofs or intermediate ideas. Without sagacity, demonstrative knowledge would be impossible. 'Illation' is another word for 'inference'. It has to do with perceiving the relations between propositions, whether mental or verbal. What is crucial for Locke is that illation cannot proceed in the absence of sagacity: it is only by perceiving the agreement of two ideas by the assistance of a third that one can form a proposition which in turn is the premise in an inference. This is true, whether one accepts the orthodox propositional account of Locke on knowledge or instead the knowledge by acquaintance view. Furthermore, Locke is adamant that inference proceeds naturally and not with reference to, or within the argument forms of, the Aristotelian syllogistic.

Unfortunately, on many occasions, when we examine ideas we do not perceive their agreement but only suppose it or, as Locke says, perceive their probable agreement. In these cases we do not have knowledge; we have judgement. Judgement, of course, is inferior to knowledge insofar as it is less certain. However, reasoning – that is, the use of sagacity and illation – is still necessary for forming judgements.

Judgements are more or less probable, depending upon the evidence that we have for them. This evidence comes from three sources. First, it can come directly from the senses. Second, it can derive indirectly from the testimony of others. And, third, it can come from beyond the senses. In the final section below, we shall discuss the evidence of the senses. In the case of the indirect evidence of testimony, Locke accepts a variety of forms of evidence, listed here in decreasing order of reliability: conformity with our experience, the number and reliability of the witnesses, their skill and expertise, the intention of the author (in the case of recorded testimony), consistency with features of the context, and contrary testimony. Indirect evidence of the senses is to be evaluated according to the principle '[t]hat any Testimony, the farther off it is from the original Truth, the less force and proof it has' (1975: 4.16.10).

Moreover, according to Locke, there is a special class of propositions about which we can form judgements that are derived from the testimony of one who cannot lie. These are the propositions of revelation that have God as their witness. Assent to these propositions is called faith. If reason is the generic faculty by which we come to know or judge the certainty or probability of a proposition by the use of our natural faculties of sensation and reflection, then faith, by contrast, has as its object propositions that both cannot be discovered by sensation or reflection and are accompanied by the testimony that they were originally revealed by God. These propositions are above reason, in the sense that they could not be discovered by any witness through sensation and reflection. And yet reason is required to evaluate the claim that God originally revealed these propositions. As Locke puts it, '*Revelation* is natural *Reason* enlarged by a new set of Discoveries communicated by GOD immediately, which *Reason* vouches the Truth of' (4.19.4; emphases in the original).

In all cases of judgement, whether about things in the world to which we have epistemic access or things beyond the senses, the supposed agreement of the ideas involved is natural. And, while Locke does not spell out what this naturalness consists in, he does provide a clear account of its contrast class – that is, non-natural associations of ideas. According to Locke, humans habitually experience the occurrence of unnatural associations between ideas. This association of ideas is a pathological condition in the understanding, and Locke warns against it in the strongest possible terms. In some cases it may appear harmless, such as a musician, who on thinking of the first notes of a tune, finds that the subsequent notes follow 'without any care or attention' (2.33.6). However, more often than not the association of ideas is pernicious, as we find when the idea Infallibility is associated with a particular person. In such cases, that person's pronouncement is 'swallowed for a certain Truth, by an implicit Faith, when ever that imagin'd infallible Person dictates and demands assent without enquiry' (2.33.17).

5. Locke on the sciences

In the very last section of the *Essay*, Locke (1975: 4.21.5) uses the expressions 'objects of knowledge' and 'objects of the understanding' to refer to the sciences and he claims that they are naturally divided into three. This tripartite division is the subject of the *Essay*'s final chapter. It clearly parallels the Stoic division of philosophy into the knowledge of nature, ethics, and logic. For Locke, the objects of knowledge are *things*, *actions*, and *signs* and these provide a convenient way in to Locke's account of the sciences. Let us begin with knowledge of things.

Knowledge of things is the knowledge we have of matter, of body, and of spirits. It encompasses knowledge of the constitution, properties, and behaviour of things that leads to knowledge of how things are 'in their own proper Beings' (4.21.2). Locke calls this division of knowledge natural philosophy, though he is aware that he is using the term 'natural philosophy' here in a broader sense than is usual, because it covers not only objects in the material world, but also God, angels, and spirits. The pursuit of this branch of knowledge will end in 'bare speculative Truth' (i.e. demonstrative science), but, as we shall see, the extent to which this can be achieved is, according to Locke, severely limited.

Even though this form of knowledge is limited, it is still enormously important. As Locke's nameless interlocutor replies to the sceptic, 'It matters not what Men's Fancies are, 'tis the Knowledge of things that is only to be prized' (4.4.1). This knowledge can only be prized, however, if there is a genuine case against the sceptic who claims that there is no difference between the propositions that a harpy is not a centaur and that a square is not a circle. What is it that guarantees we can know that there are things in the external world? On the face of it, the sceptical problem is particularly acute for Locke because for him it is ideas and not things in the external world that are the immediate objects of the understanding: 'the Mind knows not Things immediately, but only by the intervention of the *Ideas* it has of them' (4.4.3). In other words, Locke is committed to what Jonathan Bennett (1971: 69) has called the veil of perception. This, notoriously, raises the spectre of external world scepticism: if we do not have direct epistemic access to things in the world, how do we know that there really is an external world that comprises of things? Surprisingly, Locke was unperturbed by this sceptical challenge.

His response to the external world sceptic hinges on the claim that God has fitted humans with reliable sense organs. Our senses are fitted and adapted by God accurately to convey both that our ideas have external causes and the nature of these causes. In short, Locke is committed to what today we would call theological reliabilism.

Locke's (1975: 4.4.4) case is built around simple ideas which are

> the product of Things operating on the Mind in a natural way, and producing therein those Perceptions which by the Wisdom and Will of our Maker they are ordained and adapted to. From whence it follows, that *simple* Ideas *are not fictions* of our Fancies, but the natural and regular productions of Things without us, really operating upon us; and so carry with them all the conformity which is intended; or which our state requires. (Emphases in the original)

The passivity of the understanding and the accuracy of the representational nature of the ideas are crucial here: 'These *simple Ideas*, when offered to the mind, *the Understanding can* no more refuse to have, nor alter, when they are imprinted, nor blot them out, and make new ones in it self, than a mirror can refuse, alter, or obliterate the Images or *Ideas*, which, the Objects set before it, do therein produce' (2.1.25; emphases in the original). Each of Locke's arguments against external world scepticism is best seen as an argument for this form of reliabilism. Thus, he claims that we can be sure that external objects are the cause of our simple ideas because those who lack a particular sense, such as sight, also lack the ideas that arise from the proper operation of that sense – say, Blue and Red. Moreover, the sense organ is not the ultimate cause of the simple ideas it produces, because each sense requires a proper context to function: we do not acquire the idea of Red in the dark (4.11.4).

Locke also uses the phenomenology of bodily sensations to argue for reliabilism. Pain caused by an actual external object causes great disturbance, whereas the memory of pain does not. Likewise, against the sceptic who claims that we cannot distinguish between dreaming and being awake, Locke argues that 'if our Dreamer pleases to try, whether the glowing heat of a glass Furnace, be barely a wandring Imagination in a drowsy Man's Fancy, by putting his Hand into it, he may perhaps be wakened into a certainty greater than he could wish, that it is something more than bare Imagination' (4.11.8). His conclusion is that 'when our Senses do actually convey into our Understandings any *Idea*, we cannot but be satisfied, that there doth something at that time really exist without us' (4.11.9). However, to have simple ideas that are caused by external things is not to have knowledge, for knowledge, as we have seen, requires the perception of the agreement of ideas.

In the case of our knowledge of external objects, we are restricted to sensitive knowledge of those particular things that are 'actually present to our Senses' (4.3.5). This knowledge is not as certain as intuitive or demonstrative knowledge, but deserves the name 'knowledge' nonetheless. It is the perception of the agreement of the sensory idea of a thing with the idea that some thing exists here and now in the external world that is the cause of the sensory idea (Locke 1823: iv, 360). The sensory idea of that thing, what Locke calls 'the idea of actual sensation', is the occurrent idea of the thing with the 'tag' that it is an idea acquired via the senses (rather than, say, memory). So, for example, one might have both the sensory idea of White and the idea of Snow actually existing here and now in the external world and causing my sensory idea of White. If these ideas agree, then one has the sensitive knowledge 'This snow is white'. One cannot, however, have sensitive knowledge that all snow is white, or knowledge of any other general proposition about things in the world. Nor can one have knowledge of things in the world that are too small or too remote to be perceived.

These two limits to our knowledge of things have serious consequences for natural philosophy as it pertains to material bodies. Locke (1975) believes that things have inner natures, what he calls real essences, but that in every case we do not know what the inner nature is: we do not have epistemic access to real essences. The upshot is that 'natural Philosophy is not capable of being made a Science' (4.12.10).[5] The crucial point here is that 'science' has a very specific sense: to be a science is to be a body of knowledge demonstrated from principles. Because we lack knowledge of real essences, we lack the requisite principles for a science of material bodies. This is what Locke means when he says (4.3.26.) that, in spite of all the advances in experimental philosophy, '*in physical Things, scientifical* [knowledge] will still be out of our reach'.

Happily, this is not the case for Locke's second object of knowledge – namely, actions. Locke claims a number of times in the *Essay* that we can have a demonstrative science of morality: '*Morality is capable of Demonstration*.'[6] Of course, he was not the first philosopher to make this claim; however, he was the first to set such a claim in the context of a well-developed theory of how our ethical notions are formed. According to Locke, one species of complex ideas is modes. These can be simple or mixed. Simple modes are formed by the understanding through the operation of iteration on the very same idea: the modal idea Twelve is formed by iterating the idea Unity eleven times. By contrast, moral ideas are mixed modes and they are formed by combining different ideas. Locke gives the examples of Murder and Wrestling.

Another salient characteristic of modal ideas, over and above their complexity, is that they do not intimate real existence (2.12.4, 3.5.3). Rather, they are formed by the understanding and need not have any correlates in the real world. Nevertheless, the fact that modal ideas do not intimate real existence does not imply that there are no archetypes of the ideas in the real world. There are acts of murder and wrestling, but, unlike substances, such actions tend to be transient. Thus, our modal ideas are not completely detached from experience. Furthermore, mixed modes, unlike our ideas of substances, can be accurately defined because each of their constituents is a clear and distinct idea. As such, we can know the real essence of murder or property in a way that is not possible with substances such as gold.

A useful contemporary example is the idea of Same-Sex Marriage. This is a clear and distinct moral idea that is formed by the understanding and, in point of fact, was formed before there were any real world archetypes of same-sex marriage. Furthermore, it has implications for the more general mixed mode Marriage. For example, if Same-Sex Marriage is taken to be a species of the genus Marriage, then the idea Marriage needs to be redefined. Should the new mixed mode Marriage then be incorporated into a legal code, as has occurred in some jurisdictions, we can have – and in fact do have – archetypes of Same-Sex Marriage in the real world.

These features of Locke's account of moral ideas give the theory much intuitive appeal, but they do not imply that we can have a demonstrative science of morality. For that, Locke needs not only clear and definable ideas, but also a set of moral principles on which to found the science. In the *Essay* he gestures towards what this would look like, but never undertakes the task himself. The clearest passage to this effect is the following:

> The Idea of a supreme Being, infinite in Power, Goodness, and Wisdom, whose Workmanship we are, and on whom we depend; and the *Idea* of our selves, as understanding, rational Beings; being such as are clear in us, would, I suppose, if duly considered, and pursued, afford such Foundations of our Duty and Rules of Action, as might place *Morality amongst the Sciences capable of Demonstration*: wherein I doubt not, but from self-evident Propositions, by necessary Consequences, as incontestable as those in Mathematicks, the measures of right and wrong might be made out to any one that will apply himself with the same Indifferency and Attention to the one, as he does to the other of these Sciences. (4.3.18; emphases in the original)

This would then give rise to moral propositions such as '*Where there is no Property, there is no Injustice*' and '*No Government allows absolute Liberty*', which are, according to Locke, as certain as any proposition in Euclid (4.3.18). Some scholars have claimed that the theory of government set out in the second treatise of Locke's *Two Treatises of Government* provides just such a theory. However, it must be pointed out that, in spite of the tight conceptual connections between such notions as obligation, property, and rights, it is not set out as a demonstrative science.

Thus, in the final analysis, Locke's claim that morality is capable of being made a science is little more than a promissory note: he never came up with such a science. And yet this does not exhaust our interest in Locke's views on morals for his theory of knowledge. For Locke also provides an ethics of belief – that is, a set of norms that should regulate our epistemic practices. This comprises three elements. First, he articulates some general normative claims, general epistemic obligations for any rational agent. Second, he sets out regulative norms for belief formation; and, third, he applies his ethics of belief in practical contexts. Let us examine an example of each.

Locke's account of knowledge and opinion is set within a strongly normative context. He is deeply concerned with reasoning well and he regards the starting point for this to be the love of and seeking after truth. In *Of the Conduct of the Understanding* Locke (1823: iii, 230) tells us, 'We should contend earnestly for the truth, but we should first be sure that it is truth.' This should be done with an attitude of indifference, particularly with respect to the principles on which our knowledge is to be founded:

> In these two things, viz. an equal indifferency for all truth; I mean the receiving it, the love of it, as truth, but not loving it for any other reason, before we know it to be true, and in the examination of our principles, and not receiving any for such, nor building on them, till we are fully convinced, as rational creatures, of their solidity, truth, and certainty; consists that freedom of the understanding which is necessary to a rational creature, and without which it is not truly an understanding. (iii, 231)

Moreover, for Locke (1975), over and above this general alethic obligation, there are a number of more specific epistemic duties that are to be applied in belief formation. For example,

> *the Mind if it will proceed rationally, ought to examine all the grounds of Probability*, and see how they make more or less, *for or against* any probable Proposition, before it assents to or dissents from it, and upon a due ballancing the whole, reject, or receive it, with a more or less firm assent, proportionably to the preponderancy of the greater grounds of Probability on one side or the other. (4.15.5; emphases in the original)

A general orientation towards truth and a conscientious application of one's epistemic duties is not enough for Locke. For, over and above a love of truth and well-formed beliefs, we need epistemic humility. The application of epistemic humility is perhaps best illustrated in one of Locke's arguments for religious toleration. In his *Third Letter for Toleration* he argues that a magistrate who has true beliefs concerning the content and practice of religion should still be tolerant of other beliefs and practices. This is because he cannot *know* that his own beliefs are true. Thus, epistemic humility should rule, and toleration should be allowed.[7]

Signs comprise the third and final object of knowledge, according to Locke. Interestingly, he calls the science of signs 'logic'. Given that there are two types of signs – ideas and words – it follows that logic is concerned with both ideas and words. Ideas signify things in the world or in the mind, and words signify ideas. We have already treated of Locke's theory of ideas, so it remains here to make some brief comments on his view of words and language.

The purpose of the science of signs is 'the understanding of Things, or conveying its [the mind's] Knowledge to others' (4.21.4). Thus, Locke is concerned not with developing a theory of meaning, but rather with the role of language in the acquisition and transmission of knowledge. Furthermore, because people tend to think by using language rather than mere ideas, his focus on the transmission of knowledge must begin with words: 'most Men, if not all, in their Thinking and Reasonings within themselves, make use of Words instead of *Ideas*' (4.5.4). He has much to say in Book Three of the *Essay* on the dangers of the abuses of words, and elsewhere on how best to acquire knowledge that is transmitted through language.

For Locke, because people naturally avail themselves of the use of language when thinking, epistemic hygiene must begin with words: it begins with eradicating the abuses of words. These include lack of clarity and distinctness in the ideas that they signify, inconstancy of use, affected obscurity, and taking them for things (Locke cites 'substantial forms' and 'the soul of the world' as examples [2.10]). Yet circumventing the imperfections of language and the abuses of words is not sufficient for genuine understanding. For, according to Locke, there is a qualitative dimension to the transmission of knowledge that must be grasped if we are to acquire what he calls 'real knowledge'. Thus, for example, when it comes to reading, 'it is usually supposed that by reading, the author's knowledge is transfused into the reader's understanding; and so it is, but not by bare reading, but by reading and understanding what he writ' (1823: iii, 250). And this brings us back to the other type of sign – namely, ideas. For the first step to real knowledge is the examining of the relations between the ideas signified by the words that constitute the verbal propositions that the reader encounters: 'to observe the connexion of these ideas in the propositions which those books hold forth, and pretend to teach as truths'.[8] So the correct use of language will take the mind back to the ideas signified. But the mind should not stop there, for, according to Locke, 'he that will conduct his understanding right must not look for in the acuteness of invention, nor the authority of writers, but will find [them] only in the consideration of things themselves' (iii, 263). And, of course, things comprise the first of 'the three great Provinces of the intellectual World'.

So, while Locke considers the three domains of human knowledge – natural philosophy, ethics, and logic – to be 'wholly separate and distinct one from another', logic, or the doctrine of signs, is a kind of bridging science insofar as it is through its correct application that we are able to come to real knowledge of actions and things. It is both a constituent of, and the means by which we come to grasp, '[a]ll that can fall within the compass of Humane Understanding' (1975: 4.21.5, 1).

The compass of human understanding, for Locke, is the range of all that we can know. And throughout the *Essay* Locke is at pains to stress just how limited our knowledge is. Likewise, there are limits to how far the survey of this chapter on Locke on knowledge can take us into his theory; much more could be said than has been covered here. However, all of the finer details pertaining to the theory of ideas, the account of language, and the theory of demonstration are best set within the threefold account set out above. For Locke, the theory of principles, the theory of demonstration, and the account of the sciences provide the framework for an account of knowledge. And yet, for all of this, it is the normative dimensions of knowing that were his greatest concerns. Locke's desire for us his readers is that it is 'not by bare reading, but by reading and understanding what he writ' that we come to grasp what knowledge really is.

Notes

1. Locke's *Essay* is cited by book, chapter, and section number, using Arabic numerals.
2. Locke (1975: 2.33.19) and his *Second Reply to Stillingfleet* (1823: iv, 357).
3. This view is developed in Mattern (1978).
4. For this view, see Rickless (2008).
5. See also Locke (1989: 244–5).
6. See Locke (1975: 3.11.16; also 4.3.18, 4.12.8).
7. *Third Letter for Toleration* (Locke 1823: vi, 142–6).
8. *Some Thoughts concerning Reading and Studying for a Gentleman* (Locke 1823: iii, 294).

References

Aristotle. (1984), *The Complete Works of Aristotle*, 2 vols, ed. J. Barnes, Princeton: Princeton University Press.

Barrow, I. (1734), *The Usefulness of Mathematical Learning Explained and Demonstrated*, London: Stephen Austen. First published in Latin in 1683–84.

Bennett, J. (1971), *Locke, Berkeley, Hume: Central Themes*, Oxford: Oxford University Press.

Locke, J. (1823), *The Works of John Locke*, 10 vols, London: C. and J. Rivington.

Locke, J. (1975 [1690]), *An Essay concerning Human Understanding*, ed. P. H. Nidditch, Oxford: Clarendon Press.

Locke, J. (1988), *Two Treatises of Government*, ed. P. Laslett, Cambridge: Cambridge University Press.

Locke, J. (1989), *Some Thoughts Concerning Education*, ed. J. W. Yolton and J. S. Yolton, Oxford: Oxford University Press.

Mattern, R. (1978), 'Locke: "Our Knowledge, Which all Consists in Propositions"', *Canadian Journal of Philosophy*, 8: 677–95.

Newton, I. (1999), *The Principia*, ed. and trans. I. B. Cohen and A. Whitman, Berkeley: University of California Press.

Rickless, S. C. (2008), 'Is Locke's Theory of Knowledge Inconsistent?' *Philosophy and Phenomenological Research*, 77: 83–104.

8

Hume

Margaret Schabas

Until the middle of the twentieth century, David Hume (1711–76) was primarily characterized as a sceptic. Bertrand Russell and Karl Popper, for example, maintained that for Hume, knowledge in the sense of true and justified belief was not possible.[1] The primary bone to pick centred on the justification of our beliefs. Hume's brilliant analyses of both inductive inference and causal ascriptions exposed their fallibility. Our warrant for inductive inferences is also inductive; our belief in causation is based on nothing more than the habitual correlation of events. Hume retreated to the claim that all knowledge is probable rather than certain, and hence subject to revision.

The depiction of Hume as a full-blown sceptic has gradually waned to the point that virtually no one saddles him with that label. Hume is now seen as a pragmatic and common-sense thinker, one who sought to temper overly zealous claims to certainty such as those issued by the Cartesians. Insofar as Hume's primary mission was the elimination of superstition and religious enthusiasm, he was favourably disposed to the possibility of securing and augmenting secular knowledge. This 'New Hume' is even more inclined to embrace causal ascriptions and to see science in a positive light.[2] Hume believed that our stock of knowledge is growing, partly because we are able to sharpen our tools for winnowing false beliefs and partly because progressive societies are more likely to foster science. As we will see, Hume developed an extensive argument to the effect that liberal political and economic conditions contribute directly to the growth of knowledge. Conversely, knowledge for Hume (1777) has utility: it fosters social progress that in turn enables the pursuit of new knowledge. Hence, we find an 'indissoluble chain' linking 'industry, knowledge, and humanity' (271).

Hume's life coincided with the most intense outpouring of Enlightenment thought in science and the arts.[3] He benefitted from the ascent of Scotland, especially his beloved Edinburgh, as a centre of learning, and although he became acquainted with many of the leading savants across Europe, he never let his friendships with his fellow Scots take second place. As a mature man, he spent time in Paris and London, and basked in his hard-earned fame as a great philosopher, historian, and essayist. If there is a single unifying theme to Hume, however, it is the pursuit of political stability. For much of Hume's life, Britain was at war, either with France or with distant colonial powers, and he was very aware that Britain's military conquests came at a huge price to human well-being. Hume's primary fascination was with the 'science of man' and the extent to which our increased understanding of the human condition might bring more peace and happiness to the world.

His primary contribution to epistemology is Book One of his youthful but canonical *A Treatise of Human Nature* (1739–40). Because of its poor reception, he abridged and revised his arguments into a more successful *An Enquiry Concerning Human Understanding* (1748) that he then revised over the course of his life, ten editions with production numbering approximately 10,000 copies in total. Hume also offers important insights into the formation and growth of knowledge in his other works: *Essays: Moral, Political and Literary* (1741–77), *Enquiry Concerning the Principles of Morals* (1751), *Natural History of Religion* (1757), and the *Dialogues Concerning Natural Religion* (1779). These last two works were mostly drafted in the 1740s but publication was delayed because Hume feared reprisals. With the exception of his multivolume *History of England* (1754–62), the bulk of Hume's work, and in particular his epistemology, was written before 1751, and many of the core ideas can be traced back to the 1730s and 1740s when he was still a young man.

Hume is an empiricist through and through. There is no a priori knowledge, or divine revelation. Even the instincts of animals are not innate but are rather a variant of the same type of experimental reasoning that we humans undertake. Hume is clear that there are no Platonic forms, only particular ideas, which in turn are formed from single impressions. If an idea appears to be universal, it is only a figment of our imagination.

Hume's approach to the standing and prospect of human knowledge is comparatively singular for his day because of his thoroughly secular approach. He has long been labelled a naturalist in the sense that he does not invoke supernatural elements in his efforts to understand our capacity for knowledge. It is not just that he does not invoke God or the soul, as was commonplace for much of early modern philosophy; he also mounts arguments to show that our ability to know that either entity exists is beyond our reach. He traces our belief in the afterlife to our fear of death, which in turn is intrinsic to the preservation of our species (1777: 598).

Hume became the patron saint for the logical positivists precisely because he eschewed all metaphysical assertions. There are only two kinds of reasoning, one that yields formal truths concerning quantity or number, and the other that results in empirical truths grounded in matters of fact. Anything else, Hume (1748: 123) declares, should be committed to the flames since it can 'contain nothing but sophistry and illusion'. But he also tried to inject an empirical element into mathematics, in two respects. The objects of mathematics – numbers or geometrical figures – are arrived at 'by the senses and imagination' (118n), and mathematical proofs are undertaken by trial or error, and carried out in the mind's eye and are thus empirical (1739–40: 52, 121–2). Furthermore, mathematics is in the service of practical results, such as fortification, and is of no consequence without application (287–8). This serves to illustrate the more general point that, for Hume, all knowledge, even mathematical knowledge, emanates from human needs and human nature. We are not in some sense reading God's first bible in the pursuit of natural philosophy; we are reading our own human-made testament.

More importantly, the key to understanding human nature is to understand how our mind processes the world. Hume took the formation of sensory impressions as veridical, and the manner by which they cause ideas as part and parcel of our limited mental machinery. The mind is akin to a theatre whereby specific and distinct impressions occupy the mind's stage at any given time. These impressions come mostly via our perceptual apparatus, particularly vision, but can also come from our internal passions such as fear or joy.

Unlike Descartes, Hume does not see chimeras or dreams as posing serious problems for epistemology. They are authentic sensations at the moment, but we can prevail on common sense and reason to place them in the proper context. Reason tells us that the oar that appears bent in water is in fact straight. Not only do we absorb sensations reliably, but we can also take them as representational of the world or, at least, the surface of the world that we humans can access. There is no need to resort to the distinction between primary and secondary qualities on which the mechanical philosophy is based. Hume contrasts our observation of a black marble sphere with a white marble sphere, and then with a white marble cube. A so-called distinction of reason permits us to separate the form from the colour and to see a resemblance between the two marble spheres, and between the white marble and white cube. Nevertheless, it is impossible to conjure up in the mind's eye the idea of the sphere or cube without the colour, or so Hume submits (21–2).

Impressions of objects come to us wholesale, with the extension and colour content inextricably linked to one another, an argument already advanced by George Berkeley, whom Hume had read with care in his twenties (1748: xxiv-xxvi). But, rather than embrace Berkeley's immaterialism, and the subsequent move to God as the cause of all things, Hume accepts that there is a natural causal explanation for our impressions (1739–40: 115–16). The problem lies in finding these causes. There are definitely powers and forces in the world, but they will forever remain unobservable. Even if we could build better microscopes, Hume believes that we are unlikely to know more than a few of the properties of the microphysical world (1748: 50–1).

The copy principle is central to Hume's account of the human mind. Tasting a pineapple spawns an immediate impression of that taste that is then transformed by the mind into a somewhat less vivid or fainter idea. Ideas are direct copies of impressions, and they can be simple or complex. Ideas are the building blocks for the edifice of knowledge, and are processed by the mind in accordance with three basic operations – resemblance, contiguity, or causation – that unfold pre-linguistically. Certain additional capacities – memory and imagination, most saliently – facilitate our propensity towards abstract thought. Although Hume invites us to introspect on how this mental machinery functions, we may in actuality have no objective stance by which to grasp some or all of these (Garrett 1997; Owen 2005).

Hume's account has many unresolved problems. He has little to say about the critical role of memory, although it clearly demands some temporal extension and thus some additional attention to how disparate but analogous ideas are conjoined. Insofar as each impression is particular, and contains some quantitative and qualitative variants to prior impressions, there is arguably no such thing as a simple impression. Hume seems to admit as much. Blue, green, and scarlet are all simple ideas; there is more resemblance, however, between blue and green than between blue and scarlet (1739–40: 18n). The only way to make sense of this comparison by Hume is to see that green is not simple but is instead the product of blue and yellow. But if all ideas turn out to be complex, then do we consider each idea a copy of that particular variant or in some sense a composite of analogous impressions? We conjure up the idea of a triangle, Hume suggests, and our first image is of an equilateral triangle, but we might then realize that this is too limiting and expand out to include an isosceles triangle as well (19). Did this require a prior impression of each kind of triangle, or could we use the manipulations on offer in geometry to go from one kind to another? In that case, should we start with a non-equilateral and see the equilateral as a limiting case?

Hume is a philosopher of the mind and not of language, but in brief passages he offers an account of the acquisition of language. When we assign a word to an idea – say, the word 'horse' – we have annexed the idea of a particular horse – say, a black and short one – to the idea, until other variants – white, tall, and so on – crowd in as closely resembling (1748: 118n). Perhaps we are invoking a prototype that corresponds to some approximate mean of our past encounters with analogous instances (1739–40: 28). Although my prototype is likely to differ from yours, it is sufficiently similar to enable us to communicate by using that term. In fact, philosophical disputes are fundamentally semantic for Hume. If we cannot resolve a dispute by appealing to facts, then it behooves us to be more exacting with our terms and the meanings assigned.

Hume acknowledges the sense in which each of us encounters phenomena in the world along a somewhat idiosyncratic path, and thus that we are never in full agreement with others. But he also avoids the final step to solipsism, and at one point calls this 'ridiculous' (177). The very fact that we use language suggests some overlap in our experiences and mental processes. Furthermore, there are foreign languages, and we are able to translate from one to another. The fact that diverse 'languages so nearly correspond to each other' stacks the cards in favour of common experience (13).

Hume relies quite heavily on introspection and writes as if this is unproblematic (Garrett 2015). Most critics would see introspection as inviting the subjective and the idiosyncratic into the mix, both of which are antithetical to the achievement of genuine knowledge. The underlying assumption for Hume, and one that he acknowledges from time to time, is that there is great uniformity in human nature, such that introspection is likely to unearth common patterns. In his efforts to spell out the three laws of association, for example, he brilliantly shifts the burden of proof to his reader and entreats him or her to find an exception or alternative. As long as none can do so, Hume effectively reaffirms his stance of uniformity and the exhaustive set of the three laws of mental association: namely, resemblance, contiguity, and causation.

Hume also, famously, grants an exception to the copy principle with his example of the missing shade of blue. A person, having observed all but one of the shades of blue on a spectrum, is able to fill in the gap without having experienced the prior impression (1739–40: 9–10; 1748: 15–16). He admits that this poses a difficulty, but moves on in silence. Scholars have attempted multiple solutions, but no single one seems to have rescued Hume from the problem. I read the passage as one of Hume's many thought experiments, since it would not be possible to find a man of 30 years of age who had seen every shade of blue but one. To test this would undoubtedly require exposing him first to that particular shade in a way that would make it impossible to carry out the test. The thrust of Hume's exception to his principle is possibly to demonstrate the way in which we use prior knowledge – say, of colour spectra in general – to fill more quickly evident gaps in our factual ascriptions. But that prior knowledge is most certainly empirical in origin.

The missing shade of blue is a kind of test, and that is a key to understanding Hume writ large. He seeks tests for everything; that is the essence of his broad appeal to the experimental method.[4] One of Hume's favourite tests is to take an idea and trace its genealogy. If you cannot find a prior impression, try as you might, then the idea is spurious and should be discarded as a candidate for knowledge. Hume finds a number of these to put on the discard heap of illegitimate ideas: notably, soul, substance, self, and, above all, cause. Try as we might in our causal ascriptions to trace it back to a distinct impression of a cause, we invariably fail. Our belief in causation is the product of habit and custom, and must be understood as derivative of that human disposition. That, in turn, is an important piece of information to hold onto, however, since it reveals all the more the manner by which we forge our way in the world, building up expectations of patterns over time. Hume uses a thought experiment of someone arriving on planet earth with no prior experience, and emphasizes the extent to which there would be no such prior expectations. Everything would appear disconnected from everything else.

Did Hume believe in laws of nature? The answer is clearly in the affirmative, but needs qualification. The laws exist but are always mediated by human nature, our perceptual abilities, and our disposition to seek out causal patterns as a means of coping. For that reason, they may not hold universally, although Hume sometimes suggests that they do. When he wrote, there were about twenty extant laws in the physical sciences and astronomy: notably, the laws of Archimedes, Stevin, Kepler, Galileo, Descartes, Hooke, Huygens, Mariotte, and Newton. Hume believes that the principle of inertia as first articulated by Descartes (and which became Newton's first law) has become an empirical 'fact' (1748: 57–8n)[5] and he also refers to Descartes' first law of mechanics that could be recast as the conservation of momentum.

There were also about half a dozen laws in the extant discourse of economics circa 1750, such as Gresham's law or the quantity theory of money. Hume was inclined to identify these laws in his economic writings, such as the law of supply and demand, the law of one price, or the functional relation between the division of labour and the size of the market. Hume was celebrated for discovering several more laws in economics that still have merit, such as the correlation between the interest and the profit rate, the specie-flow mechanism, and the causal relationship between economic growth and an unanticipated injection of money.[6] At the start of his *Political Discourses* (1752), his set of twelve essays on economics, Hume (1777: 253-4) announced that the 'chief business of philosophers' is to spurn 'coffee-house conversation' and to ascend up to 'universal propositions, which comprehend under them an infinite number of individuals, and include a whole science in a single theorem'. He also believed that the science of politics, a synonym for economics, could become 'almost as general and certain ... as any the mathematical sciences afford us' (16).

Hume's formative years coincided with the ascent of the Newtonian system that explained the empirical laws of planetary orbits and projectile motion in terms of gravitational attraction and subsumed both under the mechanical philosophy. When the Newtonian system finally triumphed in the 1750s, Hume would have been hard-pressed to naysay its success. Nevertheless, the influence of Newton on Hume has been overblown, especially on his two seminal works that most pertain to his epistemology. There is only one mention of Newton in Hume's *Treatise* and one in his first *Enquiry*, both in footnotes (1739-40: 47n; 1748: 58n). Both notes depict a Newton purged of any metaphysical ascriptions, whether a vacuum, microphysical particles, or an ether to explain gravitational attraction.[7]

In his 1742 essay 'Of the Rise and Progress of the Arts and Sciences', Hume (1777) acknowledges the ascent of the Newtonian system and predicts that it will prevail, but also remarks that it was still legitimately challenged by the alternative grand systems of the Cartesians and the Leibnizians. Moreover, in that same section of the first *Enquiry* where he refers to Newton, Hume (1748: 60-1n) also comments on the *vis viva* controversy. He hopes that direct measurement might resolve whether force is a function of velocity (Descartes), or rather of velocity-squared (Leibniz). This suggests that Hume was still inclined, in 1748, to take the non-Newtonian systems seriously and to see them as engaging important paths of inquiry, as turned out to be the case.

Hume expresses admiration for Newton's genius, but he also presents a Newton who used 'cautious and modest' methods and never 'insisted on' the existence of gravity 'without more experiments' (58n).[8] Any casual reader of Newton would quickly refute such an account. Newton used some experimental findings to great advantage, but he also drew heavily on metaphysical assertions about the nature of physical nature (its simplicity and corpuscular composition, for example), not to mention the critical role of God. Even in his more empirical treatise, the *Opticks* (1704), Newton ventured well beyond experimental findings, positing a particle theory of light, and a property he called 'fits' to explain the problematic phenomenon of diffraction.

There is also no concrete evidence that Hume ever read or studied Newton with care, or even some of the texts that disseminated the Newtonian theory. Hume studied mathematics and natural philosophy at the University of Edinburgh from the ages of ten to fourteen. We have some idea of the content of those courses, but they did not include a reading of Newton's *Principia* (1687) or sufficient mathematical training to understand the calculus or method of fluxions in Newton's terminology (Barfoot 1990). When Hume went to France in his mid-twenties (1734–37), he had access to two excellent libraries, first at Reims and then at La Flêche; but, since Newton was just being introduced into French learned circles by Voltaire and Maupertuis in those same years, it is not obvious that this would have made its way to the provincial towns where Hume sojourned. It is absolutely certain, however, that he would have been exposed to Cartesian thought, and he frames much of his *Treatise* and, in particular, the Abstract attached to the end of Book Three, with an explicit recognition of that school of thought.

Another clue that Hume could not have read Newton's *Principia* with care when he issued his *Treatise* can be found in a remark at the close of Book Two, when Hume muses on the subject of curiosity or the love of truth. He discusses genius without giving any names, and remarks that the truths discovered by mathematicians should be useful as well as entertaining. There are certain branches of mathematics, such as the 'conic sections, … [however] few mathematicians take any pleasure in these researches, but turn their thoughts to what is more useful and important' (1739–40: 287). No one could say this if they knew Newton's *Principia*, since his system was predicated on demonstrating that a central force emanating from one body would result in another body in its vicinity describing one of the four conic sections (circle, ellipse, parabola, hyperbola). The brilliance of Newton's account rested on the fact that the extant laws of Kepler, Galileo, and Huygens demonstrated empirically that planets or projectiles describe one of the conic sections. Hence a single type of central force must exist – namely, gravitational attraction – and its mathematical formulation was then readily deduced, such that the force was inversely proportional to the square of the distance between the two bodies. If Hume ever understood these derivations, he never bothered to override his youthful dismissal of that branch of mathematics.[9]

Furthermore, Hume could hardly be viewed as sympathetic to the full Newtonian system, particularly its commitment to the mechanical philosophy.

He devoted dozens of pages to unpacking the concepts of absolute space and time, of the vacuum, and of substance. His primary aim was to expose the utter confusion that beset these concepts. He never resolves, for example, if a vacuum exists or not, a critical distinction between the Newtonian and Cartesian systems. Hume also did not endorse the theory of corpuscles or atoms. 'My intention never was to penetrate into the nature of bodies, or explain the secret causes of their operations ... Such an enterprize [sic] is beyond the reach of human understanding, and that we can never pretend to know body otherwise than by those external properties, which discover themselves to the senses' (1739–40: 46). This is reinforced in the first *Enquiry*: 'there are no ideas ... more obscure and uncertain, than those of power, force, energy, or necessary connexion' (1748: 50). We know that Hume's primary target in the *Treatise* was the Cartesians, particularly the work of Nicolas Malebranche, because he says as much, but his probing analyses could just as well have been levelled at the Newtonians.

Nevertheless, it is important to emphasize that Hume matured philosophically through the period during which the Cartesian system waned. The Leibnizian system took a different path, leading via Roger Boscovich, among others, to the concept of energy that unified mid-nineteenth-century physics.[10] Hume (1739–40: 413) suggests that one of the shortcomings of the Cartesians is 'that matter is utterly deprived of energy' and hence there is no compelling explanation of mechanical motion. But Hume steered towards Newton, not Leibniz (whom he had also read) (408). By about 1750, he had learned about some of the critical findings that supported the Newtonian system: one was the measurement of the earth's polar regions by Maupertuis (1732–37) and another was the partial solution to the lunar orbit by Alexis Clairaut (1747).[11] In the concluding chapter to his second *Enquiry*, Hume (1751: 78–9) writes that 'the bulk and figure of the earth have been measured and delineated, ... the motions of the tides have been accounted for, the order and economy of the heavenly bodies subjected to their proper laws, and infinite itself reduced to calculation'. In 1759, the return of Halley's Comet, a prediction that rested directly on assimilating the perturbation of the planets due to gravitational forces, was the most triumphant moment for the Newtonian system.

In 1750, Hume and Adam Smith became friends and subsequently chose each other as their literary executors in the event of one predeceasing the other. In their correspondence, Smith kept Hume abreast of the various revisions to his *History of Astronomy* (1795), in case of a sudden demise, so there is reason to believe that they discussed its contents in person as well. Smith probably sketched this essay in the late 1740s and had most certainly drafted it by 1752. Hume may have learned from Smith about the tipping of the balance towards Newton, but it is important to note that, even with the return of Halley's Comet, Smith remained circumspect about Newton, noting that his system, although much superior to the Cartesian, might at some point in the future be superseded. We do not know that Hume shared this view with Smith, but insofar as Hume was a less conservative thinker than Smith, and inclined to accept the fallibility of all knowledge, there is reason to think that he did. It is even possible that Smith is echoing his esteemed friend, since there are clear indications of an imprint of Hume's *Treatise*.

To summarize, Hume lived through an important period in the history of science. One key theme that Hume (and Smith) took from this is that the Cartesians had sustained for over a century a metaphysical system of thought that in hindsight appeared ridiculous. Hume and Smith both spared no mercy for the absurd ascription by Cartesians of vortices to all features of the universe. As for Malebranche's doctrine of occasionalism that places God as the proximate cause to all bodily motion, Hume (1748: 57) depicts such an account as entering a 'fairy land, long ere we have reached the last steps of our theory'. It would be hard to imagine a more pejorative denunciation of an esteemed body of thought.

Another way to view this is to paint Hume less as pro-Newtonian but most definitely as anti-Cartesian. There are marked breaks with Cartesian dualism in his youthful *Treatise*. Hume did not view the mind as a passive receptacle for the ego, or give any credence to the idea of an eternal soul. He suggests that the concepts of God, substance, and the human will are unfounded because there are no antecedent impressions from which they are drawn. There is no substance that is mind-independent, nor any mind that is without the body, without the passions, or perceptual apparatus that insinuates sensation into our very beliefs. Much has been made of the fact that, for Hume, our beliefs are the product of non-rational faculties of the mind, and these in turn depend on physiological processes of the body; belief incorporates a sensation or feeling that, if unpacked, would display a physical pathway in the past, forming customary associations.

This entanglement of the mental and the physical is also evident in Hume's account of the moral and the natural sciences. Both realms are law governed, but our minds are such that we engage the two as woven together. Hume gives the graphic example of the prisoner about to be executed by an axe. Our mind, he avers, would just as much commit to the inexorable force of the axe and the death that ensues once the head is severed, as the obedience of the executioner and guards to the law of the land. 'Here is a connected chain of natural causes and voluntary actions; but the mind feels no difference between them, in passing from one link to another' (69). This captures well a key feature of Hume's theory of knowledge – that the natural and moral realm are felt to be on the same epistemic level. There is no disembodied mind any more than there is pure body, and we are thus as much beholden to social laws and convention as to the laws of the physical world.

For Hume, knowledge is in essence the explanation of phenomena. Most phenomena are ordinary: bread nourishes, or money purchases goods. Knowledge arises most readily from those that are repeated; singular effects, such as one footprint on a desert island, prove problematic for drawing sound inferences. There are also extraordinary phenomena, such as an earthquake and others that are purportedly miraculous, because they violate the known laws of nature. The main point is that Hume sees our efforts at knowledge as reacting to what physical or human nature presents to us as discernible events or encounters that we call phenomena. There is no sense to the longstanding view that God has measured the scope of human knowledge, or that God would have made the world partially but not wholly accessible because of some divine plan. For Hume, our knowledge of the world is entirely contingent on what we, as one species among many, happen to observe or experience. The patterns that we discern and work up into scientific laws may never cohere into a unified system: there is a distinct possibility that our world is imperfect and unfinished (107). In his *Dialogues Concerning Natural Religion*, Philo considers the possibility that our universe is poorly constructed, 'so little finished in every part' and 'so coarse are the strokes with which it is executed' (1779: 73).

Hume's world is entirely non-normative. There is no intrinsic vice or virtue in the world, nor justice. Some virtues, such as benevolence or courage, are deemed natural insofar as they spring forth without external motivation. But all virtues are known *post facto*, when we judge the motives that result in our actions. Artificial virtues – justice, most notably – require additional motivation. Justice is sustained because we recognize both the social utility of respecting property and the fact that society would unravel if we did not uphold the rule of law. As Hume puts it, there would be no justice without the existence of property: they are two sides of the same coin.

Hume is also clear that there is no providence. But because we function as a species there must be some resonance between our minds and the external world, some 'pre-established harmony' that enables the contents of our mind to represent or grasp some surface similarities that are genuine, or sufficiently genuine for us to survive (1748: 44). Hume, a century before Darwin, cannot avail himself of the principle of natural selection to make sense of this, but there is reason to see Hume as a proto-evolutionary thinker, a predilection he shared with others of the eighteenth century – notably, Bernard Mandeville and the Comte du Buffon.[12] In several of his works, Hume reinforces the view that we human beings form one species and thus our kinship runs deep. It is likely that Hume knew of the *Systema Naturae* (1735) by Carl Linnaeus that gave us the binomial system of taxonomy and the appellation of *Homo sapiens*. Hume (1777: 378) conjectures that 'the universe, like an animal body, has a natural progress from infancy to old age' and that our species might not yet have reached middle age. He also believes in what we would call cultural evolution: 'It is not fully known, what degree of refinement, either in virtue or vice, human nature is susceptible of; nor what may be expected of mankind from any great revolution in their education, customs, or principles' (87–8). Some virtues – the Monkish virtues of self-denial and solitude, fasting, and penance – have been replaced by the commercial virtues of application and industry, ambition and perseverance, frugality and prudence (1751: 73–8).

Hume follows Bernard Mandeville insofar as he explores the theme of sociability. Hume believes that the family bonds into which we are born cultivate other-regarding sentiments, and that we have a strong capacity for sympathy with members of our species, both friends and strangers. Although we are governed by our passions and prone to self-deception if not knavery, we are also capable of much goodness and honesty. Much of our knowledge depends on the testimony of others and it is critical that we recognize this. We should be cautious in our acceptance of a given testimonial report, but if it accords with a number of other reports, from disparate and reliable reports, and the reports are well preserved, then we might count the claim as true. Conversely, if there is but one reporter, and from the distant past (as is the case for religious miracles), then we should be highly sceptical.

One of Hume's central maxims to achieve wisdom is to avoid hasty generalization. Always proportion one's beliefs to the evidence and, when possible, collect as much reliable evidence as possible. Hume gives as an example two hypothetical reports of events in January 1600, during the reign of Elizabeth I. One is a report that for eight days there was total darkness over the entire earth, but that this was observed by everyone in 'all languages' and was still affirmed down through the centuries. He thinks the widespread consensus is sufficient to accept that the report is true and that we must seek its cause.[13] But a different report, that some physicians and members of court attested that the queen had died on 1 January 1600 and then come back to life shortly after, should be very much doubted. There is good reason to suppose that she had reasons to simulate the death and to collude with those close by. As Hume (1748: 98) remarks, 'I should rather believe the most extraordinary events to arise from their concurrence, than admit of so signal a violation of the laws of nature.'

The source of knowledge is thus important, but so, too, is the number of inferences in a given demonstration (1739–40: 121). Hume compares the natural and the moral sciences in this respect, and proposes that, because there are more inferences in the natural sciences, there is more reason to assume that error will creep in. There is a presumption by Hume, however, that enduring truths require lengthy probing. On the opening page of his *Treatise* he remarks, 'for if truth be at all within the reach of human capacity, 'tis certain it must lie very deep and abstruse' (3). There is a sense of a long journey that demands the accumulation of many observations and the sifting through of various hypotheses before settling on the most plausible. In the science of man, the observations must be taken

> as they appear in the common course of the world, by men's behaviour in company, in affairs, and in their pleasures. Where experiments of this kind are judiciously collected and compar'd, we may hope to establish on them a science, which will not be inferior in certainty, and will be much superior in utility to any other of human comprehension. (6)

Hume is thus keen to elevate the epistemic standing of the moral sciences, and this objective, to a considerable extent, frames his entire set of writings.

Hume's essay 'Of the Rise and Progress of the Arts and Sciences' offers a brief, albeit fascinating, account of the history of human knowledge. By 'Arts' he means, as was customary at the time, artisan activities including the manufacturing of cloth or other household items. In Europe, the capitalist system had taken hold in the sixteenth century but was only to undergo industrialization in the last third of the eighteenth century, after Hume had laid down his pen. Our everyday assumption that science is applied to industry was not yet in place, but historians have found that the overlap between science and artisanal techniques was widespread, and that mathematics was primarily applied to specific problems in, for example, navigation, fortification, or surveying.[14] Hume acknowledged the importance of agricultural science and commended his own older brother for studying new techniques with considerable improvements to the yield on the family estate.

Hume is fascinated with the changing economic and political landscape of his day, the rapid rise and expansion of trade and commerce, and the sense in which political regimes were undertaking new fiscal measures, or issuing new kinds of public securities. But he also reflects on the factors that prompt scientific learning. Because avarice is a universal passion, 'it is more easy to account for the rise and progress of commerce in any kingdom, than for that of learning' (1777: 113). The latter depends on curiosity taking hold over those with 'youth, leisure, education, genius, and example' (ibid.). As a result, there are never more than a few who 'cultivate the sciences in any state'. Nevertheless, Hume believes that a pattern exists, and that 'in tracing the history of the arts and sciences', given sufficient caution, we might arrive at 'stable and universal principles' rather than 'assign causes which never existed' (ibid.).

First, Hume maintains that the question regarding the progress of science, although it stems from 'the taste, genius, and spirit of a few', 'it is impossible but a share of the same spirit and genius must be antecedently diffused throughout the people among whom they arise' (114). For this reason, the account will engage 'general causes and principles', and thus transcend the merely contingent and accidental. The first condition for Hume is that the government be free. If, conversely, tyranny or arbitrary power is prevalent, then the people are 'slaves in the full and proper sense of the word; and it is impossible they can ever aspire to any refinements of taste or reason' (117). But once the rule of law is established, in a republic, 'the sciences may raise their heads and flourish' (118). Hume grants the remote possibility of science taking root under an enlightened monarch, who governs by the law and not by arbitrary power, but thinks that this is the exception. He considered his own Britain a variant of this, with many republican tendencies since the Glorious Revolution of 1688.

Hume thus argues that one of the key 'advantages of free states', by which he means republics or civilized monarchs, is the fostering of science. Secure and liberal regimes prompt curiosity, 'eloquence', and 'emulation', and these in turn foster 'genius and capacity' (119). Another key factor that is conducive to the rise of knowledge is international trade. If there are 'a number of neighbouring and independent states, connected together by commerce and policy', this will foster emulation and hence improvement (ibid.). It is also important that these are small states that are likely to evolve into commonwealths rather than grow large and eventually resort to tyranny. One reason why the size of the republic matters is that in a small state an oppressive action could be readily known by the people, whereas in large states these can be more successfully hidden. Large states are also able to afford displays of majestic power, that fosters 'a kind of fascination on men, and naturally contributes to the enslaving of them' (ibid.).

As a discerning reader might surmise, Hume is also offering an explanation of the birth of science in ancient Greece. It was comprised of 'a cluster of little principalities, which soon became republics; and being united both by their near neighbourhood, and by the times of the same language and interest, they entered into the closest intercourse of commerce and learning' (120). Hume also attempts to explain why this happened, and he attributes much to the effect of 'mutual jealousy' that would emerge between these little principalities, 'keeps them from receiving too lightly the law from each other, in matters of taste and of reasoning' (ibid.). In short, each little island is likely to challenge and criticize the view of their neighbour rather than to accept things on authority. Hence, Hume approves strongly of the republic of letters. Modern Europe, he avers, 'is at present a copy at large, of what Greece was formerly a pattern in miniature' (121)

Hume believes that his theory is also confirmed by China, where he supposes the arts and sciences remain static. He believes that 'reputation' stifles thought and that this is more likely in a large than a small nation. As a vast nation with one language (or so he believes), Confucius has dominated and thus thwarted progress in the sciences. Geography is also important. Europe, Hume asserts, is the region on the globe most divided by 'seas, rivers, and mountains' and Greece has this in miniature and more than any other part of Europe, or so Hume asserts.

He draws important distinctions between republics and civilized monarchs. In the former, those who wish to curry political favour must look to the people, while those in the latter, to their superiors. The republic thus fosters 'industry, capacity, or knowledge', while the monarchy fosters 'wit, complaisance, or civility' (126). It is for this reason, too, that 'a strong genius succeeds best in republics; a refined taste in monarchies. And consequently the sciences are the more natural growth of the one [republics], and the polite arts of the other [monarchies]' (ibid.).

Another critical observation is that, in monarchies, mathematics and natural philosophy are 'not half so valuable' as religion and politics, and hence 'metaphysics and morals' (ibid.). The reason is that monarchies depend on a 'superstitious reverence to priests and principles', who in turn abridge genuine reasoning. In its place, politeness is fostered, because of the 'long train of dependence from the prince to the peasant' (ibid.). For this reason, the republics are renowned for their lack of good manners and politeness. Hume points to the Swiss or Dutch of his day, and extracts observations from Cicero as additional confirmation. But he also notes that what is considered polite manners is contingent on the age. In ancient times, the master would eat and drink better than his guests but in the present it is customary that the master of the feast eat last and least.

These various arguments may strike us as simplistic or superficial, but the point to grasp is that Hume is attempting to explain the rise and expansion of knowledge, both theoretical and applied, in terms of economic, political, and geographical factors. The trope of comparing ancients and moderns was commonplace, but Hume was one of the first to introduce political or economic factors into the account. One could quibble with each and every assertion but that does not undercut the very original endeavour at hand. Hume believed that the European economy was experiencing unprecedented growth, as indeed was the case, and that this would expand in tandem with the rise of political liberty and the growth of knowledge. Recollect his 'indissoluble chain' of 'industry, knowledge, and humanity' (271).

In conclusion, Hume firmly believed that we had amassed considerable amounts of knowledge about the world, in mathematics, science, agriculture, literature, arts, politics, economics, and history. He was also sanguine that there was much new knowledge yet to be discovered, particularly if enlightened regimes were sustained. His optimism rings loud and clear, consonant with many of his enlightened age. But not even Hume could have anticipated the extent to which the adjective 'Humean' is now so deeply imbedded in contemporary philosophical discourse, or the sense in which his imprint continues to be evident in virtually every branch of inquiry.[15]

Notes

1 See Schmidt (2003). For more recent assessments of Hume's standing in the philosophical canon, see Bailey and O'Brien (2015).
2 See Read and Richman (2007), Ainslie and Butler (2015), and Garrett (2015).
3 See Harris (2015).
4 See Demeter (2012: 577–99).
5 Hume did not acknowledge Galileo, who first posited a curvilinear version of the principle of inertia.
6 For a brief overview of Hume's economics, see Schabas and Wennerlind (2011: 217–30).
7 There is good circumstantial evidence that Hume was acquainted, during the 1740s, with novel theories about the electric fluid and that this was then seen as part of the ubiquitous ether. I have argued (2005: 65–74) that such ideas may have prompted some of Hume's ideas in monetary theory that drew heavily on fluid metaphors.
8 See also Hume (1754–62: vi, 542).
9 This passage is deleted in his *Dissertation on the Passions* (1757), which was his revised version of Book Two of the *Treatise*. But Hume has an implicit reference

to Newton's experiments with prisms that demonstrated the heterogeneity of light (5). And in his second *Enquiry* (1751: 27) Hume cites Newton's 'chief rule of philosophizing' that submits to the uniformity of nature, although with an odd twist because Hume introduces 'energies', a term not used by Newton. See Schliesser (2008); Hazony and Schliesser (2016).
10 See Gaukroger (2010: 345–7).
11 See Hankins (1985).
12 Hume knew the work of Mandeville before he wrote the *Treatise*, and later admired the work of Buffon (1749). It is not out of the question that Buffon took up his proto-evolutionary thinking from Hume. See Schabas (2005).
13 Hume does not offer an explanation. However, one of the worst volcanic eruptions in human times transpired in mid-February 1600, at Huaynaputina in Peru. The reform of the calendar in Hume's day allows for his ascription of January. The European harvests were severely affected by the ash and the drop in temperature. This seems the only reasonable explanation of what is otherwise a very peculiar phenomenon.
14 See, for example, Hankins (1985), Smith and Findlen (2002), and Gaukroger (2010).
15 I wish to thank David Owen and Carl Wennerlind for valuable feedback.

References

Ainslie, D. and Butler, A. (eds) (2015), *The Cambridge Companion to Hume's* Treatise, Cambridge: Cambridge University Press.
Bailey, A. and O'Brien, D. (eds) (2015), *The Bloomsbury Companion to Hume*, London: Bloomsbury.
Barfoot, M. (1990), 'Hume and the Culture of Science in the Early Eighteenth Century', in M. A. Stewart (ed.), *Studies in the Philosophy of the Scottish Enlightenment*, Oxford: Oxford University Press.
Demeter, T. (2012), 'Hume's Experimental Method', *British Journal for the History of Philosophy*, 20: 577–99.
Garrett, D. (1997), *Cognition and Commitment in Hume's Philosophy*, New York: Oxford University Press.
Garrett, D. (2015), *Hume*, London: Routledge.
Gaukroger, S. (2010), *The Collapse of Mechanism and the Rise of Sensibility*, Oxford: Oxford University Press.
Hankins, T. L. (1985), *Science and the Enlightenment*, Cambridge: Cambridge University Press.
Harris, J. A. (2015), *Hume: An Intellectual Biography*, Cambridge: Cambridge University Press.

Hazony, Y. and Schliesser, E. (2016), 'Newton and Hume', in P. Russell (ed.), *The Oxford Handbook of Hume*, Oxford: Oxford University Press.

Hume, D. (1739-40 [2000]), *A Treatise of Human Nature*, ed. D. F. Norton and M. J. Norton, Oxford: Oxford University Press.

Hume, D. (1748 [2000]), *An Enquiry Concerning Human Understanding*, ed. T. L. Beauchamp, Oxford: Oxford University Press.

Hume, D. (1751 [1998]), *An Enquiry Concerning the Principles of Morals*, ed. T. L. Beauchamp, Oxford: Oxford University Press.

Hume, D. (1754-62 [1983]), *The History of England, from the Invasion of Julius Caesar to the Revolution in 1688*, 6 vols, ed. W. B. Todd, Indianapolis: Liberty Press.

Hume, D. (1757 [2007]), *A Dissertation on the Passions* and *The Natural History of Religion*, ed. T. L. Beauchamp, Oxford: Oxford University Press.

Hume, D. (1777 [1985]), *Essays: Moral, Political and Literary*, ed. Eugene Rotwein, Indianapolis: Liberty Press.

Hume, D. (1779 [1980]), *Dialogues Concerning Natural Religion*, ed. R. H. Popkin, Indianapolis: Liberty Press.

Norton, D. F. and Taylor, J. (eds) (2009), *The Cambridge Companion to Hume*, 2nd edn, Cambridge: Cambridge University Press.

Owen, D. (2009), 'Hume and the Mechanics of Mind: Impressions, Ideas, and Association', in Norton and Taylor (2009).

Read, R. and Richman, K. A. (eds) (2007), *The New Hume Debate*, revised edn, London: Routledge.

Schabas, M. (2005), *The Natural Origins of Economics*, Chicago: University of Chicago Press.

Schabas, M. and Wennerlind, C. (2011), 'Hume on Money, Commerce, and the Science of Economics', *Journal of Economic Perspectives*, 25: 217-30.

Schliesser, E. (2008), 'Hume's Newtonianism and Anti-Newtonianism', *Stanford Encyclopedia of Philosophy* (online).

Schmidt, C. M. (2003), *David Hume: Reason in History*, University Park: Pennsylvania State University.

Smith, A. (1795 [1980]), 'History of Astronomy', in W. P. D. Wightman and J. C. Bryce (eds), *Adam Smith: Essays on Philosophical Subjects*, Oxford: Oxford University Press.

Smith, P. H. and Findlen, P. (eds) (2002), *Merchants and Marvels: Commerce, Science, and Art in Early Modern Europe*, New York: Routledge.

9

Kant

John Zammito

Immanuel Kant (1724–1804) was a man of his times (the Enlightenment) and a figure committed to the timeless ideal of rational argument that has defined the Western philosophical tradition from its outset. His essential concern was that humans live up to their rational endowment, notwithstanding their material embodiment and finite cognitive capacities. He sought to confirm rationally grounded moral freedom as the destiny and the dignity of humankind, both in this world and in the ideal 'kingdom of ends'.[1] Thus, he meant to salvage the heritage of Western metaphysics – a divinely sanctioned order in the universe, human moral freedom and responsibility, and the immortality of the individual soul – within the parameters of critical inquiry that the Enlightenment had come to demand. He placed metaphysics within the 'limits of human understanding' but elaborated grounds for 'rational belief' in metaphysical ideas, indispensable for human hopes, as well as for 'rational obligation', indispensable for human moral and political action.[2] Thus, he consummated his lifelong 'love affair' with metaphysics even as he endeavoured to clip the wings of dogmatic metaphysicians and drastic sceptics before him.[3]

Born the son of a saddle-maker in Königsberg, East Prussia, Kant attended the local university (1740–46), where he studied under Martin Knutzen (1713–51). From his Pietist family Kant derived moral assiduousness, and, from Knutzen, a thorough grounding in the currently fashionable Leibniz-Wolff 'School Philosophy', especially as canonized in the writings of Christian Wolff (1679–1754).[4] By the 1740s, this school had come to be challenged by Pietist philosophers like Christian August Crusius (1715–75) on the grounds of human rational finitude and dependence on divine grace.[5] For many Wolffian revisionists, sensibility demanded a greater stature in accounts of human experience than the 'obscurity' to which it was confined, as against the 'clarity and distinctness' of reason and demonstrative logic, in 'School philosophy'.[6] Still more important was a European-scale dispute between Leibnizian and Newtonian thought, crystallized in the *Leibniz-Clarke Correspondence* (1716) and propagated by the newly revitalized Berlin Academy after 1746 (Clarke 1956). Kant's philosophical thinking evolved from these two tensions – Pietism versus Wolffianism, and Newtonianism versus Leibnizianism (Laywine 1993). But he came increasingly to incorporate into his thinking new impulses from the French and Scottish Enlightenments – most crucially, Jean-Jacques Rousseau and David Hume. Rousseau rescued him from intellectual elitism with the dramatic claim that moral conscience was the defining dignity of *all* human beings.[7] Hume, as we will observe, awakened Kant to the metaphysical hubris of conventional philosophy.

In 1755, after years of service as a tutor, Kant became unsalaried lecturer at the University of Königsberg, teaching at this rank until 1770, when he was finally promoted to Professor of Logic and Metaphysics. Over the intervening years, Kant gradually came to wider notice, particularly through his entry for the Berlin Academy Prize contest of 1763 (published 1764), and through his popular essay *Observations on the Feelings of the Beautiful and the Sublime* (1764). The Prize contest proved a decisive moment for the revisionist challenge to Wolffian philosophy in Germany, querying the universal applicability of the 'mathematical method' in human reasoning, and opening the way for the intrusion of more 'empiricist' approaches from Britain (and, in a lesser measure, France) (Tonelli 1959). While Kant's submission did not win the competition (it was won by the Berlin philosopher, Moses Mendelssohn [1729–86]), nevertheless it achieved sufficient notice to be published alongside the winning essay. The *Observations* represented Kant's effort to refashion his philosophical style and topicality along the lines of the more literary and popular models provided by Rousseau and Hume. It became the most widely published and read of all of Kant's works in his lifetime. Kant's celebrity gradually escalated, especially through his 'pragmatic' course offerings on physical geography (and later anthropology), aimed to develop his students' urbanity (*Weltkenntnis*).[8]

His foremost student and eventual rival Johann Gottfried Herder (1744–1803) (1877: 324–5) has left us with a magnificent portrait of the Kant of those years:

> Playfulness, wit, and humour were at his command. His lectures were the most entertaining talks. His mind, which examined Leibniz, Wolff, Baumgarten, Crusius and Hume, and investigated the laws of nature of Newton, Kepler, and the physicists, comprehended equally the newest works of Rousseau … and the

latest discoveries of science. He weighed them all, and always came back to the unbiased knowledge of nature and to the moral worth of man. The history of men and people, natural history and science, mathematics and observation, were the sources from which he enlivened his lectures and conversations. He was indifferent to nothing worth knowing. No cabal, no sect, no prejudice, no desire for fame, could ever tempt him in the slightest from broadening and illuminating the truth. He incited and gently forced others to think for themselves; despotism was foreign to his nature.

Several of Kant's works were reviewed by Mendelssohn (1991) in the key Enlightenment journal *Letters Concerning the Latest in Literature* (1764–65), and the two men entered into a lifelong correspondence and friendship. Another important Berlin philosopher, Johann Heinrich Lambert (1728–77), began corresponding with Kant at the same time. But Kant alarmed both with the caustic scepticism of his bizarre text, *Dreams of a Spirit-Seer Elucidated by the Dreams of Metaphysics* (1766).

Provoked by the outright mystagoguery of Emanuel Swedenborg (1688–1772), and stung by criticisms of metaphysics from the Western Enlightenment (especially Hume and Rousseau), it seemed that Kant meant to repudiate the whole tradition. Around 1769, however, he underwent a famous 'upheaval' (*Umwälzung*), ushering in his so-called critical period. One leading explanation for this dramatic turn is that Kant discovered the problem of the mathematical 'antinomies' – that is, the inescapable propensity of human reason to develop internally consistent but mutually contradictory arguments about space and time (Hinske 1965). A second hypothesis is that he was, in his famous phrase from 1783 (1902ff: iv, 274), 'awakened from his dogmatic slumber by the reminder of David Hume' – that is, the contention that causal inference could only be inductive and contingent, not deductive and necessary, in human cognition. In any event, in his *Inaugural Dissertation* (1770) Kant enunciated two crucial positions of his 'critical' philosophy: the radical distinction of sensibility from understanding as features of human consciousness, and the claim that space and time were subjective though necessary forms of sensible intuition.[9] Kant's *Dissertation* remained transitional; its shortcomings were pointed out in letters from Lambert and Mendelssohn. Kant took the ensuing decade (1771–81) to work out his considered position.

In 1781 he published his most famous and daunting work, the *Critique of Pure Reason*. This propounded his 'transcendental' or 'critical' philosophy as a decisive innovation that for the first time raised and answered the question of the warrant for metaphysics, given the 'limits of human reason'. In this endeavour, Kant had two negative objectives and one positive one. The negative objectives were to debunk what he had come to regard as untenable 'dogmatic metaphysics' (roughly, the Leibniz-Wolff system) and to overcome equally untenable all-out scepticism about objective – especially natural-scientific – knowledge (roughly, Hume's challenge to the idea of causal necessity). The positive objective, stated in Kant's own famous terms, was 'to limit knowledge to make room for faith' – that is, to carve out scope for, and give strength to human hopes for, righteousness and redemption against the twin threats of materialist determinism and utter doubt.[10] This complex agenda accounts for the difficulties in both the composition and the reception of his argument.

The key to the critical turn was an analogy to the Copernican Revolution: it systematically relocated the vantage-point of inquiry.[11] Instead of seeking to warrant knowledge-claims by verifying the conformity of a mental construct to the object itself, Kant proposed that objects had to conform to the mind's fundamental structures to qualify as even possible experience. In service to this strategy, he undertook to reconstruct the history of Western philosophy into a contest between 'empiricists' and 'rationalists'.[12] From Aristotle through Locke and beyond, the 'empiricists' contended that 'there is nothing in the mind that was not first in the senses'. The 'rationalist' rejoinder from Leibniz was to affirm most of the claim, with the decisive supplement 'except the mind itself'.[13] That is, the essential thrust of German rationalism was to affirm the active role of the mind in the organization and warrant of knowledge. Kant's transcendental philosophy or 'critique' entailed the epistemological investigation of the necessary structures in the mind that made coherent experience possible.[14] Since the mind could only govern what was present to consciousness, Kant distinguished between this 'phenomenon' and the essentially unknowable 'thing-in-itself' (noumenon) which the mind inferred as its source.[15] While Kant could offer warrant for knowledge-claims regarding phenomena (against Hume), he also demonstrated why there could never be warrant for knowledge-claims regarding noumena (against Leibniz), even as he could further demonstrate that one could still think, without contradiction, many things about noumena (God, freedom, immortality) which were of urgent human concern: that is, there was room for rational faith.

Kant's argument presumed a fundamental distinction of sensibility (receptivity) from understanding (spontaneity), which he took to define human finitude. While he was prepared to hold, with Leibniz, that the mind is capable of generating and coupling concepts spontaneously, he insisted that this agency could only be actualized when confronted with intuition: that is, something immediately and concretely given.[16] In the human case, Kant held with Locke that such intuitions could only be sensible: that is, occasioned by involuntary reception of sense data. However, sense perception was insufficient, albeit necessary, for the experience of an object. The manifold of sensations had to be imaginatively coordinated into a unity within the intuitive forms of space and time. This unity then needed to be subordinated to the logical rules for cognitive judgement, the 'categories of the understanding', and thereby related to other objects in a coherent causal order, which was Kant's notion of experience. The warrant of an objective experience – namely, one that claimed intersubjective validity (indeed, a priori or universal necessity) – was thus a matter of these successive, active syntheses by the mind. For Kant, the crucial problem was that of how and why the given sensations, even as mediated through formal intuition, should be amenable to 'constitution' by the categories.[17] This was the crux of his famous 'transcendental deduction', which he singled out as the most important and demanding part of his book.[18] Kant claimed that the coherence of experience as *my own* – that is, the very possibility of accompanying this complex congeries of syntheses with an identical 'I think' (the 'transcendental unity of apperception'), necessitated the constitutive authority of the concepts over sensation.[19]

The urgent issue that Kant then faced was to set strict limits upon what this transcendental deduction authorized. At the very same time that it warranted knowledge-claims about phenomena, it restricted them *to* phenomena. Even the 'I think' which made objective validity possible presented one of the crucial limits of human knowledge, since the 'I' that thinks belonged to the realm of the noumenal for theoretical reason.[20] All that could be known determinately about the 'I think' was just that it accompanied all of one's representations – not what or why it was. All the grand hopes of Wolffian rational psychology to achieve speculative knowledge of an immortal soul were dashed. That was the first of the enormous restrictions that Kant introduced into metaphysics in the second part of the *Critique of Pure Reason*, the 'Transcendental Dialectic'. Next, he proceeded to lay out fully the 'antinomies' of reason, demonstrating the futility of speculation in the sphere of cosmology, then the conundrum of freedom and necessity, and finally the inadequacy of speculative proofs of the existence of God. In place of these grand metaphysical conceptions, Kant allowed only a 'regulative' interest of reason in achieving totality, which permitted the postulation of an 'ideal' of pure reason. Still, that allowed the conjecture of God from a 'practical' point of view. Kant maintained that belief in God only served to supplement the moral project which reason entailed upon humans, so that no speculatively warranted theological dogma (and equally no revelation) was required. As rational beings, even if finite ones, Kant held humans to be governed by an ineluctable obligation, a 'categorical imperative', which commanded that all maxims of human choice conform to the principle of universalizability. Kant's critical philosophy secured the 'primacy' of this 'practical' use of reason against the twin dangers of strict determinism and unrestricted scepticism in theoretical philosophy.[21] Thus, Kant answered the three essential questions that he believed humans confront: 'What can I know? What must I do? What may I hope?'[22]

Reception of the *Critique of Pure Reason* was not what he had hoped. Lambert, to whom he wished to dedicate it, had died, and Mendelssohn could make no sense of it. The most significant review, in the *Göttingische Gelehrten Anzeigen* (January 1782), authored by the popular philosopher Christian Garve (1742–98) but drastically revised by the editor Johann Georg Heinrich Feder (1740–1821), outraged Kant by accusing him of impenetrable obscurity and Berkeleyan idealism. He set about rectifying these misconceptions in *Prolegomena to Any Future Metaphysics* (1783), and a revised version of the *Critique of Pure Reason* (1787). Between the *Prolegomena* and the revised version of the first *Critique*, Kant also published two other works of substantial importance, the *Foundations of the Metaphysics of Morals* (1785) and *Metaphysical Foundations of Natural Science* (1786). These works began to fulfil a commitment that Kant had made in the first *Critique* – namely, to derive a defensible metaphysics from the transcendental framework of the 'critical philosophy', both in natural and in moral philosophy. In 1786 Kant's work finally achieved the popularity that he craved, with the appearance of a series of influential essays on his work by Karl Leonhard Reinhold (1757–1823): *Letters on the Kantian Philosophy* (2005), which appeared originally in the key German Enlightenment journal, *Teusche Merkur*.

As Kant maintained in *Foundations of the Metaphysics of Morals*, even if no empirical evidence for its actuality could be found, the only thing that could deserve the characterization 'good' was a will whose intention was entirely formed by adherence to the principle of right. Kant sought to prove that reason could of itself constitute a sufficient motive for the will. He found evidence for this in the experience of duty, or necessary obligation, even and especially when this contravened palpable material interests in the agent. While morality was thus essentially a matter of intention, actualization of moral duty remained imperative. This created the core tension between the freedom of the will, required in order to be answerable to this duty, and the determinism of the phenomenal world under natural laws, which theoretical reason had established.

Assigning freedom to the noumenal realm in his 'Third Antinomy' allowed Kant to escape a bald contradiction, but the problem of the actualization of moral will in the phenomenal world remained a significant problem to be taken up in his later works.[23]

Kant's breakthrough to prominence in the German Enlightenment arose in the context of three controversies. The first took place in 1784 in the pages of the key Enlightenment journal *Berlinische Monatsschrift*, as German thinkers tried to define for themselves what the movement of Enlightenment signified (Schmidt 1996). Kant's contribution – 'Answer to the Question: What is Enlightenment?' – is one of the texts most frequently cited to represent the entire (German) Enlightenment. Kant (1902ff: viii, 35) opened that essay with the proposition, 'Enlightenment is man's emergence from his self-incurred immaturity.' To be enlightened, Kant explained there and also in the essay 'What Is Orientation in Thinking?' (1786), is to *think for oneself*. Hence Kant's maxim, *sapere aude!* – dare to know (ibid.). Enlightenment was essentially a 'negative principle in the use of one's cognitive powers', testing everything by the standard of universality (viii, 146-7n). This was a project both for each individual and for humanity as a whole. The latter constituted historical progress, in which Kant expressed firm confidence tempered by the sober realization that 'to enlighten an era ... is a very protracted process, for there are numerous external obstacles' (ibid.). Kant granted that he did not yet live in an 'enlightened age', but insisted that he lived 'in an age of enlightenment' (viii, 40). His was an age in which the 'public use of reason' – freedom of expression – could no longer be denied, and it supplied 'all that is needed' for the triumph of enlightenment (viii, 38). The essence of this public use of reason was critique: 'Our age is properly the age of critique, and to critique everything must submit', he wrote. Neither church nor state could pretend exemption.

The second context for Kant's breakthrough was the 'Pantheism Controversy' (1785-89), triggered by the sensational report – circulated by Friedrich Heinrich Jacobi (1743-1819) – that, shortly before his death, the great hero of the German Enlightenment, Gotthold Ephraim Lessing (1729-1781), admitted that he was a 'Spinozist'.[24] Jacobi labelled that 'atheism'. Lessing's friend, Mendelssohn, sought to rebut the charge. An ugly disputation followed, climaxing with Mendelssohn's death. Both sides called upon Kant for support. Reluctantly, he published 'What Is Orientation in Thinking?' in which he advocated, against both protagonists, the idea of 'rational faith' developed in his own critical philosophy.

The third context was a quarrel with a longer history – Kant's hostility to the flamboyant 'Storm and Stress' movement in German literature and cultural criticism, especially as propagated by his former student Herder.[25] In 1784, Herder published the first volume of his greatest work, *Ideas for a Philosophy of the History of Mankind*, and Kant took the unusual step – for him – of writing a (withering) review. It appeared in a new journal, the Jena *Allgemeine Litteratur-Zeitung*, which would become the flagship of German Kantianism. Concurrently, Kant published 'Idea for a Universal History from a Cosmopolitan Perspective' in the *Berlinische Monatsschrift*. These publications pitted against one another the two most important spokesmen of the later German Enlightenment. Kant emerged victorious. Ironically, the man who initially leaped to Herder's defence against Kant's hostile review, Karl Leonhard Reinhold, quickly converted to Kant's side, publishing the crucial *Letters on the Kantian Philosophy* which brought Kant to public prominence.

Caught up with his own system, Kant elaborated it with redoubled intensity in the wake of his new popularity. In 1787 he published a revised version of his first *Critique*, in 1788 the *Critique of Practical Reason*, and in 1790 the *Critique of Judgment*. The thrust of the second *Critique* was to expound what Kant called the 'fact of pure reason' – namely, the ineluctable claim that the moral law imposed upon humans – and the concomitant necessity of human freedom in light of this 'categorical imperative' – *ought* implies *can*, to put it simply. The second *Critique* also defended the notion that the sensible world governed by *natural laws* could be 'thought' without contradiction as a realm amenable to the actualization of *supersensible law* (morality) by virtue of their common *lawfulness*, the essence of reason. Kant developed this idea further in the third *Critique*, under the rubric of 'moral teleology'. In both *Critiques*, Kant endeavoured to show the importance of 'postulating' for 'practical' reason the Providence of God and the immortality of the soul in order to promote the actualization of moral obligation, achievement of the 'highest good' in this world.[26] For Kant, this would entail substantive political-historical outcomes, leading ultimately to the establishment of an ethical commonwealth of mankind, a 'kingdom of God on earth'.

The third *Critique* addressed these concerns only after carrying out two other inquiries. First, Kant developed a transcendental aesthetics. He held the 'judgment of taste' concerning the beautiful was 'disinterested'.[27] Hence, it made a universal claim that achieved transcendental warrant via the subjective 'harmony of the faculties'. Imagination freely conformed to the rules of the understanding in playful reconfiguration ('purposiveness without purpose'), thereby eliciting aesthetic pleasure, an ongoing 'liveliness' of the mind.[28] But beauty and sublimity also offered powerful intimations of more ultimate human concerns. Beauty served as a 'symbol of morality', and the sublime, properly understood, registered the 'destiny of mankind' (*Bestimmung des Menschen*) in transcendental freedom.

Second, Kant argued that organisms could never be explained mechanistically, and he therefore elaborated a teleological methodology for the life sciences, a significant intervention especially into the ongoing inquiry into 'vital forces' (*Lebenskräfte*). He sought to impose philosophical sobriety on what he feared were speculative excesses, stimulated, in his view, by the rampant vitalism of his rival, Herder. As Kant (1902ff: xii, 31–5) observed in a comment on an essay in neurophysiology by Samuel Thomas Soemmerring in 1795, he considered himself 'someone not unacquainted with the natural sciences'. He took himself very seriously as a *Naturforscher*, and therefore as being authorized to assert himself in these matters (Adickes 1924–25). In particular, he addressed problems about speciation and variety which had arisen in the controversies between Buffon and Linnaeus over taxonomy and then, more particularly, in the critique launched by Lord Kames against the monogenism of the human species. In a series of essays, Kant took up the question of human variation, and he introduced the notion of 'race' as his concept for permanent variations in human population, expressing the innate potentialities (*Keime* and *Anlagen*) in the species and establishing irreversible racial division as humans spread across the globe.[29]

Kant published three essays primarily concerned with this theory of 'race'. The first appeared initially in 1775 as an announcement for his university students of his course in physical geography and especially his new course in anthropology, which he began to offer in 1772 but submitted to significant revision by 1775. That course, especially in its revised form, addressed what humans made of themselves, whereas the question of 'race' belonged properly in his course on physical geography, since it was something that nature made of humankind.[30] Kant's second essay on 'race' appeared in 1785. Behind these published works, transcripts from Kant's lectures and his unpublished notes reveal an unpleasant set of views about the hierarchy of cultural capabilities and the consequent historical fates of the various human 'races' which has kindled important debates about Kant's role in the rise of so-called scientific racism.[31]

In the narrower context of the emergent life sciences, Kant believed that his theory of race offered a key context for the elaboration of a properly *historical* or developmental study of nature – *Naturgeschichte* in the literal sense – as contrasted to conventional natural history, which was only descriptive classification (*Naturbeschreibung*). These ideas provoked a controversy with the distinguished naturalist Georg Forster (1754–94) in the mid-1780s, in part occasioned by Kant's harsh critique of Herder, whom Forster (1786) admired.[32] Kant's response to Forster's criticism was the important essay 'On the Use of Teleological Principles in Philosophy' (1788), which anticipated the key concerns and arguments of the third *Critique*.

In that *Critique*, Kant discerned in both aesthetics and life-science the operation of a new transcendental faculty – *reflective judgement* – which projected purposeful order onto the natural world yet at the same time found this projection *accommodated* by nature. This 'favour' nature showed that human attentiveness (aesthetic, as well as theoretical) provided the crucial accommodation for Kant between the noumenal order of reason, with its obligation of the moral subject to actualize that order, and the phenomenal world. Both nature and morality appeared to manifest purposive order. This fulfilled Kant's greatest aspiration for systematic coherence. At the same time, by bringing the spheres of living nature and human artifice together and gesturing to a conceivable 'supersensible substrate' unifying the noumenal order with human subjectivity, this work captured the imagination of the new generation of German Idealism and Romanticism.[33]

Just as Kant came to prominence, the whole Enlightenment in Germany entered into eclipse. After the death of the Prussian king Frederick II (1712–86), his conservative successor, Frederick William II (1744–97), sought to curb the Enlightenment. The new king's Minister of Culture, Johann Christoph von Wöllner (1732–1800), issued an Edict in 1788 enforcing orthodoxy in Prussia's churches and universities. In 1789 the outbreak of the French Revolution intensified conservative anxiety linking cultural criticism with political unrest. With the radicalization of the French Revolution, the reception of a key polemic against it – *Reflections on the Revolution in France* (1791), by Edmund Burke (1729–97) – and the outbreak of war with France, the climate in the Germanies became distinctly inhospitable to Enlightenment by 1793.

Meanwhile, counterattacks from both of Kant's main philosophical opponents finally came to be mounted with full force. From the side of the orthodox Leibniz-Wolff school, the attack came in the so-called Kant-Eberhard Controversy of 1790, wherein Kant was held to be merely repeating the original insights of Leibniz. From the side of the sceptics, 'Aenesidemus' (Gottlob Ernst Schulze [1761–1833]) began the still-resounding chorus of claims that Kant had not really 'answered' Hume (Beiser 1987). Important young figures were nevertheless declaring their allegiance to Kant's thought, notably Wilhelm von Humboldt (1767–1835) and Friedrich Schiller (1759–1805).[34] Another young enthusiast burst upon the scene in 1792 with an anonymous text entitled

Attempt at a Critique of All Revelation, issued by Kant's own publisher. The public, awaiting Kant's work on religion, presumed that it was his. Kant had to disavow authorship while graciously praising the newcomer for his insights. Johann Gottlieb Fichte (1762–1814), the author of the text, became famous overnight (La Vopa 2001). Kant hastened to publish his own treatment, *Religion within the Limits of Reason Alone* (1793), only to have it run afoul of the Wöllner Edict. Admonished by the king himself to desist from publishing on religion, Kant dutifully complied. Meanwhile, Fichte, appointed in 1794 to the chair in philosophy at Jena, the cockpit of German Kantianism, quickly exacerbated the fears of the conservatives as he became Germany's most outspoken defender of Jacobinism. Within a few years he was hounded from his chair on the charge of atheism, once again fulminated by the witch-hunter F. H. Jacobi. By 1797, at the latest, Enlightenment was over in Germany.

Kant honoured his commitment to the king of Prussia, but he continued to publish on other questions – notably, history and political theory, linking these quite explicitly to the events taking place in France. His key essays in this vein were 'Theory and Practice' (1793) and 'Perpetual Peace' (1795). Kant remained firm in the view that the enthusiasm that greeted the outbreak of the French Revolution among foreign observers was the decisive empirical confirmation of the destiny of the human race to achieve ethical commonwealth, accompanied by world peace. His ideas of universal republicanism and cosmopolitan world government have become mainstays in subsequent political theory. Upon the king's death, Kant even took up the question of religion again, especially to dispute the authority of the theology faculty to suppress free expression in philosophy (*Conflict of the Faculties*, 1798).

In 1797, at the age of 73, Kant published a major, two-part *Metaphysics of Morals*, detailing his position not only on concrete moral practice but also on political right. Yet this work aroused little excitement. Over the 1790s, even those who called themselves Kantians came to believe that others were in a better position than Kant himself to elaborate his system. At first, Reinhold played this leading role; then it passed to Fichte. In some ways, Kant seemed to have outlived his own system. He gave vent to his exasperation in his public letter to Fichte (1799), denouncing the latter's thought. Meanwhile, he sought furiously to fill the notorious 'gap' that he and everyone else perceived in his system. As a complement of the *Metaphysics of Morals*, Kant's 'transition project', as he called this last, unfinished work, was an effort to complete a 'metaphysics of nature', thus rounding out the full philosophical system Kant had envisioned in the first *Critique*. In many ways, these manuscripts of his resonate with the concurrent endeavours of his successors – most prominently, Friedrich Schelling – to create a *Naturphilosophie*, the distinctive German Idealist vision of a self-generative whole of nature – a *natura naturans*, in Spinoza's famous terms. Death intervened in 1804, however, leaving the fragmentary *Opus postumum* to decipher.

By the time of his death, Kant was ubiquitously celebrated as the glory of German culture – indeed, its crowning gift to Western civilization – even as the actual leadership of German philosophy came quite firmly into the hands of others: the succession of Idealists Fichte, Schelling, and Hegel. But Kantianism had its revenge. Insurgents overthrew German Idealism by the mid-nineteenth century under the battle cry 'Back to Kant!' (Beiser 2014). Philosophy has been going back to Kant ever since, if only to try to find a way beyond him. His legacy is one of the principal treasures of modern Western philosophy, and no more recent philosopher in that tradition can with impunity neglect to engage with his challenging propositions.[35]

Notes

1. Kant characterizes the kingdom of ends as 'a whole of all ends in systematic connection (a whole of both rational beings as ends in themselves and also of the particular ends which each may set for himself)': *Foundations of the Metaphysics of Morals* (1902ff: iv, 113).
2. The 'limits of human understanding' proved the overarching theme of philosophical consideration in the Enlightenment, starting with Locke's *Essay Concerning Human Understanding* (1690), which set forth the agenda, and culminating in the works of David Hume and Immanuel Kant. 'Rational belief' will prove a crucial notion in Kant, to be explored further below. 'Rational obligation' is the core idea of Kant's 'deontological' ethics – namely, that reason is a sufficient and necessary force guiding moral action.
3. In his *Prolegomena*, Kant (1902ff: iv, 274) wrote:
   Wearied then of a dogmatism that teaches us nothing as well as of a scepticism that promises us nothing, not even the peace of a permissible ignorance, led on by the importance of the knowledge we need, yet rendered mistrustful by long experience regarding all knowledge that we believe ourselves to possess or that offers itself in the name of pure reason, we still face our critical question: *is metaphysics possible at all*? (Emphasis in the original)
4. For a current English-language account of Kant's life, see Kuehn (2001).
5. For this backdrop, see Beck (1969).

6 From Descartes through the Leibniz-Wolff school philosophy in Germany, 'clarity and distinctness' characterized the operations of the (higher) rational faculty. Sensibility was construed in that tradition as 'obscure' and 'confused'. In the rising critique of Wolff's rationalism, key philosophers in Germany began to take sensibility more seriously. The key figure was Alexander Baumgarten (1714–62).

7 In *Remarks in the 'Observations on the Feelings of the Beautiful and the Sublime'*, Kant (1991: 38) wrote of Rousseau 'setting him right'. See Velkley (1989).

8 Kant made a fundamental pedagogical distinction between 'knowledge for the school' and 'knowledge for the world'. Thus, he always taught courses designed to equip his students for active careers in the world, and these courses did a great deal to enhance Kant's stature as a teacher in the German Enlightenment.

9 Kant (1998: A 15/B 29) spelled this out more clearly in his *Critique of Pure Reason*: '[T]here are two stems of human knowledge, namely, sensibility and understanding, which perhaps spring from a common, but to us unknown root. Through the former, objects are given to us; through the latter, they are thought.'

10 Kant (1998: B xxx) wrote of the need to 'limit knowledge to make room for faith', in the Preface to the revised edition of the *Critique of Pure Reason*.

11 Kant (1998: B xx, note) drew this famous analogy in the Preface to the second edition of his *Critique of Pure Reason*: 'The transformation in the way of thinking [in metaphysics] which I set forth in the *Critique* is analogous to the Copernican hypothesis'. And

[h]itherto it has been assumed that all our knowledge must conform to objects. But all attempts to ascertain anything about them *a priori* by concepts, and thus to extend our knowledge, came to nothing on this assumption. Let us try, then, whether we may not make better progress on the task of metaphysics if we assume that objects must conform to our knowledge. (B xvi)

12 For a provocative reading of this, see Park (2013: 11–30).

13 See Leibniz (1981), his detailed response to Locke's original text of 1689, completed in 1705 but published only in 1765.

14 'I entitle *transcendental* all knowledge which is occupied not so much with objects as with the mode of our knowledge of objects in so far as this mode of knowledge is to be possible *a priori*' (Kant 1998: A 11–12/B 25).

15 'By that is meant a something = X, of which we know, and with the present constitution of our understanding can know, nothing whatsoever ... [T]he concept of a *noumenon* ... is not indeed in any way positive, and is not determinate knowledge of anything' (Kant 1998: A 250–2).

16 'Without sensibility no object would be given to us, and without the understanding no object would be thought. Thoughts without content are empty, intuitions

without concepts are blind ... It is only from the united cooperation of the two that knowledge can arise' (Kant 1998: A 51/B 75).

17 That objects of sensible intuition must conform to the formal conditions of sensibility which lie *a priori* in the mind is evident, because otherwise they would not be objects for us. But that they must likewise conform to the conditions which the understanding requires for the synthetic unity of thought is a conclusion the grounds of which are by no means so obvious (Kant 1998: A 90/B 122–3).

18 Kant (1998: A xvi) signalled the importance of this section in his original Preface to the *Critique of Pure Reason*: 'I know of no inquiries more important ... than those I have undertaken in the second chapter of the Transcendental Analytic, under the title of *Deduction of the Pure Concepts of Understanding*. They are also the ones that have cost me the greatest effort.'

19 'It must be possible for the "I think" to accompany all my representations' (Kant 1998: B 131). 'For any combination to take place, all the elements in the manifold must belong to *one* consciousness' (ibid.; emphasis in the original).

20 '[I]n the synthetic original unity of apperception, I am conscious of myself, not as I appear to myself, nor as I am in myself, but only that I am ... I exist as an intelligence which is conscious solely of its power of combination' (Kant 1998: B 157).

21 On the project of *Kritik* to defeat materialism and scepticism, see the Preface to second edition of the first *Critique* (Kant 1998: B xxxiv).

22 Kant (1992: 538) described his philosophical concerns under these three queries in his *Jäsche Logic*.

23 The union of causality as freedom with causality as the mechanism of nature, the first being given through the moral law and the latter through natural law, and both related to the same subject, man, is impossible unless man is conceived by pure consciousness as a being in itself in relation to the former, but by empirical reason as appearance in relation to the latter. Otherwise the self-contradiction of reason is unavoidable.

Therefore, we face a 'paradoxical demand to regard one's self, as subject to freedom, as noumenon, and yet from the point of view of nature to think of one's self as a phenomenon in one's own empirical consciousness' (*Critique of Practical Reason*: Kant 1902ff: iv, 6).

Now even if an immeasurable gulf is fixed between the sensible realm of the concept of nature and the supersensible realm of the concept of freedom, so that no transition is possible from the first to the second (by means of the theoretical use of reason), just as if they were two different worlds of which the first could have no influence upon the second, yet the second is *meant* to have an influence on the first. The concept of freedom is meant to actualize in the world of sense the purpose proposed by its laws. (v, 175–6)

24 For the texts of this crucial controversy, see Scholz (1916).
25 Over the course of his 'silent decade', Kant expressed his growing irritation in a number of *Reflexionen*. See Zammito (1992: 33–41).
26 Kant characterized man's 'final purpose' (*Endzweck*), 'the highest task nature has set mankind', as a 'moral whole', 'a completely *just civic constitution*' ('Idea for a Universal History', 1902ff: viii, 22). 'For in fact the moral law ideally transfers us into a nature in which reason would bring forth the highest good were it accompanied by sufficient physical capacities; and it determines our will to impart to the sensuous world the form of a system of rational beings' (iv, 43). The realization of the 'highest good' would accordingly achieve the 'Kingdom of God in this world'.
27 The importance of 'taste' and the idea of 'disinterestedness' both originated in writings of the Scottish Enlightenment, grounded in the earlier writings of Shaftesbury.
28 The key ideas of the 'Critique of Aesthetic Judgment' have been extensively analysed (e.g. Guyer 1979; Zuckert 2007).
29 All of these key ideas were presented in 'Of the Different Races of Human Beings', published in 1775 (Kant 1902ff: ii, 429–43).
30 Kant (1902ff: vii, 119–20) explained this difference in orientation in his approach to anthropology – a 'pragmatic' as opposed to a 'physiological' one – in the opening remarks of his published *Anthropology* (1798), but he already signalled this distinct orientation in a letter to Marcus Herz in winter of 1773 (x, 145–6).
31 See Larrimore (1999). For two instalments in the ongoing debate, see Bernasconi (2001) and Kleingeld (2007).
32 See my discussion of this controversy (Zammito 2011).
33 'There must, therefore, be a ground of the *unity* of the supersensible, which lies at the basis of nature, with that which the concept of freedom practically contains' (*Critique of Judgment*: Kant 1902ff: v, 176).
   [T]he antinomies, both here [i.e. in the *Critique of Judgment*] and in the *Critique of Practical Reason*, compel us, whether we like it or not, to look beyond the horizon of the sensible, and to seek in the supersensible the point of union of all our faculties *a priori*: for we are left with no other expedience to bring reason into harmony with itself. (v, 341)
34 See Schiller (1962).
35 See, for example, Guyer (2006).

References

Adickes, E. (1924–25), *Kant als Naturforscher*, 2 vols, Berlin: de Gruyter.

Beck, L. W. (1969), *Early German Philosophy*, Cambridge, MA: Harvard University Press.
Beiser, F. (1987), *The Fate of Reason: German Philosophy from Kant to Fichte*, Cambridge, MA: Harvard University Press.
Beiser, F. (2014), *The Genesis of Neo-Kantianism, 1796–1880*, Oxford: Oxford University Press.
Bernasconi, R. (2001), 'Who Invented the Concept of Race? Kant's Role in the Enlightenment Construction of Race', in R. Bernasconi (ed.), *Race*, Malden, MA: Blackwell.
Clarke, S. (ed.) (1956 [1716]), *The Leibniz-Clarke Correspondence, Together with Extracts from Newton's* Principia *and* Optics, Indianapolis: Hackett.
Forster, G. (1786), 'Noch etwas über die Menschenrassen', *Teutsche Merkur* (October), 57–86 (November): 150–66.
Guyer, P. (1979), *Kant and Claim of Taste*, Cambridge, MA: Harvard University Press.
Guyer, P. (ed.) (2006), *The Cambridge Companion to Kant and Modern Philosophy*, Cambridge: Cambridge University Press.
Herder, J. G. (1877), *Briefe zu Beförderung der Humanität*, in *Herders Sämtliche Werke*, ed. B. Suphan, vol. 18, Berlin: Weidmann.
Hinske, N. (1965), 'Kants Begriff der Antinomie und die Etappen seiner Ausarbeitung', *Kant-Studien*, 56: 485–96.
Kant, I. (1902ff), *Gesammelte Schriften Herausgeben von der Preussischen Akademie der Wissenschaften zu Berlin*, Berlin: de Gruyter.
Kant, I. (1991), *Bemerkungen in den 'Beobachtungen über das Gefühl des Schönen und Erhabenen'*, Hamburg: Meiner.
Kant, I. (1992), *Jäsche Logic*, in *Lectures on Logic*, trans. J. M. Young, Cambridge: Cambridge University Press.
Kant, I. (1998), *Critique of Pure Reason*, ed. and trans. P. Guyer and A. Wood, Cambridge: Cambridge University Press.
Kleingeld, P. (2007), 'Kant's Second Thoughts on Race', *Philosophical Quarterly*, 57: 573–92.
Kuehn, M. (2001), *Kant: A Biography*, Cambridge: Cambridge University Press.
La Vopa, A. (2001), *Fichte: The Self and the Calling of Philosophy, 1762–1799*, Cambridge: Cambridge University Press.
Larrimore, M. (1999), 'Sublime Waste: Kant on the Destiny of Races', in C. Wilson (ed.), *Civilization and Oppression*, Calgary: University of Calgary Press.
Laywine, A. (1993), *Kant's Early Metaphysics and the Origins of the Critical Philosophy*, Atascadero, CA: Ridgeview.
Leibniz, G. W. (1981), *New Essays Concerning Human Understanding*, ed. and trans. P. Remant and J. Bennett, Cambridge: Cambridge University Press.
Locke, J. (1975 [1690]), *An Essay Concerning Human Understanding*, ed. P. H. Nidditch, Oxford: Clarendon Press.

Mendelssohn, M. (1991), *Briefe, die neueste Literatur betreffend* 280 (1764–65), reprinted in Mendelssohn, *Gesammelte Schriften: Jubiläumsausgabe*, Stuttgart/Bad Vanstatt: Frommann-Holzboog, 5: 604–60.

Park, P. K. (2013), *Africa, Asia, and the History of Philosophy: Racism and the Formation of the Philosophical Canon, 1780–1830*, Albany: SUNY Press.

Reinhold, K. L. (2005), *Letters on the Kantian Philosophy*, Cambridge: Cambridge University Press.

Schiller, F. (1962), *Der Briefwechsel zwischen Friedrich Schiller und Wilhelm von Humboldt*, 2 vols, Berlin: Aufbau.

Schmidt, J. (ed.) (1996), *What Is Enlightenment? Eighteenth-Century Answers and Twentieth-Century Questions*, Berkeley: University of California Press.

Scholz, H. (ed.) (1916), *Die Hauptschriften zum Pantheismus Streit zwischen Jacobi und Mendelssohn*, Berlin: Reuther and Reichard.

Tonelli, G. (1959), 'Der Streit über die mathematische Methode in der Philosophie in der ersten Hälfte des 18, Jahrhunderts und die Entstehung von Kants Schrift über die "Deutlichkeit"', *Archiv für Philosophie*, 9: 37–66.

Velkley, R. (1989), *Freedom and the End of Reason*, Chicago: University of Chicago Press.

Zammito, J. H. (1992), *The Genesis of Kant's* Critique of Judgment, Chicago: University of Chicago Press.

Zammito, J. H. (2011), 'History of Philosophy vs. History of Science: Blindness and Insight of Vantage Points on the Kant-Forster Controversy', in R. Godel and G. Stiening (eds), *Klopffechtereien – Missverständnisse – Widerspruche?*, Paderhorn: Fink.

Zuckert, R. (2007), *Kant on Beauty and Biology: An Interpretation of the* Critique of Judgment, Cambridge: Cambridge University Press.

10

German Idealism

Dean Moyar

1. Four problems from Kant's critical project

German Idealism is a philosophical movement originating in Kant's critical philosophy that aimed to explain objectivity through a complete system of knowledge grounded in the unity of self-consciousness (Dudley 2007). For the three major post-Kantian figures whom I discuss in this chapter – J. G. Fichte, F. W. J. Schelling, and G. W. F. Hegel – the systematic form of Kant's philosophy was of paramount importance, yet they all worried that Kant had not done enough to actually unite the parts of the system.[1] Perhaps the most serious issue was that Kant left reason in an oddly self-defeating position, doomed to dwell on questions that it could not answer. Kant had set out to limit theoretical knowledge to the realm of *appearances* in order to make room for moral freedom and moral religion. This project seemed to leave a good deal simply *unknowable* – known as important, but a matter of faith rather than of objective cognition. The subsequent idealists all aimed to expand the domain of the cognizable and to employ a new understanding of knowledge and its limits to reconcile theoretical knowledge of necessity with practical certainty of freedom.

The argument of the *Critique of Pure Reason* turns on Kant's distinction between knowledge of appearances and knowledge of things in themselves. He argues in his 'Transcendental Aesthetic' that space and time are pure forms of sensible intuition, which means they are subjective conditions. This dependence on intuition means that our knowledge is restricted to the domain of appearances, yet it allows us to cognize a priori the necessity in appearance that had been subject to such devastating attack by Hume.[2] Kant's 'Transcendental Analytic' provides the positive story of how we arrive at such knowledge through the 'pure concepts' or categories. He argues in the 'Metaphysical Deduction' that the forms of *judgement* give rise to the *pure concepts* that determine the objects of appearances. The key move in the 'Transcendental Deduction', emphasized especially in the B edition, is to locate the ground of the unity in 'the original *synthetic* unity of apperception' (Kant 1998: B137; emphasis in the original). Indeed, 'the whole of the rest of the understanding's use is grounded' (ibid.) on this original synthesis in self-consciousness – 'the supreme principle' (B136) that grounds the categories.

The negative counterpart to the 'Transcendental Analytic' is the 'Transcendental Dialectic', in which Kant analyses the main ways in which reason seeks to go beyond the realm of experience and to make claims about things in themselves. This leads to what he calls 'transcendental illusion', an ineliminable tendency of reason to extend itself beyond the limitations of sensible intuition. The *antinomies* result from the requirement of reason to seek the 'totality of conditions' for every condition, or, in other words, to seek *complete* explanations. In the third antinomy, Kant presents a thesis and antithesis that differ on the issue of the necessity and possibility of a free cause that can initiate a new series of appearances. According to the thesis, there must be a causality through freedom outside of natural laws because otherwise no *complete* series, and thus no sufficient cause, can ever be found. According to the antithesis, everything is simply caused by prior events in accordance with natural laws, because the idea of a free cause with no preconditions makes no sense. That is, such a cause would not allow a judgement connecting different states of affairs, and thus it 'cannot be encountered in any experience, and hence is an empty thought-entity' (A 447/B 475). Kant argues that, given transcendental idealism, both thesis and antithesis could be true. If the necessity of natural laws is valid only for appearances, there *could* be a noumenal world in which the initiation of a causal series from scratch is possible.

In his moral philosophy, Kant aims to move beyond the mere possibility of freedom and morality *in theory* to the positive reality of both *in practice*. In the 1785 *Groundwork of the Metaphysics of Morals* he argues, from the necessity of acting under the idea of freedom, to the reality of the moral law. Yet in the *Critique of Practical Reason* he argues that the consciousness of the moral law, as the 'fact of reason', announces itself to us and gives us reason to believe in the reality of freedom. This is no ordinary fact, but is rather the awareness of universal lawgiving as an active principle within the agent that is capable of generating an interest in morality and of overcoming even one's love of life (Allison 1990). It is a special kind of *judgement*: 'he must admit without hesitation that it would be possible for him. He judges, therefore, that he can do something because he is aware that he ought to do it' (Kant 1996: 163). The *Critique of Practical Reason* also has a dialectic in which Hegel considers the role of reason's demand for the *unconditioned*. In the case of practical reason, the unconditioned is a demand (to take the most important case) of uniting virtue and happiness, or our character as moral beings with our happiness as sensible beings. This demand serves as the basis for the three 'postulates of practical reason', which are immortality, freedom, and God. Immortality allows us to think of the endless striving for moral perfection, and the postulate of God is the thought of a supremely good being who could create the intelligible world in which happiness follows in proportion to virtue, thus achieving the highest good. Once again, Kant demonstrates only the possibility of thinking of this unconditioned or complete object of reason through the noumenal world. We cannot know that it will follow on our actions, but we can hope for it.

Kant (2000) typically thinks of freedom as the causality of the will in originating a new causal series, but in the *Critique of Judgment* he turns to the causal relation of parts and wholes. After treating aesthetic judgements in the book's first half, in the second half Kant addresses the nature and status of *teleological judgements*. He argues that while we do have to think of the living organism in terms of its organization through its purpose or functioning, such judgements do not *constitute* the objectivity of the organism, but are merely subjective in the sense that humans have to think that way, given the nature of our finite intellects. Once again, the issue of cause and effect, condition and conditioned, stands at the fore. In his initial description, a natural purpose 'must relate to itself in such a way that it is both cause and effect of itself' (244). More specifically, Kant proposes two requirements: '*First*, the possibility of its parts (as concerns both their existence and their form) must depend on their relation to the whole', and 'the parts of the thing combine into the unity of a whole because they are reciprocally cause and effect of their form' (245). The knowledge of the 'inner purposiveness' of a '*self-organizing* being' (ibid.) is not what Kant calls 'a constitutive concept' (247), but is rather 'a regulative concept for reflective judgment' (ibid.) that we form through a kind of analogy with our own action on purposes. Kant takes his point one step further in conceiving of the kind of intellect that contrasts with ours in order to give meaning to the merely regulative role of these judgements. He writes that 'we can conceive of an *intuitive* understanding' that would have 'a power of *complete spontaneity* [as opposed to *receptivity*] *of intuition*' (275) and thus not a contingent relation between universal concepts and singular intuitions. Such an understanding 'proceeds from the *synthetically universal* (the intuition of a whole as a whole) to the particular, i.e. from the whole to the parts' (276; emphases in the original). The tantalizing claim here is Kant's link of the teleological organization of living beings to a methodological issue about the structure of knowledge.[3] If there were knowledge in which the universal and the singular stood in this relation, it would provide the answer to the problem of the third antinomy as well, for it would be a self-grounded knowledge that was also complete.

We can now name four main issues in Kant's critical philosophy for the development of German Idealism. (1) How are the multiple forms of judgement and categories related to the unity of transcendental self-consciousness? Call this the *Unity of the Categories* problem. (2) If self-consciousness really is the supreme condition, why is it not simply the unconditioned itself? The immediate answer is that self-consciousness is *formal*, whereas the causal *completeness* that we seek through reason is supposed to actually determine a new series. The issue, then, is that of how there can be a principle or act or entity that is both unconditioned and the source of complete explanations. Call this the *Unconditioned Completeness* problem. (3) What can be inferred about freedom and the highest good from consciousness of the moral law? Is practical reason authorized to make claims that transcend the boundaries of theoretical reason, and, if so, does that require a revision in our overall conception of reason? Call this the *Primacy of Practice* problem. (4) Why are we barred from thinking of objects as constituted through the principle of teleology (viz., through the reciprocal explanation of part and whole)? If such thinking could give us a model of a complete explanation, why can we not affirm such explanations as real? Call this the *Constitutive Teleology* problem.

2. Fichte's transformation of transcendental idealism

Beginning already in the late 1780s, philosophers attracted to Kant's idealism were frustrated by his use of the table of judgements as the basis of the categories. Given the revolutionary potential of Kant's new framework, and in particular of the principle of the transcendental unity of apperception, why is the *necessity* of these categories made to depend on an old list of twelve forms of judgement? For Karl Reinhold, whose early *Elementarphilosophie* did a great deal to set the program for the movement, a truly scientific idealist system would derive the categories from an indubitable first principle. Reinhold's revision of the Kantian system based on 'the principle of consciousness' ultimately succumbed to sceptical objections and was abandoned by Reinhold himself, but it proved pivotal for Fichte's development of idealism.

In proposing his own version of a first principle of philosophy, Fichte is very much concerned to address the *Unity of the Categories* problem. In order to show that his principle presupposes nothing, he takes up the challenge of grounding even the most basic laws of logic.[4] In his 1794 *Foundations of the Entire Science of Knowledge*, he begins with the proposition that A is A, or A=A, which he interprets as '*If* A exists, *then* A exists' (1970a: i, 94, 1970b: 94). In turning the proposition into a hypothetical judgement, Fichte asks us to focus on the *necessary connection* between the two sides, and he then writes that this necessary connection 'is at least *in* the I, and posited *by* the I, for it is the I which judges in the above proposition' (1970a: i, 93; 1970b: 95). He calls this necessary connection 'X' and shows that it depends on the identity of the I:

> Thus the I asserts, by means of X, that *A exists absolutely for the judging I, and that simply in virtue of its being posited in the I as such;* which is to say, it is asserted that within the I – whether it be specifically positing, or judging, or whatever it may be – there is something that is permanently uniform, forever one and the same; and hence the X that is absolute posited can also be expressed as *I = I*; I am I. (1970a: i, 94; 1970b: 95–6; emphasis in the original)

In this way, Fichte demonstrates that the unity or identity of self-consciousness is the first principle upon which all other judgements, even those of formal logic, are grounded. He insists that this is not simply a fact, but rather an act, or a fact-act (*Tathandlung*). The I exists only insofar as it is active, where 'positing' is the most generic term for that activity. This original act is the root of the *a priori synthesis* that explains the necessity of our knowledge of the world. Fichte calls this act an 'intellectual intuition', though he attempts to reconcile his view with Kant's by aligning this act with the transcendental unity of apperception (1970a: i, 472; 1997: 56). Kant had written of the 'I think' that can accompany all representations, and Fichte is making the point that there must be an original unity of that 'I think' in order for the representations to be united.

Fichte's strategy of deriving the categories gets going with his second fundamental principle, the principle of *opposition*. In order for the synthetic activity of the I to be *determinate*, and for it to *come to consciousness*, there must be some kind of opposition to the I's activity. This principle immediately raises the problem of whether the mere presence of such a not-I would simply eliminate the I's activity. That is, doesn't the not-I make the identity of self-consciousness *impossible*? Fichte's answer is both 'yes' and 'no'. By itself, as an original and fundamental opposition, the not-I is a threat to the unity of the I=I. But the not-I is a necessary threat, for without it the pure I=I could not come to consciousness. In order to maintain the second principle while subordinating it to the first, Fichte introduces his third (and final) main principle, called the principle of *limitation* or *ground*. He asserts that the I and not-I can be *reciprocally determined* because each is considered as divisible, or limited through the other, and the I can therefore be considered as the ground of a determinate reality. The third principle is in essence the determinate synthesis, a *reciprocal determination* (Wechselbestimmung) that is the basic synthetic form of every category. He also identifies this category with Kant's category of *relation*, the category that Fichte held to be *the* fundamental category.

The procedure of deducing categories through the reciprocal determinations of I and not-I is what is usually described as 'the dialectic' or 'the dialectical method'. While it represents Fichte's attempt to replace the project of the Transcendental Analytic, it also involves a transformation of Kant's Transcendental Dialectic. In its main form, Kant's Dialectic examines the illegitimate extension of the conceptual beyond the conditions of objective experience. In Fichte, this demand for the unconditioned is built into the first principle itself. In the derivation process we establish the conditions for objective knowledge, but the process *as a whole* only continues because there is an unconditioned demand within it, a demand that is not satisfied by the limited knowledge of any one category, but aims at totality or a *complete* set of conditions. He writes,

> *It shows that what is postulated as the first principle and immediately established within consciousness is not possible unless something else occurs as well, and that this second thing is not possible apart from the occurrence of some third thing. It continues in this manner until all of the conditions of the first principle have been completely exhausted and its possibility has become completely comprehensible.* (1970a: i, 446; 1997: 31)

This goal of completeness, built into the starting point, is evident in Fichte's claim that the first principle is only really justified as the first principle of science once we have successfully deduced the entire system of science from it. He thus, despite his evident foundationalism, also endorses a version of holism or coherentism, a point that will be important for appreciating Hegel's debt to Fichte (see below).

For Fichte, the activity of the I is conceptually prior to space and time, and therefore Kant's main justification for restricting knowledge to the realm of appearances falls away. Fichte is happy to embrace this conclusion, and declares with great confidence that knowledge has no use for the 'thing in itself', which he holds to be 'a pure invention which possesses no reality whatsoever' (1970a: i,

428; 1997: 13). The consequences of this move are profound, for Kant's restriction was essential to saving the possibility of freedom, God, and immortality. If the necessity of objectivity constitutes the only domain that there is, it seems that the possibility of immortality, freedom, and God will be foreclosed. But such an impossibility is itself rather hard to think through within Fichte's idealism, for it would stem from a necessity that originates in the self-determined activity of the I. Everything is explained through the I, so there can be no explanation through, say, mechanical causality that could threaten the freedom of the I's self-determination.

That is, Fichte's whole philosophy takes off from a certain answer to the *Primacy of Practice* problem. He is quite explicit that the only evidence that we have for the reality of the first principle (I=I) is the awareness of the moral law as a command of self-determination.[5] This has led to a debate about just how 'practical' Fichte's first principle is, with scholars dividing over the issue of whether the entire system is premised on morality or on a thinner conception of self-consciousness.[6] Fichte's basic insight is that *all* claims to knowledge and to morality share a common root in the idea of normativity as self-imposition. His rejection of the given in all of its forms is an affirmation of the requirement to be *active* in relation to the world, to be free in imposing norms of thought and action on oneself (Brandom 1979). The self-determination of morality is just the most explicit version of the activity that lies behind all of our rational relations to the world. The theoretical knowledge of necessity cannot infringe upon the practical freedom of moral activity because the same basic thought – the spontaneity of self-consciousness – underlies both.

In applying the first principles of his system to the political domain, Fichte came up with a groundbreaking argument for *mutual recognition*, an argument that spawned not only Hegel's famous master-servant dialectic but a flood of work on the self and the 'other' in twentieth-century philosophy. The basic thrust of the argument (and especially the argument for 'summons' to freedom that precedes the main recognition argument) is that one only becomes free, and one can only be free, through a certain relation that one has with other free agents. An important element of this argument that often goes unremarked is that Fichte utilizes Kant's conception of *reflective judgement* from the third *Critique* in order to make his inference to the recognition of another free being. He thereby connects his answer to the Primacy of Practice problem to an answer to the Constitutive Teleology problem. To set up the key move, Fichte asks when it is that we can attribute purposiveness to appearances. He thinks that we can do so when we not only reflectively judge that an appearance was produced according to a rational purpose, but *also* when we judge that the purpose is intended to produce our cognition itself (1970a: iii, 37–9; 2000: 36–7). In a few pages, Fichte thus replaces traditional arguments for purposiveness in nature with a bold claim that purposiveness is manifested objectively only in and through the intentions of agents to summon other agents to free activity. Generalized, this becomes the claim that normativity is a social product.

Fichte's idealism remains uncompromisingly on the side of the subject's activity, of the subject's norm-governed freedom. This leaves him with little to say about nature or God, beyond citing them as reflections of our freedom. The text that led to the 'Atheism Controversy' and his dismissal from Jena is an account of moral religion in which God seems to be reduced to a placeholder for our hope that the highest good will be realized if we do what conscience dictates regardless of the consequences for our happiness. Given his unwillingness to follow Kant in placing God in an ineffable beyond, Fichte's argument does shade towards a reduction of the divine to the human moral vocation. He argued on Kantian grounds (reading faith in God as faith in Providence, which he interprets as faith in the Highest Good); yet, without the noumenal realm, he seems to leave little room for the claims of theology.

On the question of nature, Fichte declares a standoff with the 'realist' who would attempt to explain nature and human activity from the starting point of 'things'. He associates the realist with Spinozism, and argues that the consistent realist is a materialist and fatalist. Fichte's system focuses exclusively on the necessary acts of thought, and it is liable to the charge that it makes nature in general into a blank, generic 'not-I' to be consumed by the syntheses of the I. Nature becomes only what we need it to be in order to establish the system of human freedom. He derives the categories through his principle of reflective opposition, but he does not really derive the structure of the natural world except insofar as it shows up for us in activity or resistance to activity.

3. Schelling's attempt to unite Spinoza and Kant

While the precocious Friedrich Schelling embraced Fichte's emphasis on activity, he aimed to unite thinking and nature in a more primordial unity. He thus attempted to conceive of the absolute I as a quasi-Spinozist absolute substance. Such an original substance, conceived along the lines of the demi-urge of neo-Platonism, could be viewed as unfolding *itself* into subject and object, mind and nature. In terms of judgement, it seems reasonable to hold that the forms of judgement, especially when taken in terms of a subject-predicate form, seem to depend on a prior unity of the terms that are asserted in judgement to stand in a necessary connection. If judgements connecting subjects to predicates are true, then they connect in thought what was already connected in nature, and the latter unity would seem to be more fundamental than the former. Schelling thus sought to fill out the Fichtean program by adding a philosophy of nature to complement the transcendental philosophy. In his early period, Schelling worked out his philosophy of nature and transcendental philosophy separately, basically taking there to be two answers to the Unity of the Categories and Unconditional Completeness problems, one Fichtean and one that developed Kant's theory from the 1785 *Metaphysical Foundations of Natural Science* and the *Critique of Judgment* account of teleology.

Of the many system drafts and outlines that Schelling produced between 1795 and 1809, his 1800 *System of Transcendental Idealism* stands out for its comprehensiveness and clarity of presentation. It almost reads like a reconstruction of Kant's three *Critiques* on a Fichtean basis (something that Fichte himself never managed), with Schelling's own original contributions emerging at certain key junctures. Michael Vater alludes to the suppressed originality of the work in

> its muted voicing of certain themes which elsewhere attain their proper development – themes such as the reality and ultimacy of nature in an idealistic perspective, nature's function as the ground and anti-type of spirit, the self-identity of the Absolute within dispersed finite being, the conceptual though unconscious element in art, and philosophy's task of constructing a general metaphysics upon the model of human freedom. (Schelling 1978: xi)

While the work does contain a characteristic 'deduction of matter' and a discussion of teleology, the philosophy of nature takes a back seat to the question of the knowing and acting subject's relation to the world. The most striking claims come at the end in the discussion of art and genius. Schelling attempts to answer the question of how the subject can know the original unity of subject and object (i.e. the absolute) without its thereby ceasing to be a unity. Within ordinary action, the conflict between freedom and necessity cannot be resolved: 'Man is forever a broken fragment, for either his action is necessary, and then not free, or free, and then not necessary and according to law' (1856–61: iii, 608; 1978: 216). Schelling is here agreeing with Kant in a curious way in emphasizing that freedom and nature are irreconcilable within human action. Schelling's ultimate goal in the *System of Transcendental Idealism* is to find a completed expression of the absolute that can be intuited as such. Only the artist, the genius, is capable of this: 'as soon as the product is completed, all appearance of freedom is removed. The intelligence will feel itself astonished and *blessed* by this union, will regard it, that is, in the light of a bounty freely granted by a higher nature, by whose aid the impossible has been made possible' (1856–61: iii, 614; 1978: 221; emphasis in the original). What is realized is 'none other than that absolute which contains the common ground of the pre-established harmony between the conscious and the unconscious' (ibid.). In this sense, art becomes the organ of philosophy, for it alone reconciles the freedom of transcendental philosophy and the necessity of mechanical nature.

Schelling (1856–61) took a further turn in 1801 to a 'philosophy of identity' that moved more forcefully away from Fichte's transcendental philosophy. He conceives of philosophy as a single theory of the absolute, where the philosopher's job is to exhibit the particular in the universal through a certain kind of intuition. His even more emphatic Spinozism is evident in his claim that '[n]ot I know, but only totality *knows* in me, if the knowledge that I consider my own is to be a real, true knowledge. Yet this *One* that knows is also the only thing known, and neither difference nor correspondence exist here, for the *knowing* and the known are not different but the same' (vi, 140; 1994: 143; Förster 2012: ch. 10; emphases in the original). Taking direct aim at Fichte's subject-oriented idealism, Schelling (1856–61: vi, 142; 1994: 144) writes, 'We claim that reason is the self-knowledge of the eternal identity. With this proposition, we have simultaneously defeated forever all subjectivization [*Subjektivierung*] of rational knowledge.' The philosopher intuits the absolute unity in a way that transcends the discursive limitations of the ordinary finite intellect. The philosopher himself thus must be seen as a kind of genius, for only a rare capacity for such intuition is capable of access to the absolute. On this point I concur with the scepticism of Daniel Breazeale (2014: 118), who writes,

> If construction in intuition comes down in the end to nothing but entertaining a certain *immediate vision of reality*, accompanied by the heartfelt assurance that *every* properly qualified person can and must share this vision, then what happens when this simply proves not to be the case? What happens if others report a *different* intellectual vision of the absolute and of the ideas of reason? Or what if they report no 'vision' of these at all? (Emphases in the original)

On the pivotal question of moral freedom, Schelling makes his most original contribution in his final published text from his early career, the 1809 essay *On the Essence of Human Freedom*. Much of the essay is an attempt to explain the possibility of evil, and though he takes aim at Fichtean optimism about human freedom, in his own way he is giving an answer to the *Primacy of Practice* problem by speculating on the origin of our freedom to do good and evil. Schelling (1856–61: i/7, 388; 2006: 53) defends original sin as an original act of the subject that represents the 'dark principle of evil'. He criticizes Fichte for thinking that the source of evil is the lethargy or laziness of man,[7] and he further criticizes Fichte for taking the shallow view that our consciousness of freedom is a transparent window to the reality of those actions. Schelling in one sense returns to Kant's view on radical evil, for Kant, too, thought that evil stems from a choice that takes place outside of temporal conditions. But, unlike Kant, Schelling aims to give an account of this original act through an account of the original constitution of the universe, and he is thus squarely in the traditional domain of a theodicy, attempting to justify God's creation in light of the evil in this world. He aims to explain the origin of evil without explaining it away as something other than our own activity. The view is essentially mystical and religious, as one can see in his claim, 'As man is now, the good as light can be developed only from the dark principle through a divine transformation [*Transmutation*]' (ibid.). Schelling aims to go back behind consciousness, mere appearance, to the origins of both good and evil, and in doing so he pushes up against the limits of intelligibility.[8]

4. Hegel's *Phenomenology of Spirit*

Hegel's first publication was an exposition of the difference between Fichte's and Schelling's philosophies, with a clear defence of Schelling's perspective of identity against the merely subjective identity of Fichte's system. Yet, when Hegel settled on his philosophical position in the *Phenomenology of Spirit*, he had arrived at a position that is much closer methodologically to Fichte's *Wissenschaftslehre* than to Schelling's philosophy of identity. Indeed, Hegel (1968ff: ix, 17; trans. 2013: ¶16) famously writes in the *Phenomenology* Preface that the emphasis on the identity of the Absolute led to a formalism akin to the night in which 'all cows are black'. The Preface contains a number of other slogans that indicate Hegel's distance from Schelling's project. Recall that Schelling retained the idea of the importance of the starting point, yet he argued in Spinozistic fashion that the starting point has to be a kind of substance from which the system, and indeed the world, flows. When Hegel (1968ff: ix, 18, 2013: ¶17) writes that 'everything hangs on apprehending and expressing the truth not as *substance* but also equally as *subject* [das Wahre nicht als *Substanz*, sondern ebensosehr als *Subjekt* aufzufassen und auszudrücken]', we can see him as moving back in the direction of Fichte's emphasis on the subject. But an even more striking departure from Schelling's view comes in the following passage: 'The true is the whole. However, the whole is only the essence completing itself through its own development. This much must be said of the absolute: It is essentially a *result*, and only at the *end* is it what it is in truth' (1968ff: ix, 19; 2013: ¶20; emphases in the original). In this switch from beginning with substance to beginning with an 'essence' that has to 'complete itself', Hegel is returning to the holistic dimension of Fichte's strategy. While Fichte emphasized the foundational role of the I=I, he also claimed that the first principle is a presupposition that is only redeemed or validated once the system has been successfully developed from it. Hegel is taking this holism a step further in claiming that there simply is no absolute starting point, for the absolute is in the result. Modifying Fichte's approach, Hegel aims to establish an unconditioned ground and then to investigate the conditions for the realization of that ground in a fully determinate world. He calls reason 'purposive activity' because he reinterprets the process of mutual conditioning as a process of realizing an initially abstract purpose (1968ff: ix, 20; 2013: ¶22).

Hegel came to believe that the problem of the idealist *starting point*, in the pure I=I or in the Absolute, was not a problem that could be solved by postulating the most basic activity or the most basic substance. The validity of the categories of idealism, and of the supreme principle itself, has to be established for, demonstrated to, the knowing subject. Hegel calls his demonstration a 'ladder' (1968ff: ix, 23; 2013: ¶26) and a 'deduction' of the concept of science through a proof that ordinary consciousness is already thoroughly implicated in idealism.[9] In the *Phenomenology* Hegel thus undertakes an essentially epistemological project in the service of *introducing* a metaphysical system that could begin again, as it were, from a pure basis in thought. That second beginning comes in *The Science of Logic*, the first part of a three-part system presented comprehensively in outline in the *Encyclopedia* (recall that Schelling had a two-part system of nature and transcendental philosophy). In *The Science of Logic* he develops the categories of thought within the element of thought alone, purified of the relation to intuition and human psychology generally. In what follows, I will outline Hegel's answers to the four Kantian issues only with reference to the project of the *Phenomenology*, adding a few comments at the end on how *The Science of Logic*'s perspective raises further issues about the nature of Hegel's idealism.

We can see Hegel addressing the Unity of the Categories problem in his strategy, within the *Phenomenology*, of extracting the categories from ordinary practices of judgement and of showing that they are all grounded in what he calls the absolute concept (hereafter: simply 'the Concept'). The Concept is Hegel's version of the transcendental unity of self-consciousness in the sense that it is a principle of unifying different elements (e.g. identifying a singular object as the instantiation of a universal through identifying and uniting particular properties). The Concept itself is not primarily a psychological activity, but rather a *logical* structure that is the heart of Hegel's answer to the *Unity of the Categories* problem. The validity or authority of the Concept (and of idealism generally) is demonstrated by showing that ordinary consciousness is already implicitly relying on the pure concepts or categories, and that ultimately those categories themselves depend on the Concept. He calls this project a 'self-completing scepticism', by which he means that the ordinary or 'natural consciousness' undermines its own claims to immediate knowledge in the very process of making them. The process also thereby reveals the ground of knowledge in the Concept and answers the Unity of the Categories problem.

Hegel's method of testing what he calls 'shapes of consciousness' can be formulated in terms of *judgement* and compared to the Kantian and Fichtean projects.[10] The unity of the initial judgement in a shape is provided by the shape's specific concept, but in the process of experience multiple conflicting judgements arise, and the question is that of what further concept would provide the unity of those judgements. This process is clearest in the work's opening three chapters, which Hegel together calls 'Consciousness', covering our access to the world through our senses, perception, and the understanding. In the first 'shape', the *singular* judgement of 'Sense-certainty' is shown to depend on a *universality* that can unite the diverse judgements in a single form. Hegel then goes through the 'thing of many properties' of perception, showing that the object consists of relations and that the unity of the object founders on the divergence of its self-identity and relation to others (what he calls 'for-itself' and 'for another'). Finally, Hegel considers the unity of appearances through the understanding's conception of force and lawfulness, the 'essence' of objects behind their appearances. This form of unity also proves insufficient, and ultimately dependent on what Hegel calls 'simple infinity' and 'the absolute concept' (1968ff: ix, 99; 2013: ¶162). Hegel concludes the first main part of the *Phenomenology* ('Consciousness') by identifying this ground with self-consciousness, thereby aligning his Concept with the Kantian unity of self-consciousness.

Returning to the *Unconditioned Completeness* problem, in what sense can we say that, for Hegel, self-consciousness or the Concept is an unconditioned activity that can provide the kind of completeness that mere laws of nature cannot? Let us return to the claim that the absolute is a result. Hegel implies that the Concept and self-consciousness are constituted by the conceptual development that has led to this conclusion. So, properly speaking, the result of the first three chapters is not the mere form of simple infinity, but rather the entire object of consciousness *constituted by the inferences* that led to the Concept. We have to begin from judgements, but objectivity consists of the inferences of reason that result from the dialectical development of the judgements. This move to a constitutive use of inferential reasoning is just what Kant denied, but he denied it primarily on the grounds that a manifold of sensible representations needs to be given for the categories to apply. Hegel, along with Fichte, jettisoned this restriction, and in the *Phenomenology*'s opening chapters Hegel justifies this rejection by showing that the contributions of sense and perception can be reduced to their role in making judgements. The judgemental form then is taken up into inferential form, and the unity of the object is taken up into an inferential totality of a system of relations that sustain individual objects.[11] An individual planet, for instance, is what it is only in relation to the sun and can be specified only in terms of laws of motion and a theory of gravitation. But the point holds for many kinds of objects, as Hegel thinks that laws or universals are only meaningful through their determinate instantiation, and that singular objects only count as objects insofar as they can be described and evaluated within networks of rules and relations.

When we move to the famous chapter IV account of 'Self-consciousness' in the *Phenomenology*, we not only get another complication with Hegel's response to the Unconditioned Completeness problem, but also the beginning of his response to the remaining two problems as well. Having derived self-consciousness (with the structure of the Concept) as the ground of consciousness of objects of experience, Hegel turns the question around and sets up an inquiry into the conditions of the objectivity of self-consciousness itself. His first move is to take self-consciousness as a capacity of living, desiring creatures. Hegel begins the account of the conditions of self-consciousness as a story of the emergence of freedom and subjectivity from the substantial element that he identifies with *life*. His question is one of how, from merely desiring creatures, indistinguishable within the process of the life of the species, the human individual emerges as a thinking, valuing, worshipping creature. Hegel thus adopts as his starting point a naturalism that takes on board Schelling's assertion that there must be a unity of nature and mind prior to the judgements of mind about nature. It is an answer to the Constitutive Teleology Problem; but, as with many answers in Hegel, it is a provisional one. In the compressed account of life in chapter IV (¶¶69–173), Hegel describes life as a biological process with the inferential structure that had been the result of chapters I–III. To the extent that there is a primal unity of nature and mind, Hegel thinks that we can make, and that we must have *already made, sense* of the unity as a self-sustaining totality (rather than as an undifferentiated original substance). Further, the idea that Hegel employs to make the transition out of life is mutual recognition, an account of *intersubjectivity* that he adapts from Fichte's *Foundations of Natural Right* to play a more basic role in the constitution of the human mind.

The opening sections of 'Self-consciousness' have generated scores of interpretations because of the fecundity and generality of Hegel's claim of mutual recognition: '*Self-consciousness attains its satisfaction only in another self-consciousness*' (¶175). The simplest interpretation of the claim is that an individual can only develop a sense of her subjectivity through the affirmation of another individual, where that second individual must also be affirmed by the first as a subject. We cannot just assume that the human being is free through conscious awareness of herself as free, but rather we have to view freedom as a social category, an 'achievement' of human interaction.[12] Hegel does not simply postulate mutual recognition, but rather derives it by starting from the most basic form of contestation over who deserves to be recognized as free. The first move is a struggle to the death between two individuals who aim to prove their freedom to each other by proving that they value freedom more than mere life. The productive resolution of the struggle is the surrender of one individual to be the servant of the other. The servant is the ultimate winner because, by treating life as essential, or valuable, the servant develops an intelligible relation to the world, an opening to the objectivity of the world, albeit one mediated through the recognition of the master. This is a point about the development of our capacities for effective thinking and reasoning, for Hegel takes it that only in this 'desire *held in check*' (¶195; emphasis in the original) do we come to understand that concepts are essential for objectivity, and that our own identities are constituted through thinking rather than through mere desire.

When Hegel introduces mutual recognition as the satisfaction of self-consciousness, he also links it to the key concept of *Geist*, translated as 'mind' or 'spirit'. This concept, which became (in the process of writing the book) Hegel's master concept for the project, clearly represents a structure of human *sociality*. An important debate about Hegel's philosophy as a whole concerns the extent to which the account of reason, religion, and philosophy itself is just an account of forms of human sociality. The extreme version of the 'social' interpretation would read Hegel as claiming that there is nothing to objectivity above and beyond what we make of it through social practices, a kind of knowledge by agreement. A moderate version of the sociality thesis, defended elegantly by Terry Pinkard in *Hegel's Phenomenology: The Sociality of Reason*, leans on the idea of giving and asking for *reasons* in order to emphasize that our concepts are developed both through interaction with each other and through interaction with the world. The key issue here is that of what Hegel's account of Spirit allows us to say about the Primacy of Practice problem. If we can read all claims to knowledge, both theoretical and practical, as dependent on social forms, we would be in a good position to make sense of the value of certain kinds of knowledge relative to others. That would in turn show why we need systematic philosophy to incorporate the results of natural science and the human sciences into an overall ethical vision.

Hegel's treatment of moral freedom in the *Phenomenology* nicely encapsulates his transformation of Kantian and Fichtean idealism. True to his idea that the absolute is a result, moral freedom comes at the end of the 'Spirit' chapter. He shows how moral agency is structured by the Concept, and how our dependence on the Concept in the practice of morality thereby confirms the objectivity of the Concept and completes the proof of the Concept's actuality. Hegel (1968ff: ix, 239; 2013: ¶440) shifts Kant's argument for the highest good from the idea of an all-powerful God in a noumenal realm to the social context of action, to spirit as 'shapes of a world'. His aim is to show how the modern morality of individual autonomy develops from a long history of attempts to unite individuality and universality (represented by the characters of Antigone and Creon in Hegel's famous interpretation of Sophocles' tragedy). Somewhat surprisingly, Hegel ends up celebrating the concept of conscience, though he departs from the Fichtean idea that we can defer happiness or the highest good to God conceived of as providence.[13] Instead, he thinks of conscience as a holistic process of practical reasoning structured by the Concept. While Hegel does situate conscience in a social context, he thereby also places demands on the context (i.e. on the state) to live up to the ethical demand of integrating the individual and universal. In the end, the mutual recognition of finite subjects who confess their finitude is the 'appearing God' (1968ff: ix, 362; 2013: ¶671), the model for the religious community in which our ethical vocation is affirmed. The mutual recognition in conscience forms the basis, for Hegel, of modern Christian community, but also of the modern secular State. In the *Philosophy of Right*, Hegel's main book of practical philosophy, he thus follows the account of conscience with an account of modern social institutions in which the ethical conscience is realized.

The *Phenomenology* remains an introduction to Hegel's system, whose merits can be judged in the end only through an examination of the *Encyclopedia*, and in particular through an assessment of its expanded first part, *The Science of Logic*. In that text Hegel 'starts over', as it were, with the bare concept of being, and develops a wide range of metaphysical, mathematical, and epistemological concepts. He revisits all four of the Kantian problems that I have used to frame German Idealism, giving them logical solutions that are supposed to swing free of questions about their natural and psychological embodiment. There are ongoing debates about specific moves in *The Science of Logic*, but there also remains a more general debate about just what kind of project this is. One can argue that the Logic is an account of the thinkability of various concepts, so that the work as a whole could be read as a priori cognition of the conditions of possibility of determinate objects.[14] However, insofar as Hegel is clearly intent on eliminating every gap between thought and being/reality/actuality, one could argue that he is really claiming that the categories emanate from being, or perhaps from the absolute negativity of essence. Yet it is clear that Hegel was very concerned to separate the Logic from the 'real philosophy' of nature and spirit, so that the logic does not directly constitute spatiotemporal reality. A neutral reading could take the logic to be developing the forms of intelligibility, with the assumption that these forms are not merely the product of a limited human standpoint. The controversial idea of a dialectic of the forms of intelligibility can only be redeemed by establishing its completeness at the end of the account, when the result has shown the later categories to incorporate the lower (or to render them superfluous).

Hegel's defence of teleology as superior to mechanism is one of the highlights of the account's late stages, for he thinks that freedom stands or falls with teleology.[15] His answers to all four of our Kantian problems converge in the work's closing section, 'The Idea', which begins with an account of life. The structure of the organism thus comes to be a master concept for the systematicity of our concepts, for showing how an account of those concepts can be complete and thereby unconditioned. *The Science of Logic* ends with the idea of the Good and an account of the dialectical method. The overall claim is that philosophy can account for its own value, its own right to legislate the conditions of intelligibility to nature and human practice, because only philosophy can completely justify itself, be the 'cause of itself', account for all of its own conditions.

Notes

1. There are a host of other important figures active in the period, and much important research has been done over the past decades to unearth their work and its influence on the principal figures in the movement. See Beiser (1987).
2. Kant (1998: A 94/B 127–8) writes of Locke and Hume: 'The empirical derivation, however, to which both of them resorted, cannot be reconciled with the reality of the scientific cognition *a priori* that we possess, that namely of *pure mathematics* and *general natural science*, and is therefore refuted by the fact.'
3. See Förster (2012) on this point.
4. For informative accounts of Fichte's philosophical approach, see Pippin (1989), Neuhouser (1990), Wood (1991), Martin (1997), and Breazeale (2013).
5. Fichte (1970a: i, 446, 1997: 49) writes:
   We have here presupposed the fact of this intellectual intuition ... It is, however, an entirely different undertaking to confirm, on the basis of something even higher, the *belief* in the reality of this intellectual intuition, with which, according to our explicit admission, transcendental idealism must commence, and to show the presence within reason itself of the very interest upon which this belief is based. The only way in which this can be accomplished is by exhibiting the ethical law within us, within the context of which the I is represented as something sublime and elevated above all of the original modifications.
6. See Ameriks (2000) and Franks (2005).
7. This is not entirely fair to Fichte. For a discussion of Fichte's view, see Ware (2015).
8. See Kosch (2010) for an excellent discussion of this essay. See also Kosch (2014).
9. For the statement that the *Phenomenology* is a deduction of science, see Hegel (1968ff: xxi, 33; 2010: 29).
10. I go into this in much greater detail in Moyar (2015). On the role of inferences in these chapters of the *Phenomenology*, see also Brandom (2002).
11. See Hegel's (1968ff: ix, 423; 2013: ¶789) important description of 'the object as a whole'.
12. For helpful accounts of this chapter, see Pinkard (1994) and Pippin (2014).
13. I have gone into this theme in detail in Moyar (2011).
14. See Pippin (1989) for the classic account along these lines.
15. The most prominent issue here is the mechanism versus teleology issue that Hegel treats towards the end of the *Science of Logic*. See Yeomans (2011) and Kreines (2015).

References

Allison, H. (1990), *Kant's Theory of Freedom*, Cambridge: Cambridge University Press.
Ameriks, K. (2000), *Kant and the Fate of Autonomy: Problems in the Appropriation of the Critical Philosophy*, Cambridge: Cambridge University Press.
Beiser, F. (1987), *The Fate of Reason: German Philosophy from Kant to Fichte*, Cambridge, MA: University Press.
Brandom, R. (1979), 'Freedom as Constraint by Norms', *American Philosophical Quarterly*, 16: 187–96.
Brandom, R. (2002), *Tales of the Mighty Dead: Historical Essays in the Metaphysics of Intentionality*, Cambridge, MA: Harvard University Press.
Breazeale, D. (2013), *Thinking through the* Wissenschaftslehre: *Themes from Fichte's Early Philosophy*, Oxford: Oxford University Press.
Breazeale, D. (2014), '"Exhibiting the Particular in the Universal": Philosophical Construction and Intuition in Schelling's Philosophy of Identity (1801–1804)', in L. Ostaric (ed.), *Interpreting Schelling*, Cambridge: Cambridge University Press.
Dudley, W. (2007), *Understanding German Idealism*, London: Acumen.
Fichte, J. G. (1970a), *Fichtes Sämmtliche Werke*, ed. I. H. Fichte, Berlin: de Gruyter.
Fichte, J. G. (1970b), *The Science of Knowledge*, ed. and trans. P. Heath and J. Lachs, Cambridge: Cambridge University Press.
Fichte, J. G. (1997), *Introductions to the* Wissenschaftslehre *and other Writings (1797–1800)*, ed. and trans. D. Breazeale, Indianapolis: Hackett.
Fichte, J. G. (2000), *Foundations of Natural Right*, ed. F. Neuhouser, trans. M. Baur, Cambridge: Cambridge University Press.
Förster, E. (2012), *The Twenty Five Years of Philosophy: A Systematic Reconstruction*, trans. B. Bowman, Cambridge, MA: Harvard University Press.
Franks, P. (2005), *All or Nothing: Systematicity, Transcendental Arguments, and Skepticism in German Idealism*, Cambridge, MA: Harvard University Press.
Hegel, G. W. F. (1968ff), *Gesammelte Werke*, ed. Rheinisch-Westfaelischen Akademie der Wissenschaften, Hamburg: Felix Meiner.
Hegel, G. W. F. (2010), *The Science of Logic*, ed. and trans. G. di Giovanni, Cambridge: Cambridge University Press.
Hegel, G. W. F. (2013), *Phenomenology of Spirit*, trans. T. Pinkard, http://terrypinkard.weebly.com/phenomenology-of-spirit-page.html.
Kant, I. (1996), *Practical Philosophy*, ed. and trans. M. Gregor, Cambridge: Cambridge University Press.
Kant, I. (1998), *Critique of Pure Reason*, ed. and trans. P. Guyer and A. Wood, Cambridge: Cambridge University Press.
Kant, I. (2000), *Critique of the Power of Judgment*, trans. P. Guyer and E. Matthews, Cambridge: Cambridge University Press.
Kosch, M. (2010), *Freedom and Reason in Kant, Schelling, and Kierkegaard*, Oxford: Oxford University Press.

Kosch, M. (2014), 'Idealism and Freedom in Schelling's *Freiheitsschrift*', in L. Ostaric (ed.), *Interpreting Schelling*, Cambridge: Cambridge University Press.

Kreines, J. (2015), *Reason in the World: Hegel's Metaphysics and Its Philosophical Appeal*, Oxford: Oxford University Press.

Martin, W. (1997), *Idealism and Objectivity: Understanding Fichte's Jena Project*, Stanford: Stanford University Press.

Moyar, D. (2011), *Hegel's Conscience*, Oxford: Oxford University Press.

Moyar, D. (2015), 'The Inferential Object: Hegel's Reduction and Deduction of Consciousness', *Internationales Jahrbuch des Deutschen Idealismus*, 11: 119–44.

Neuhouser, F. (1990), *Fichte's Theory of Subjectivity*, Cambridge: Cambridge University Press.

Pinkard, T. (1994), *Hegel's* Phenomenology*: The Sociality of Reason*, Cambridge: Cambridge University Press.

Pippin, R. (1989), *Hegel's Idealism: The Satisfactions of Self-Consciousness*, Cambridge: Cambridge University Press.

Pippin, R. (2014), *Hegel on Self-Consciousness: Desire and Death in the* Phenomenology of Spirit, Princeton: Princeton University Press.

Schelling, F. W. J. (1856–61), *Sämmtliche Werke*, ed. K. F. A. Schelling, Stuttgart: Cotta.

Schelling, F. W. J. (1978), *System of Transcendental Idealism (1800)*, trans. Peter Heath, intro. Michael Vater, Charlottesville: University Press of Virginia.

Schelling, F. W. J. (1994), *Idealism and the Endgame of Theory: Three Essays by F.W.J. Schelling*, ed. and trans. Thomas Pfau, Buffalo: SUNY Press.

Schelling, F. W. J. (2006), *Philosophical Investigations into the Essence of Human Freedom*, trans. Jeff Love and Johannes Schmidt, Buffalo: SUNY Press.

Ware, O. (2015), 'Agency and Evil in Fichte's Ethics', *Philosophers' Imprint*, 15: 1–21.

Wood, A. (1991), 'Fichte's Philosophical Revolution', *Philosophical Topics*, 19: 1–28.

Yeomans, C. (2011), *Freedom and Reflection: Hegel and the Logic of Agency*, Oxford: Oxford University Press.

Whewell, Mill, and the Birth of the Philosophy of Science

Stephen Gaukroger

1. Introduction

The philosophy of science as a methodological and epistemological discipline emerged in the middle decades of the nineteenth century. It was prompted not by developments in science or in epistemology as such, however, but rather by new and unprecedented claims to scientific standing in what were termed the moral sciences, particularly economics and political theory. The expansion of science into the areas of morality and politics was highly contentious, particularly in France, with the social theory of August Comte, and in England, with developments in political economy. The topic of this chapter is the rise of philosophical investigation into the nature of science in England, as manifested in two projects. The first, that of William Whewell (1794–1866), set out a comprehensive philosophy of science designed to avoid the naturalization of the humanities. The second, that of John Stuart Mill (1806–73), was initially concerned with political questions, responding to Whewell's perceived conservatism, but Mill came to realize that he needed to devise a philosophy of science to counter that of Whewell if he was to be convincing in this.

2. The problem of the moral sciences

The core question that prompted much philosophy in the early to mid-nineteenth century in England was the naturalization and/or quantification of human motivation and behaviour. By 'naturalization' here I mean subjecting these phenomena to empirical investigation, on the model of the sciences but without reduction to the physical or life sciences, as in various form of materialism, for example. By 'quantification' I mean the application of mathematical (algebraic, arithmetical, or statistical) techniques to human behaviour and motivation. Such approaches called into question traditional metaphysical and religious treatment of these questions, particularly in the case of moral, and by extension political, questions.

Naturalizing projects that did not involve quantification included attempts to understand human psychology through its medicalization, and the attempt, notably in Herder, to investigate language as an empirical manifestation of states of mind. Those that also occasionally involved quantification include attempts to consider human nature in comparative terms, whether anatomical, geographical, or historical. Some projects of a statistical nature essentially involved both, such as the biometric and more specifically anthropometric attempts to understand individual behaviour on the model of collective or aggregate behaviour.

Two kinds of project focused on quantification, with only a tangential concern with naturalization, and it is these that will concern us. The first was Ricardo's formulation of a 'scientific economics'.[1] It presented arguments rigorously, in terms of basic assumptions and the deduction of conclusions from these. The conclusions it drew conflicted with traditional conservative political views, particularly on the relationship between landlords and tenants, but the scientific status of the arguments looked strong. As a result, there arose, among those who wished to defend the conservative position, notably Whewell and his colleagues, a questioning of just what science was, what it could and could not achieve. Whewell's interest was initially methodological, but his reading of Kant encouraged him to think in more epistemological terms, and what emerged was what might be called the first philosophy of science.

The second quantification project emerged with Bentham's consequentialist moral theory. The problems to which this was a response can be traced back to Mandeville's *Fable of the Bees*. Mandeville (1714) had argued that the qualities, such as avarice, that encouraged the kind of successful commercial society which was to everyone's benefit were the opposite of those that were universally lauded in the case of individual morality.[2] The basic dilemma was that the demands placed on individual behaviour, by those collective goals that bring with them economic and political well-being, were in conflict with the moral demands that shape the individual behaviour that we value most. One solution to this conflict was the revision and broadening of the scope of individual morality through the advocacy of forms of moral pluralism, and Hume and Smith followed this path. This is in line with the traditional view which, if only implicit, had been that only individual behaviour has a moral dimension. Individuals are able to form intentions and to act upon these, and this would seem to be a prerequisite of moral behaviour. By contrast, the role of intentionality in collective behaviour is difficult to fathom. The natural home of morality, so to speak, lies in the realm of the individual. On such a view, while it is true that empires, nations, and states can act in various ways that attract moral sanction or approval, and can be subject to moral maxims such as that of the doctrine of just war, moral responsibility is properly ascribed not to a state as such but to the ruler. For the kind of approach taken by Mandeville, by contrast, collective activity has a moral dimension, one that conflicts with individual morality, and it is far from clear that the language of intentionality is applicable to collective or aggregate behaviour.

Unlike distributive properties – those properties of the whole that are the properties of each of the parts – collective properties are not mirrored at the individual level, and they cannot be arrived at by abstraction from individual behaviour. An increasing number of writers recognized this in the eighteenth century, particularly those composing 'philosophical' histories such as Voltaire, Montesquieu, and Hume. Hume (1793), for example, in developing the idea that the relation between cause and effect is a matter of inference rather than direct perception, argues that such connections are more easily established when changes in human conditions produce changes in large-scale human behaviour, as in the case of the rise and progress of the arts and sciences, or that of the rise and progress of commerce, rather than on an individual level, and he distinguishes two forms of history corresponding respectively to cultural change and to individual actions. Montesquieu (1949: ii, 39), likewise, writes that causes become less arbitrary to the extent that they have a more general effect: we know better what shapes the achievements of societies that have adopted a given way of life than we know what shapes the lives of individuals. Note the stress on causal explanation here. If one wants to account for social, political, or economic questions in causal terms, one has in effect to abandon individual behaviour and turn instead to the behaviour of collective or aggregate entities. And to the extent to which rendering phenomena amenable to causal explanation is part of a process of naturalization, then, in the shift from understanding behaviour at the personal level to the aggregate level, one is moving to a different kind of understanding of human behaviour.

Bentham's solution to how an account of morality could cover both individual and collective behaviour was to abandon individual morality as a norm. Unlike the traditional accounts, which attempted to extrapolate from the case of individual morality, his was a theory having universal application, in that it covered collective and individual morality without distinction. To do this, it had to reverse the core case: an account perfectly fitted to resolving problems in the collective case was applied to the individual case. It marked a radical departure from traditional conceptions of morality, in that questions of intentions and character, not to mention divine and natural law accounts, were jettisoned in favour of something far more straightforwardly observable – namely, the consequences of acts. It had two distinctive features. First, it opened up morality to a quantitative assessment. The assessment of whether an action is right or not is simply a function of the consequences of that action. It was no longer a straightforward question of right versus wrong, for consequences could be assessed in comparative terms, in terms of a calculation. Second, with its abandonment of a role for intention and character, moral decision-making began to look decidedly more scientific than it had ever done. It was an empirical and transparent matter what the consequences of actions were, and, at least in principle, much more of an empirical matter (when divorced from considerations of intention and character) which of these consequences deserved praise or condemnation. Moreover, unlike traditional understandings of morality centred on intentionality, moral decision-making was no longer something to which the language of cause and effect was alien.

This is the context within which the dispute between Whewell and Mill took place. The issues are stake were complex but they can be summed up as being between 'intuitionism' – Mill's term for what he took to be Whewell's position – and a form of positivism which Mill himself developed. Intuitionism and positivism, at least as understood here, share the belief that what holds for science must hold for morality. Simplifying somewhat, although both Whewell and Mill were advocates of inductivism, for Whewell morality and science-cum-mathematics ultimately depend on deep and unchallengeable intuitions, whereas for Mill the legitimacy of both science-cum-mathematics and morality must solely depend on their appeal to external criteria.

3. Whewell on science

In a series of breakfast meetings in Cambridge in 1812–13, Whewell, with the astronomer John Herschel, the mathematician Charles Babbage, and the economist Richard Jones, discussed how to revive a programme of scientific discovery in the physical sciences in England on a par with the late-seventeenth-century work of Newton. They sought the answer in a commitment to what they considered to be the Newtonian methodology of induction. But it was not just a question of fostering the physical sciences. There was also a newly developed scientific approach to economics, in Ricardo's economic theories, which worked on the basis of deduction from postulates, which was not inductive, but at the same time not that different from the procedure adopted in much of Newton's *Principia*.

John Herschel's *A Preliminary Discourse on the Study of Natural Philosophy* (1830) was one of the first steps in the metatheory of science. Its ranking of the sciences set the stage for an account of what the success of the various sciences consisted in, and his schema was built on by Whewell (1831a) in a long review that appeared soon afterwards. Botany, mineralogy, and chemistry were identified as the lowest level of science, at 'the outset of their inductive career'. Next came the branches of 'physics' (notably, electricity and magnetism), then optics, and at the apex mechanics and astronomy, fully mathematized disciplines that had successfully combined induction and deduction. Induction stood at the basis for the sciences and, as they advanced and became increasingly subject to mathematical treatment, deductive relations could be established.

Induction plays a key role, but what Whewell means by 'induction' needs clarification. Bacon had treated induction as the construction of theories on the basis of extensive observation of nature, and this remained a core meaning, providing a contrast with deduction. In his *Philosophy of the Inductive Sciences* (1840), however, Whewell does not allow that bare induction of this kind could be enough for scientific discovery. Rather, 'discoverer's induction', as he termed it, could not be a passive response to nature but must involve both objective experience and ideas, which the enquiry brings to the investigation of nature, and which provide it with direction. His recognition of the need for the latter derives from his reading of Kant. The basic question that Whewell takes over from Kant is that of how universal and necessary laws, of the kind that one finds in mechanics and astronomy, can be generated simply on the basis of induction from observation and experiment. Kant, he argued, had stressed 'ideas' over 'perceptions', thereby ridding science of its objective connections with nature, whereas Locke and the 'sensationists' had implausibly reduced science to passive observation.

The fundamental ideas that he set out, while influenced by Kant, served a different purpose from concepts such as Kant's 'forms of the intuition' – space, time, and causation. Whewell was interested not just in something that was a permanent and fixed feature of the mind, but he also wanted to include ideas fundamental to particular scientific disciplines. So, while space and time figure in his fundamental notions, so too do chemical affinities, because he believes that chemistry could not proceed without these. These discipline-specific fundamental ideas might well form some unified scientific understanding at some stage in the future, but the crucial thing is that they are discovered, not innate.

Since fundamental ideas are what guide our empirical investigation of nature, and since, at least in some cases, they are formed in response to prior investigation of nature, it might seem that they must initially come from some kind of induction from basic observations. But Whewell does not allow this, and it is in this context that he makes room for hypotheses. He recognizes neither the inductive versus hypothetical nor the ideal versus sensationalist as absolute dichotomies. Moreover, the hypotheses that become fundamental ideas are objective, not just in the sense that they capture something in nature, but because they do this in virtue of corresponding to archetypical ideas existing independently of any particular beliefs that humans have. Here Whewell departs radically from Kant.

In the final edition of his *The Philosophy of the Inductive Sciences*, he added a section arguing that the divine mind contains many archetypical ideas and that God created the universe in accordance with these ideas. Space is such an archetypical idea, in that God created physical objects with spatial characteristics and existing in spatial relations to one another. God gave us access to these ideas by which he created the universe. He created 'germs' in our minds which, when developed, match or represent divine archetypical ideas. We come to know the natural world by developing these ideas in tandem with observation and experiment. It is not unlike discovering natural kinds in an area like natural history, where we gradually refine our classifications of families, genera, and species finally to reveal the divisions there in nature. But Whewell makes it clear that this is not a process that the individual can carry out. Rather, it is the process that scientists undertake in their routine work: it requires discussion and debate based on the evidence, for only this can lead to clarification and progress in identifying and grasping the archetypical ideas.

In a context in which it was believed that scientific inquiry produced moral effects in the minds of its cultivators,[3] Whewell (1833) stressed the moral consequences of inductive and deductive habits of thought. The former, the procedure of 'discovers', he associated with a natural-theological process of discovering God's purpose in the world. Proponents of the idea that deduction was constitutive of scientific enquiry, by contrast, dealt with remote abstractions, treating the truth of basic laws as necessary, never considering that they could have been different and so overlooking the possibility that they had been ordained by God.

4. Whewell on political economy

The moral standing of induction for Whewell was nowhere more evident than in his discussion of the new economic theories of Ricardo. In his 1817 *On the Principles of Political Economy and Taxation*, Ricardo offered a purely deductive account of rent, wages, and profit that started from a number of seemingly uncontentious basic assumptions, and worked out deductively from these. The quasi-geometrical procedure could be defended in Newtonian terms, but more specifically it resembled that of eighteenth-century mechanics, where the deduction proceeds from basic definitions of physical concepts. It is in fact close to what Whewell had identified as the highest stages of scientific enquiry, in mechanics and astronomy. But on Whewell's account these areas had gradually been built up from inductive foundations, whereas what Ricardo was proposing was something that ignored induction altogether.

For Whewell, the more successful a science became, the more it tended to take a deductive form. Could it be, then, that economics had simply bypassed the inductive stage? Whewell and his circle set out to show the failings that resulted from attempting to do this. The issue was crucial to Whewell. His economist colleague Richard Jones opposed what he and Whewell considered to be the way in which Ricardo applied the label 'science' to his economics, which they considered was merely a way of presenting this theory as dogma. In reviewing Jones' *Essay on the Distribution of Wealth and on the Sources of Taxation* (1831), Whewell uses Jones' discussion of different kinds of rents to criticize Ricardo's extrapolation from one kind of rent, farmers' rent, to its universal form. This, Whewell (1831b: 51–2) writes, provides 'the most glaring example of the false method of erecting a science which had occurred since the world has had any examples of the true method'. True principles, he argued, cannot be obtained by 'some transient and cursory reference to a few facts of observation or of consciousness' (53).

Whewell was particularly concerned with the way in which Ricardians compared their strict definitions of rents, wages, and capital with the procedures of geometry. Relations were explored in geometry on the basis of 'first principles' which made no reference to experience, but were purely the product of thought.

By contrast, in the physical sciences, definitions were helpful only if they captured relations that had been discovered to be there in nature. For example, in mechanics and optics, one does not simply start with precise definitions; rather, the definitions emerge as disputes are resolved and new theories established. Exact definitions are not the causes, but the consequences, of scientific progress. Understanding of the different stages of development of the sciences, and how they achieved a particular standing was crucial; political economy could not claim the status of a mature deductive science. Indeed, on Whewell's account, economics was at the bottom of the scientific hierarchy because the complexity of the social realm required extensive empirical research, whereas this process had only just begun.

But there was another element in Whewell's criticisms. If Ricardo's account of value and rent is taken in moral terms, then, since labour produces the entire product, rent is an unjust institution and landlords are simply parasitic. Ricardo eschewed such a moral reading, at least publicly, considering his work something that could only be judged on its scientific merits. But, for Whewell, questions of rent, taxes, wages, and capital involved passions and interests distancing economics from the canonical forms of scientific enquiry – whether the mathematical or the physical sciences – that must form the standard for scientific enquiry.

Whewell rejected the implicit moral criticism inherent in Ricardo's theory of rent. He denied that Ricardo employed a scientific method, and wondered whether the complexity of the mass of empirical work that would need to be done for economics to start on the road to science could ever be achieved. Moreover, he doubted that, even if this could be achieved, it could ever have the scientific standing to which it aspired, given that, unlike the other sciences, it was not a purely factual or conceptual enterprise, caught up as it was in moral and political questions that lay outside its purely empirical basis.

Nevertheless, the physical sciences and morality did have some structural similarities for Whewell.[4] In his *Lectures on the History of Moral Philosophy in England*, Whewell saw the issue in terms of 'the arbitrary or necessary nature of moral truth', and, although moral knowledge could not be arrived at by induction, it was like scientific knowledge in that it was regulated by general rules which in his *Elements of Morality* he tells us 'must be necessary truths'. The rules regulating duty and affections are necessary truths that are as fundamental to human thought as are our understanding of space and time. This does not mean that we grasp them immediately, however. Rather, we come to understand them, if only imperfectly at first, through a cultivation of the mind, but once grasped they are self-evident. In mechanics, he explains in a letter to Frederic Meyers of 6 September 1845,

> although we now have axioms, defined conceptions and vigorous reasonings, we can point to persons, and to whole ages and nations, who did not assent to those axioms because the mechanical ideas of their minds were not sufficiently unfolded. In this we have, it seems to me, an answer to the objection that what I assert as moral axioms are not evident to all men. They are as much evident to all men as the axiom that a body will not alter its motions without a cause, or the like. They become evident to men in proportion as all men have their conceptions of the terms of science rendered clear and distinct. (Douglas 1881)

The comparison with mechanics here is not accidental. Whewell is offering a general theory of knowledge that accounts for both scientific and moral knowledge, which establishes the objectivity of both. There are two ingredients in his account. Induction and general ideas play the crucial role in the empirical sciences, but it is 'fundamental ideas' alone that establish objectivity in non-empirical areas such as pure mathematics and morality. Self-evident fundamental ideas cannot be identified by seeking 'the casual opinion of individual men any more than we can determine the axioms of geometry by polling schoolchildren' (Whewell 1846: 34–5).

But while it was relatively uncontentious to have induction playing this role, 'fundamental ideas' ideas were an entirely different matter. Here is the major point of conflict between Whewell and Mill. The fact that Whewell's 'necessary truths' of morality matched the prevalent Anglican conservatism suggested to Mill that it was not so much a question of Ricardo dressing up his economics as dogma, as it was of Whewell dressing up conservatism as dogma.

5. Mill versus Whewell

Mill's original concern was not with questions of science but instead with political questions: in particular, the elaboration and defence of a radical politics. Whewell was just an apologist for the status quo, in Mill's view. This raises the question of how one should discuss morality. Whewell had located his discussion of morality in the context of knowledge generally, and had contrasted it with scientific knowledge in crucial respects. In taking up questions of scientific knowledge, Mill engages the issues on the terrain that Whewell sets out. At stake is the standing of 'fundamental ideas' and induction.

Mill seeks objectivity in our moral and scientific judgements, as much as does Whewell. One basic reason behind this agreement is that both see morality in terms of the exercise of reason – not sensibility, as Hume and Smith advocated, for example. Consequently, questions of objectivity and truth are paramount. The contrast between the two lies in the fact that induction appeals to an external standard, whereas Whewell's 'intuitionism' seeks a priori support for moral ideals. Mill (1969: 168) advocates abandoning the latter and making the whole of knowledge subject to external standards:

> The contest between the morality which appeals to an external standard, and that which grounds itself on an internal conviction, is the contest of progressive morality against stationary – of reason and argument against the deification of mere opinion and habit. The doctrine that the existing order of things is the natural order, and that, being natural all innovation on it is criminal, is as vicious in moral, as it is now at last admitted to be in physics, and in society and government.

Induction is the external standard in the case of the sciences, consequentialism in the case of morality. Like Whewell, Mill believes in objective standards generally. Consequently, the answer to problem of moral diversity and conflict – between different societies or between individual morality and commercial culture – cannot lie in the kind of moral pluralism advocated by Hume and Smith, for example. There must be a single moral code. But to specify this moral code in terms of a particular content, as Whewell does, seemed to Mill to involve an unjustified, and indeed unjustifiable, choice of content. How, then, could objectivity be secured? Certainly not by induction, or by taking a poll, which Whewell presents as the alternative. Rather, it consists in eschewing questions of content and elaborating a rule. Kant had proposed such a rule – universalizability, the criterion of the morality of an action being that your action could become one that everyone could act upon in similar circumstances – but this was an internal rule, whereas Mill, following the utilitarian tradition of Bentham and his father, James Mill, wants something external – namely, the consequences of the act – to serve as the criterion by which to decide morality. It was not the character of the person acting, the person's intention, or the universalizability of the act that mattered; instead, it was the observable consequences that did so. If the act had harmful consequences, then it was immoral. A great deal of fine-tuning was necessary to establish the plausibility of consequentialism between its initial formulation and Mill (and his successors such as Sidgwick), but the crucial point was that consequences were external and observable. This, combined with the fact that they were calculable, in that one could compare actions in terms of the amount of benefit or harm that they caused, gave consequentialist morality a quasi-scientific standing: an independence from particular habits, prejudices, or ill-formed beliefs, and a decision procedure that was not unlike a form of economic calculation. Moreover, since both Whewell and Mill saw an intimate connection between morals and politics, what was at stake was not just differing theories of how moral judgements should be made, but also the standing of the traditional conservative land-owning politics, and radical political reforms.

A great deal was at stake, and what was novel was the way in which the standing and application of science lay at the foundation of the debates. Bentham and James Mill had not connected their programmes for moral and political reform with science, nor had defenders of conservative morality and politics. Whewell changed this, propelling the epistemological and methodological standing of science into the centre of the question of how we are to live our lives.

Mill's strategy was to demonstrate that fundamental ideas were not needed either in the physical or the mathematical sciences, and so that Whewell's proposed justification for his moral theory in the role of fundamental ideas in the sciences fell flat. But Whewell's account had two apparent strengths. First, bare induction, from particular facts to general conclusions, is unlikely to yield fruitful scientific results: the idea that induction might be guided by 'fundamental ideas', indistinctly grasped at first but gradually coming to light in the course of the enquiry, provides a means by which induction might be led along fruitful paths. Second, for Mill, while it is external standards that secure objectivity in the cases of the natural sciences – in the form of induction – and morals and politics – in the form of consequentialism – it is not clear what provides these standards in a deductive discipline such as pure mathematics. Whewell can rely on a variety of 'fundamental ideas' to secure mathematical truths, maintaining that they correspond to ideal archetypes. But these are internal criteria, as is Kant's construal of mathematical truths as synthetic a priori. If Mill wants to make a general case for external criteria, then he has to provide an account of what these would be in the case of an apparently purely deductive endeavour such as mathematics or logic.

6. Induction

For Mill (1973: 163), inference is the process by which we move 'from known truths, to arrive at others really distinct from them'. Logic 'is the entire theory of the ascertainment of reasoned or inferred truth' (7), and it divides into two forms, induction and deduction (which he usually calls 'ratiocination'):

> Induction is inferring a proposition from propositions *less general* than itself, and Ratiocination is inferring a proposition from propositions *equally* or *more* general. When, from the observation of a number of individual instances, we ascend to a general proposition, or when, by combining a number of general propositions, we conclude from them another proposition still more general, the process, which is substantially the same in both instances, is called Induction. When from a general proposition, not alone (for from a single proposition nothing can be concluded which is not involved in the terms), but by combining it with other propositions, we infer a proposition of the same degree of generality with itself, or a less general proposition, or a proposition merely individual, the process is Ratiocination. When, in short, the conclusion is more general than the largest of the premises, the argument is Induction; when less general, or equally general, it is Ratiocination. (162–3; emphases in the original)

Both induction and deduction share fundamental characteristics on this conception, and both fall under Mill's general account of truth, whereby 'truths are known to us in two ways: some are known directly, and of themselves; some through the medium of other truths. The former are the subjects of Intuition, or Consciousness; the latter, of Inference' (6).

Directly known truths are sensory experiences, unlike Whewell's archetypical ideas, which are purely intelligible: that is, non-sensory. They allow scientific inference to meet an external criterion of objectivity. But, while they provide the raw material on which induction works, this material is a little too 'raw' to explain how induction might lead to the generation of general theories. Many of the problems here are artificial, and disappear once we stop thinking in terms of a sharp contrast between inductive and hypothetical methods. In the polemical disputes between Newtonians and Cartesians beginning in the last decade of the seventeenth century, the sharpness of this distinction was stressed by Newtonians, who viewed the use of hypotheses as violating objectivity (Laudan 1981), and to some extent both Whewell and Mill are heirs to this. But induction, as it had been conceived from Bacon onwards, had never been simply a matter of directly inferring general theories from particular facts, which Bacon dismissed as childish. Rather, the crucial role was played by eliminative induction. Here, the idea is that reflection on the facts suggests several possible explanations, and one goes through these, invoking evidence to eliminate them one by one, until one arrives at an explanation that cannot be eliminated in this way. Such a procedure serves the same function as an explicitly hypothetical method, except that one can give an account of how the hypotheses are generated – namely, from facts established on the basis of observation.

But this does not settle the question of whether Mill's conception of induction reflects scientific discovery accurately. Whewell, who had a far greater command than did Mill of the history of science and actual practice in the physical sciences, had no difficulty in identifying cases that fit his model of discovery. Taking the example of Kepler's discovery that planetary orbits were elliptical (as opposed to circular), Whewell argues that the discovery of new facts was not what was at issue. Rather, it was a question of bringing the data under the appropriate idea. The data in this case had already been collected by Tycho Brahe, who hadn't made sense of it. It was only when Kepler successfully fit the data into the shape of an ellipse that the true shape of orbital motion was discovered. Mill would have to argue here that the data themselves suggested an ellipse, but this is contrary to the details of how the discovery was made: it didn't occur to anyone that orbits could be anything but circular. Whewell (1849) treats Kepler's idea of the ellipse as a 'fundamental idea', something purely intelligible rather than sensory, and discovery arises, on his view, in the application of the intelligible ideas to sensory data.

7. Deduction

Whatever the problems with his account of induction, however, it is Mill's account of deduction that has been the most controversial part of his account of knowledge. We can in fact identify two different views of deduction in Mill (1973). One is that it is a particularly abstract form of induction; the other is that logic is a branch of psychology. While there are significant difficulties in reconciling these, to some extent they play different roles – a practical one and a theoretical one:

> Our object, then, will be to attempt a correct analysis of the intellectual process called Reasoning or Inference, and of such other mental operations as are intended to facilitate this: as well as on the foundation of this analysis, and pari passu with it, to bring together or frame a set of rules or canons for testing the sufficiency of any given evidence to prove any given proposition. (12)

Logic as an art of reasoning provides rules by which to guide our reasoning, rules that cover both truth (and so evidence) and validity. Logic as a science of reasoning analyses the mental processes involved in reasoning, and falls under the rubric of an empirical psychology.

The idea that deduction is a particularly abstract form of reasoning, by contrast with inductive reasoning, which is more concrete, ties deduction and induction together closely. The relation is set out in the *System of Logic* in these terms:

> All inference is from particulars to particulars. General propositions are merely registers of such inferences already made, and are short formulae for making more. The major premise of a syllogism, consequently, is a formula of this description; and the conclusion is not an inference drawn *from* the formula, but an inference drawn *according* to formula; the real logical antecedent or premise being the particular facts from which the general proposition was collected by induction. Those facts, and the individual instances which supplied them, may have been forgotten; but a record remains, not indeed descriptive of the facts themselves, but showing how these cases may be distinguished, respecting which, the facts, when known, were considered to warrant a given inference. According to the indications of this record we draw our conclusion; which is, to all intents and purposes, a conclusion from the forgotten facts. For this it is essential that we should read the record correctly; and the rules of the syllogism are a set of precautions to ensure our doing so. (193; emphases in the original)

If induction and deduction are so closely related, and we know that induction rests upon empirical foundations, the question arises as to what deduction rests upon. From what do we derive our knowledge of a general truth? Mill asks this, and answers thus: 'Of course, from observation. Now, all which man can observe are individual cases. From these all general truths must be drawn, and into these they may again be resolved; for a general truth is but an aggregate of particular truths; a comprehensive expression, by which an indefinite number of individual facts are affirmed or denied at once' (186). He gives the example of geometry, asking 'what is the ground for belief in axioms – what is the evidence on which they rest? I answer, they are experimental truths; generalizations from observation' (231).

To appreciate what is at issue here, we need to remember that there was a long tradition of thinking about inference, stretching back at least to Descartes, in which deductive inference was considered trivial (Gaukroger 1989). In particular, it was considered that the premises are always contained in the conclusion in a formally valid inference, and so that the deduction can never go beyond the premises, can never tell us anything new. This account mirrored contemporary views of syllogistic, but it made deductions in geometry, which seemed to be an informative discipline, beg the question. One solution (Descartes) was to argue that in geometry it was the analytical problem-solving inferences that did the work, not the synthetic deductive presentation (of the kind that one gets in Euclid's *Elements*), which was merely a presentational device. Mill moves in the opposite direction, arguing that geometrical proofs are informative, but he cannot invoke either Kant's account of geometry as synthetic a priori, or Whewell's archetypes. Informativeness, for Mill, means meeting an external standard, and observation is the only such standard. But the informativeness of geometrical theorems is limited because all that they can secure is compression of masses of particular truths at varying levels of abstraction. This is revealing because it indicates that Mill's way of thinking about deduction here is really about geometrical truths – what makes them true – not about deductive inference as such. Their truth derives from their compression of many truths in an economical and fruitful way. The traditional question of logicians – namely, that of which inferences are truth-preserving, and why – is not really addressed here. Kant and Whewell had both attempted to account for how the truths of mathematics could be at the same time both informative and necessary. Kant thought of our grasp of geometrical theorems in terms of features of the human mind that were not merely universal but were necessary, in that they were a condition of possibility of how we conceive of the world. Whewell, by contrast, thought, in Platonist terms, of their necessity as deriving from their correspondence to divine ideal archetypes. Mill effectively abandons necessity and accounts for informativeness.

The second strand in Mill's (1973) account is his 'science of reasoning'. But there is a connection between the two strands, for, despite the great gap between them, he moves from the core thesis of his art of reasoning, that 'the sole object of Logic is the guidance of one's own thoughts' (6) to the core thesis of his science of reasoning, that logic is a branch of psychology:

> I conceive it to be true that Logic is not the theory of Thought as Thought, but of valid Thought; not of thinking, but of correct thinking. It is not a Science distinct from, and coordinate with, Psychology. So far as it is a science at all, it is a part, or branch, of Psychology; differing from it, on the one hand as a part differs from the whole, and on the other, as an Art differs from a Science. Its theoretic grounds are wholly borrowed from Psychology, and include as much of that science as is required to justify the rules of the art. (359)

In other words, the laws of logic are dependent on contingent facts about human psychology. That these are *contingent* facts is not a worry for Mill. By contrast with those who held that logical truths were analytic and necessarily true, Mill held that they are contingently true. That is to say, they could have been different, but not in the sense that there is variation from person to person, or society to society: contingency in logic doesn't entail relativism, any more than the facts of physics being contingent entails relativism in physics. It is these universal but contingent facts that explain the objectivity of reasoning processes: that is, the objectivity in moving from premises to conclusion by means of a particular chain of reasoning. Objectivity lies here in something about the mind, but the mind is to be accounted for in terms of psychology, an empirical discipline.

How does this empirical psychology proceed? Psychology studies thought, and it attempts to discover the laws that regulate thought, and if it is to have a scientific standing then it must be subject to external criteria of evidence. But could what is involved in mathematical operations – calculations or proofs – be captured in empirical psychological laws of thought? To claim that what we treat as valid proofs or correct calculations is a fact about how our minds work perhaps makes sense in Kantian terms, where the fact is a conceptual one about what it is to think, but it is hard to see what rationale there could be for it as an empirical feature of thought. Moreover, it is difficult to understand what justification there could be for Mill's claim that we discover logical, geometrical, and arithmetical truths experimentally.

8. The birth of the philosophy of science

The interest in the nature of scientific knowledge that we have been concerned with in this chapter was very much an early-nineteenth-century phenomenon. Although it was certainly shaped by questions about the nature of understanding that the reception of Kant's work had generated, the source of the concern with metascientific questions – centring on methodology and epistemology – lay neither in developments in philosophy, nor with those in the physical or life sciences. It lay, rather, in the emergence of the human sciences, which threatened central tenets of human behaviour and motivation. Political economy and consequentialist ethics were not the only forms of the human sciences that changed the intellectual landscape at the beginning of the nineteenth century (Gaukroger 2016), but in the context of English philosophical thought of the period they were undeniably the most questioned. What emerged from this questioning was a new discipline, a form of metascience in which the credentials of scientific reasoning and practice in general were analysed. It was not simply a question of one preferred methodology being opposed to another, as was the case with the earlier disputes over Newtonian induction versus Cartesian hypothetical method. The questions were now lifted to the metalevel, so that it was the standing of scientific enquiry that provided a deeper and much enriched context in which the questions needed to be discussed. It is here that we witness the birth of the philosophy of science.

Notes

1 See Henderson (1996) and Schabas (2005).
2 See Hundert (1994).
3 See Yeo (1993).
4 See Snyder (2006).

References

Douglas, J. M. (1881), *The Life and Selections from the Correspondence of William Whewell*, London: Kegan Paul and Co.
Gaukroger, S. (1989), *Cartesian Logic*, Oxford: Oxford University Press.
Gaukroger, S. (2016), *The Natural and the Human*, Oxford: Oxford University Press.
Henderson, J. (1996), *Early Mathematical Economics; William Whewell and the British Case*, Lanham, MD: Rowman & Littlefield.
Herschel, J. (1830), *A Preliminary Discourse on the Study of Natural Philosophy*, London: Longman et al.
Hume, D. (1793), 'Of the Rise and Progress of the Arts and Sciences', in *Essays and Treatises on Several Subjects*, 2 vols, Edinburgh: Cadell.
Hundert, E. (1994), *The Enlightenment's Fable: Bernard Mandeville and the Discovery of Society*, Cambridge: Cambridge University Press.
Laudan, L. (1981), *Science and Hypothesis*, Dordrecht: Reidel.
Mandeville, B. (1714), *The Fable of the Bees*, London: Edmund Parker.
Mill, J. S. (1969), 'Whewell on Moral Philosophy' [1852], in *Collected Works of John Stuart Mill*, vol. 10, *Essays on Ethics, Religion, and Society*, Toronto: University of Toronto Press.
Mill, J. S. (1973), *A System of Logic* [1872] in *Collected Works of John Stuart Mill*, vol. 7, *A System of Logic Part I*, Toronto: University of Toronto Press.
Montesquieu, C. de Secondat, Baron de (1949), 'Essay sur les causes qui peuvent affecter les esprits et les caractères (1734)', in R. Caillois (ed.), *Oeuvres complètes*, 2 vols, Paris: La Pléiade.
Schabas, M. (2005), *The Natural Origins of Economics*, Chicago: University of Chicago Press.

Snyder, L. (2006), *Reforming Philosophy: A Victorian Debate on Science and Society*, Chicago: University of Chicago Press.
Whewell, W. (1831a) 'Modern Science – Inductive Philosophy', *Quarterly Review*, 45: 374–407.
Whewell, W. (1831b) 'Jones – on the Distribution of Wealth and the Sources of Taxation', *British Critics*, 10: 41–61.
Whewell, W. (1833), *Astronomy and General Physics Considered with Reference to Theology*, London: Pickering.
Whewell, W. (1846), *Lectures on Systematic Morality*, London: J.W. Parker.
Whewell, W. (1849), *Of Induction*, London: J.W. Parker.
Yeo, R. (1993), *Defining Science: William Whewell, Natural Knowledge and the Public Debate in Early Victorian Britain*, Cambridge: Cambridge University Press.

Index

active and passive 47–59
Adorno, Theodore 7
animal spirits 52
animals 47, 57–8
Archimedes 134
Aristotle 1, 7, 11–14, 23, 28, 64, 73, 85–6, 111–12, 119, 150
Arnauld, Antoine 85, 100
atomism 10
attributes 63–77
Augustine of Hippo 21

Babbage, Charles 188
Bacon, Francis 2, 7–26, 189, 196–7
Balling, Pieter 66
Bardout, Jean-Christophe 89
Barrow, Isaac 112
Bentham, Jeremy 186, 194
Berkeley, George 3, 152
Bernoulli, Johann 105
body, the 47–62, 122
Buffon, Comte de 140, 155
Burke, Edmund 156

causation 63–4, 68–73, 90, 101, 132–4
certainty 33–4
China 143
Cicero 143
Clairaut, Alexis 137
clarity and distinctness 29–30, 66–9, 84, 123, 126
Comte, August 185
conatus 64
Condillac, Étienne Bonnet de 3
consciousness 45–62, 105
conservation laws 90–1
Corneanu, Sorana 21
Crusius, Christian 147
Cynics, the 10

D'Alembert, Jean le Rond 4
deduction 189–201

Descartes, René 1–3, 21, 28–34, 45–62, 64–5, 68, 73, 85–6, 90–1, 109, 131, 134
determinism 101–2, 152–3
Diderot, Denis 3
doubt 45–62
dreaming 45–62, 122

Elisabeth, Princess (Descartes' correspondent) 52
empiricism 1–5, 7–8, 15, 102–3, 129–46
Enlightenment, the 147–64
Euclid 112
experiment 7–8, 16–26, 114

Feder, Johann Georg Heinrich 152
Fichte, Johann Gottlieb 5, 156, 166, 168–72, 173, 175, 176, 178, 179
Forster, George 155
foundationalism 3, 108, 113–14
freedom 147, 171–2, 174–5
Frege, Gottlieb 2

Galileo Galilei 10, 134, 136
Garber, Daniel 56
Garrett, Don 64
Garve, Christian 152
Gassendi, Pierre 27–44
Gaukroger, Stephen 20
Gellibrand, Henry 103
God, activity of in the world 86–8, 90–3
  existence of 4, 88–9, 151–2
  nature of 63–77
Gresham's law 134
Grotius, Hugo 66

Hatfield, Gary 56
Hegel, Georg Wilhem Friedrich 2, 5, 165, 175–82
Herder, Gottfried 148, 154, 155, 156, 186
Herschel, John 188–9
Hobbes, Thomas 27–44, 65

Hooke, Robert 134
Horkheimer, Max 7
Humboldt, Wilhelm von 156
Hume, David 1, 3, 80–3, 129–44, 148, 149, 150, 165, 186, 187, 194
Huyghens, Christianne 90, 136

idealism, classical German 1, 5, 158, 165–82
imagination, the 9, 47–8, 66, 71, 122
induction 189–201

Jacobi, Friedrich Heinrich 153, 157
Jones, Richard 188, 191

Kames, Lord 155
Kant, Immanuel 1–5, 147–63, 165–82, 189, 194, 199, 200
Kepler, Johannes 134, 136, 197
Knutzen, Martin 147

Lambert, Johann Heinrich 149
language 58, 126–7, 132, 186
Leibniz, Gottfried Wilhelm 2, 90, 97–110, 137, 147, 150
Lessing, Gotthold Ephraim 153
Linnaeus, Carl 140, 155
Locke, John 2–3, 65, 111–28, 151
logic 40, 65, 108, 115–20, 168–72
logical positivism 131

Maimonides 65
Malebranche, Nicolas 2, 79–96, 137
Mandeville, Bernard 140, 186–7
Mariotte, Edme 90, 134
mathematics 1, 39, 112, 131, 136, 148, 186
Maupertuis, Pierre Louis 136, 137
memory 9, 105–6, 132
Mendelssohn, Moses 148, 152, 153
mental states 45–62
Merchant, Caroline 7
Mersenne, Marin 27
metaphysics 1, 5, 9, 16, 40, 63–77, 79–96, 97–110, 147–64, 186–8
Mill, James 194
Mill, John Stuart 5, 186, 188, 193–201
mind, the 45–62, 63–4, 132–4
modes 63–77, 80
Montesquieu, Charles-Louis 187

morality 123–5, 157–8, 185–8
motion 86–7

Newton, Isaac 114, 134–7, 189, 191

occasionalism 91–3

passions of the soul 53–5, 74
perception 36–7, 47–9, 105–6, 122
pietism 148
Pinkard, Terry 180
Plato 1, 7, 16, 64, 73
poesy 9
Popkin, Richard 30
Popper, Karl 129
probability 33–4
prophecy 66
psychology 197–201
Pufendorf, Samuel 65
Pythagoreans 16

race 155
rationalism 1–5, 79–96, 102–3, 150–1
reason 9, 32–3, 54, 63–78, 93, 147–64
Régis, Pierre-Sylvain 2
Reinhold, Karl Leonhard 152, 154, 168
relations 66–9, 82, 84, 97
representation 47, 50–1
Ricardo, David 5, 186, 189, 191–3
Robinet, André 87
Rohault, Jacques 2
Rousseau, Jean-Jacques 148, 149
Russell, Bertrand 129

scepticism 3, 30–2, 35, 45–51, 122, 177
Schelling, Friedrich Wilhelm 165, 172–5, 176
Schiller, Friedrich 156
Schulze, Gottlob Ernst 156
science 2, 5, 7–27, 37–40, 84, 120–7, 135–7, 150, 168, 185–202
self, the 45–62
sensation 1, 3–4, 32–3, 45–9, 58, 108–28, 129–46
Sidgwick, Henry 194
Sleigh, Robert 99
Smith, Adam 137–8, 186, 194
Soemmerring, Samuel Thomas 155
soul, existence of 89–90

Spinoza, Benedict 2, 63–77, 172
statistics 186
Stevin, Simon 134
Stoics, the 21
substance 63–78, 85–6, 99–101, 103–5, 172
Swedenborg, Emmanuel 149

teleology 156, 168, 172, 179–82
thought, nature of 45–62

truth 46, 56, 106–8, 118
   Spinoza's theory of 67–8

Vater, Michael 173
Velthuysen, Lambertus 65
virtue 58, 140
Voltaire, François-Marie Arouet 136, 187

Whewell, William 5, 186, 188–95
will, the 47, 51–3
Wolff, Christian 147–8